Voice in the Darkness

The Apostle Paul:
His Extraordinary Story Retold

Della Letkeman

with initial research by R.E. Harlow

Everyday Publications Inc.
310 Killaly St. W.
Port Colborne ON L3K 6A6
Canada

To my granddaughters
LINDSAY, KARA,
MADISON, and MELISSA

And my grandsons
DANIEL, DREW, JAMES,
MATTHEW, and JOSHUA

Table of Contents

Maps, Charts, Illustrations, and Photos

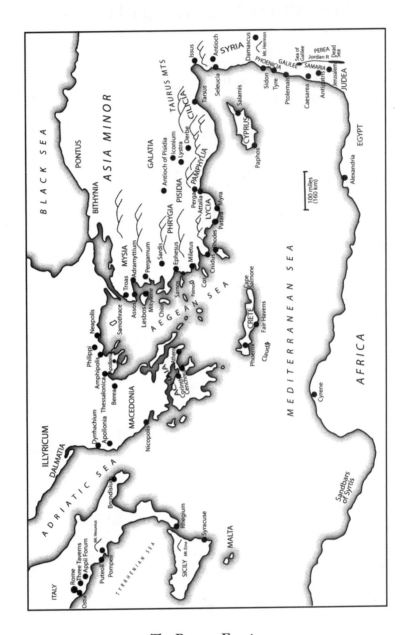

The Roman Empire

Acknowledgments

Special thanks to my husband Bill for listening as I read the manuscript on road trips. I am grateful to Ric and Tülin Munro who graciously met with me and shared photos of Ephesus, Miletus, Tarsus, Cilicia, Syrian Antioch, Rome, and Pompeii. Gertrud Harlow's wise suggestions were much appreciated as well as early editing by Eunice Free. Some helped along the way by offering to proofread the manuscript: Duncan Maxwell, Ruby Letkeman, Harry Koops, and Irene Herbert.

Marilyn MacMullen's contributions were invaluable – thank you, Marilyn, for using your expertise to fine-tune the wording in the final manuscript. What an encouragement you are to me! I am indebted to those who contributed to the final stages of the book: our son Ron, who used his talent to do the cover; Harold MacDougall, who worked quickly and tirelessly at Everyday Publications to typeset the manuscript; and Sara Townsend, who gave it a final review. The prayers of so many have been a help and a support. I pray that the re-telling of God's work in the life of the apostle Paul will bring glory to God.

Preface

"He is a chosen vessel unto Me, to bear My name before the Gentiles, and kings, and the children of Israel," Acts 9:15 KJV.

Why write another book about the apostle Paul? Dr. R.E. Harlow had hoped to write the story of Paul's life. He prepared a seven-page chart that listed people, events, places, history, and Bible references. However, he passed into the Lord's presence in 2003. So, with God's help, I undertook the project.

Except for the two opening chapters, the events in this story are written in chronological order – as they would have happened. All persons named are either mentioned in the Bible or in history books. However, I have taken some artistic license when recreating scenes.

Scripture was my first source of information. I also relied heavily on the *New Bible Dictionary*, Third Edition, InterVarsity Press, as well as the writings of F. F. Bruce. He was professor of Biblical criticism at the University of Manchester in England. To view the Scripture passages used and other sources of information, see "Notes" on pages 253-270.

I have included approximate dates throughout Paul's life to indicate whether an event took place over a number of days – or months or years. Dates have been taken from the "Chronology of the New Testament" (some dates are more approximate than others), pages 193-199, *New Bible Dictionary*.

A chronology of the lives of Jesus and Paul

The birth of Jesus occurred before the death of Herod the Great, Mathew 2:1; Luke 1:5, and therefore before March/April of 4 B.C. (*Ant.* 17.167, 191; 14.487-490[1]). Jesus may have been born in the spring or summer of 5 B.C.

John the Baptist's ministry began in the fifteenth year of Tiberius (Jan.-Dec., A.D. 29, if based on the Julian calendar, or Aug., A.D. 28-Aug., A.D. 29, if based on Roman dating). Thus John's ministry began in either A.D. 28 or 29.

---

[1] *Ant.* refers to *Antiquities of the Jews* by Josephus. The series of numbers following the abbreviation *Ant.* refers to the volume and page numbers of the writings.

Jesus' public ministry began when He was about thirty years of age, Luke 3:23. If He was born in 5 B.C. and baptized in A.D. 29, He would have been around 33 years of age.

The year of Jesus' death can be narrowed down by considering the following:

Three officials were involved in His trial. They were:

- Caiaphas, the high priest, John 18:13,14,24,28. Caiaphas was high priest from A.D. 18-37 (*Ant.* 18.35, 90-95).

- Pilate, prefect of Judea, Matthew 27:2-26, governed from A.D. 26-36 (*Ant.* 18.89).

- Herod Antipas, Luke 23:6-12. Herod was tetrarch of Galilee and Perea from 4 B.C. until A.D. 39 (*Ant.* 18.240-56; 19.351).

From this we learn that Jesus' trial must have occurred between A.D. 26 and 36.

The Passover at the time of Jesus' death: Astronomy helps identify the years in which Passover took place on a Thursday or Friday. Between A.D. 26 and 36, the years that qualify are A.D. 27, 30, 33, 36.

History confirms the death of Jesus in A.D. 33. Pilate is portrayed by his contemporary Philo (*Embassy to Gaius*, 301-302) and later by Josephus as being greedy, inflexible, and cruel. This is in keeping with Luke 13:1. Yet during Jesus' trial, Pilate is seen as caving in to the pressures of the religious leaders. Pilate had probably been appointed by Sejanus, an anti-Semite and trusted friend of Tiberius. Sejanus was executed by Tiberius in A.D. 31. From that time Pilate no longer had the protection of Rome. Herod Antipas would most likely have been the one who reported that Pilate caused a riot, probably at the Feast of Tabernacles in A.D. 32. When it was reported that Jesus stirred up trouble in Judea and Galilee, Luke 23:5, Pilate was eager to allow Herod Antipas to try Jesus, Luke 23:6-12. In this context, A.D. 33 is the most probable date. Luke 23:12 states that Pilate and Herod Antipas were friends from that day forward. This would be inaccurate if the crucifixion had taken place in A.D. 30, since they were at odds in A.D. 32. Thus, A.D. 33 best fits the historical evidence.

The date of Paul's conversion is based on two passages of Scripture:

• Galatians 1:17-18 states he went to Jerusalem three years after his conversion[2]. When Paul escaped from Damascus, Nabataean Aretas IV was in power, 2 Corinthians 11:32. Aretas reigned from A.D. 37-39, so Paul's conversion would have been between A.D. 34 and 36.

• Galatians 2:1 indicates that Paul went up to Jerusalem 14 years later (the famine visit he made with Barnabas in Acts 11,12), which is dated A.D. 47-49. Subtracting 14 years from these dates shows his conversion would be A.D. 33-35. Paul's conversion is estimated to have taken place in the summer of A.D. 35 and his return to Jerusalem in A.D. 37.

Exact dates in secular history that are linked to events in the book of Acts:

• The death of Herod Agrippa I - A.D. 44. See Acts 12:20-23.

• Porcius Festus succeeded Felix - A.D. 59. See Acts 24:27.

Probable dates linked to the story of Paul:

• Junius Gallio was proconsul of Achaia from the summer of A.D. 51 until A.D. 52. He dealt with Paul's case. See Acts 18:12-17. There is also a small probability Gallio took office on July 1, A.D. 52.

Paul's early life: No one agrees as to the exact events in Paul's early life. I combined existing Scripture with the customary schooling for young Hebrew boys raised in Jerusalem.

Letters of Paul: I have quoted brief excerpts of Paul's letters to give the reader a taste of his writings in the context of the events of his life. Missing verses or words in his letters are indicated by an ellipsis (...). In order to present the letters of Paul in an easy-to-read style, the verses have been taken from the *Holy Bible, New*

---

[2]Parts of years are equivalent to a whole year.

Living Translation (NLT). My hope is that the short summary of Paul's letters will give the reader a desire to carefully study these books of Paul's writings in their entirety as inspired by the Holy Spirit of God, 2 Timothy 3:16,17.

Physical appearance of Paul: Any mention of Paul's physical appearance is taken from a description by Thecla. She was a member of a notable family in Iconium and most probably a disciple of Paul (*St. Paul: The Traveler and Roman Citizen* by William M. Ramsay, pp. 46,127; *New Bible Dictionary,* "Paul", p. 880.)

Events in Paul's life after the Book of Acts closes: It becomes more difficult to follow Paul's activities, but scholars have reconstructed his final years from the references to trips and planned trips in his letters.

Della Letkeman

The Early Years – Tarsus, Jerusalem, Damascus

Chapter ONE

Approving Bystander

Jerusalem

A.D. 34, Jerusalem (Roman province of Judea)

The courtroom exploded in an uproar. Council members in charge of the trial ground their teeth in rage and rose to attack Stephen like a pack of hungry wolves. "How dare you speak against our people and our Temple!" one of them shouted.

Stephen, a deacon at the church in Jerusalem, sat calmly in the face of their anger. The highest court of the Jews, the Sanhedrin Council, had listened to lying witnesses accuse Stephen of blasphemy against Moses, God, and the Temple. While these men stared at Stephen, his face shone like the face of an angel. Earlier he had reminded them of their past and how God's voice had spoken to the Hebrew people throughout history. God had promised to send them a Deliverer. This Deliverer had recently come among them and His name was Jesus. "You are responsible," Stephen continued, "for persecuting God's prophets and for betraying and crucifying Jesus the Nazarene, the Just One sent by God."

The Council members fought to defend their beliefs. "The Nazarene is not the Promised One," a member shouted. "You have insulted our Temple by saying that God does not live in man-made buildings."

The Jewish Council continued to shout insults at Stephen, but he seemed unaware of their words. He was looking up instead toward heaven. Suddenly he spoke aloud with amazement. "Look, heaven is wide open and the Son of Man is

A street in the old city of Jerusalem

standing in the place of honor at God's right hand."

"What blasphemy!" shouted one of the Council members, his face turning red with fury. "How can that crucified man, Jesus, be standing next to God in a place of honor! Can there be another way into God's presence besides going through the Temple rites?"

Without waiting for a reply, Stephen's accusers covered their ears and yelling loudly, drowned out Stephen's voice. Rushing toward him, they dragged him into the street. Carts clattered by and people hastily moved aside to let them pass. The hot sun beat down mercilessly as a messenger ran ahead announcing: "Stephen will be stoned…He has spoken blasphemy…Members of the Sanhedrin are witnesses of what he has done."

People stopped to stare as the group moved through the city gate and outside the high stone wall. The steep precipice to the east lay threateningly before them. "Confess your crime," one of the Council shouted at Stephen. "If you confess, you will share in the age to come."

Stephen did not reply. His captors responded by pulling him closer to the edge of the slope. Without warning, one of the witnesses pushed him. With a gasp of surprise, Stephen lost his balance and fell down into the ravine.

Two official witnesses picked up large, sharp stones and threw them. Stephen held up his arms to protect himself. Others prepared to join in the stoning by removing their loose, outer garments. A young, bright-eyed Council member named Saul stood near the edge.

"Saul," one of the men called, "take care of our clothes." As he spoke, he tossed his outer garment into Saul's arms.

"With pleasure," Saul nodded. "I would do anything for the God of Israel." His intense eyes darkened and a hot rush crept up the back of his neck. "I hope you finish off that troublemaker."

"Stephen is going to die," another rejoiced as the pile of clothing at Saul's feet grew.

"I agree with this decision," Saul said between clenched teeth. "There is no room for compromise between our Jewish faith and these new fanatics. I will gladly help to preserve the purity of our religion!"

The Council members returned to the edge of the cliff. Bending down, each one chose his weapon from the rocky ground and hurled one stone after another at Stephen. The clatter of stone hitting stone and the thud of stone meeting human flesh echoed harshly through the valley.

Bruised and bleeding, Stephen tried to stay on his feet. With a pale face and trembling lips, he called out to God, "Lord Jesus, receive my spirit." His words stirred up the fervor of the angry mob even more. As the missiles found their mark, Stephen swayed and dropped to his knees amidst the rocks. The people above him seemed dark and distant. Although in great agony, he cried out with a loud voice, "Lord, do not charge them with this sin."

A well-aimed stone struck him and knocked him to the ground. He struggled to rise again, but could not. The stones continued to fly through the air until the men were sure that Stephen would never move again.

One by one the men dropped the remaining stones and turned away from his lifeless body. Casually rubbing their hands together to dust off the grit, the attackers returned to Saul to pick up their clothing.

"Well done," Saul told the men one after another. "May the God of our fathers honor you for defending the traditions of our people."

"Stephen's words against the Temple were blasphemy," a Council member reminded him. "Emperor Tiberius and Governor Pilate are usually in charge of ordering the death penalty, but they occasionally allow our Council to carry out these exceptions."

"Good," Saul said as he stretched taller and a smile played on his lips. "The Council's actions were right." He swelled with pride as he remembered the beautiful Temple with its shining gold and polished marble. There could be nothing more important than the traditions of his religion and his family.

Chapter
⇒TWO⇒

Passionate Pharisee

Tarsus, Jerusalem

About A.D. 1, Tarsus (Roman province of Cilicia)

In Tarsus, joy filled the home of a young, moderately wealthy couple. They were celebrating the birth of a son. The midwife washed the crying baby and wrapped him tightly in strips of cloth.

"Our son will follow the Law of God," his father said. "One day he will be a Pharisee, a separated one, as I am. He will be a Hebrew of Hebrews, one who speaks our Hebrew language and keeps our customs. He will be circumcised by the priest to show his separation from all other nations and as our gift back to God. His name must be chosen by the eighth day."

"Yes," his mother added, "but its meaning must be right."

"Saul is a good name. It was the name of Israel's first king. He came from the tribe of Benjamin, and so do we."

*   *   *   *   *   *   *

As Saul grew, he willingly helped his mother with household chores. He swept the house and carried water. With his parents and sister, he often walked the narrow stone streets of Tarsus to attend services at the synagogue. Open-minded Hebrew families living in Tarsus used the Greek language in both everyday life and in the synagogue, but not Saul's family. They spoke Hebrew.

More than half a million people lived in Tarsus, the capital city of Cilicia in Asia Minor. One of the larger cities in the Roman Empire, it was located near the northeast coast of the Mediterranean. Known as a city of culture, it had a university-style school for advanced learning.

A smooth, fertile plain surrounded the city. During the summer, pale-blue flax blossoms filled the countryside with color. At harvest-time, workers pulled the plants and tied the 3-foot[3] stalks together to dry. In time, the flax straw would be ready for spinning and then for weaving into linen clothing.

Herds of bleating, black goats grazed in the countryside, and workers used this hair to make a coarse cloth called cilicium. Saul liked to watch his father's skillful hands weave the goat's hair into coverings to make various products, such as tents for protection in cold, wet climates.

Cleopatra's Gate, on the west side of Tarsus, built shortly after Anthony and Cleopatra entered there in 41 B.C.

And in the distance soared the snow-covered Taurus Mountains. What lay beyond them? Travelers used the Cilician Gates, a narrow mountain pass 30 miles north of the city, to cross the Taurus range into central Asia Minor.

On summer days Saul and his parents had opportunities to walk to the always cold, winding Cydnus River. It ran through a deep ravine before finding its way into the middle of this bustling city. Saul squinted in the bright sunlight as smaller vessels made their way up the river from the Mediterranean Sea. The oars beat a rhythm in the water as rowers fought against the strong current.

---

[3]See Appendix, page 276 for conversion to metric.

Larger ships docked six miles below Tarsus where the river widened into Lake Rhegma. On shore, workers unloaded goods from Greece, Italy, Tyre, and Sidon. They worked in the hot sun strapping burdens for delivery onto hard-working donkeys. Occasionally, the loud, harsh cry of a donkey would fill the air. Sailors pulled ropes through creaky pulleys, lifting bundles of cloth made from goat's hair from the bank of the river onto the ship. Each bundle rocked back and forth as it swung across the side of the vessel before dropping into the ship's hold with a thud. The cloth would be delivered to another part of the Roman Empire.

While Emperor Caesar Augustus ruled the Roman Empire from 27 B.C. to A.D. 14, the entire Mediterranean area, including Tarsus, was under his control. He had restored peace and order to the Empire after one hundred years of civil war. He encouraged free trade among the provinces, developed a good postal system, and improved the harbors. He built highways that connected Rome to all parts of the Empire.

A person born in Tarsus did not automatically qualify for Roman citizenship. However, since Saul's father was a citizen of Rome, Saul, too, claimed this liberty by right. He would be able to call on this privilege later in life to help him through difficult situations.

"I am concerned about raising Saul here," his father worried.

"This is a fine city of art and culture," his mother responded. "While at one time we would have been expected to teach him ourselves, now boys of six and over can attend school at the synagogue. There a paid instructor will teach Saul to read, write, and memorize Scripture."

"Our Saul is bright and full of energy. He shouldn't be raised like the pagan children of Rome who learn to worship gods such as Vesta, the goddess of fire. Neither should he study the Law at a synagogue that promotes the use of the Greek language and culture, as does the one here in Tarsus. He should have a traditional education in the Hebrew language. He needs to go to Jerusalem for his schooling."

*   *   *   *   *   *   *

Approximately A.D. 6 to A.D. 28, Jerusalem
(Roman province of Judea)

Saul hurried along the cobblestone streets in the gray darkness of early morning. It seemed he had waited forever for this first day of school. After saying good-bye to his parents, he entered The House of the Book.

"Peace to you," his teacher greeted, as he showed him across the room to where the other boys sat in a semi-circle. Saul's heart raced with excitement as he joined other boys waiting for school.

His teacher, a married man with a good reputation, adjusted his long flowing robes and sat down cross-legged on a raised area in front of them. "Today the lesson is about Moses and how he received God's Law." The children faced the teacher with a look of wonder on their eager faces. A low table filled with scrolls stood in front of the teacher for ready reference when needed. "Listen carefully," he said clearing his throat, "and you will learn about Moses. On the first day of the third month after the Israelites left Egypt, they came to the Wilderness of Sinai. There the people camped at the foot of the mountain. Moses climbed the mountain to meet with God.

"The LORD called to him, 'Remind the people of Israel what I did to the Egyptians, and how I carried you as an eagle carries her young on her wings. Now if you will obey Me and keep My covenant, you will be a special treasure to Me. And you will serve Me as a kingdom of priests and a holy nation.'

"Moses climbed down from the mountain and told the elders of the people the words of the LORD. The people answered, 'All that the LORD has spoken, we will do.'

"Moses returned to the mountain and the LORD again spoke to him. 'I am going to come to you in a thick cloud so the people will hear when I speak with you and will believe all your words from Me. Go down to the people. Tell them to purify themselves both today and tomorrow. On the third day, I will come down upon Mount Sinai. Warn the people not to go up to the mountain or to touch its base. Anyone who sets foot on the mountain will certainly die. When there is one long blast from the ram's horn, the people must gather at the foot of the mountain.'

"Again Moses went to the people with God's words.

"Then in the morning of the third day, God sent His thunder and lightning. A thick cloud rested on the mountain. A loud blast sounded from the ram's horn. All the people trembled with fear. Moses led them out of the camp to the foot of the mountain to meet with God.

"True to His word, the LORD came down. He came in the form of fire, and smoke completely covered the mountain. The billows rose into the sky like the smoke of a furnace, and the whole mountain shook with a violent earthquake. The sound of the horn grew louder and louder. Moses spoke, and the voice of God thundered out of the darkness. The LORD then came to rest on the top of Mount Sinai and called Moses to come up. Moses climbed the mountain to meet with the LORD.

"And the LORD said to Moses, 'Go down and warn the people to not come up and look at Me. And when you return, bring your brother Aaron with you.'

"Moses obeyed. Then God spoke to the people:

I am the Lord your God, who brought you out of the land of Egypt....

1. *'You shall have no other gods before Me.*

2. *'You shall not make for yourself a carved image — any likeness of anything that is in heaven above, or that is in the earth beneath, or that is in the water under the earth; you shall not bow down to them nor serve them. For I, the Lord your God, am a jealous God....*

3. *'You shall not take the name of the Lord your God in vain....*

4. *'Remember the Sabbath day, to keep it holy....*

5. *'Honor your father and your mother....*

6. *'You shall not murder.*

7. *'You shall not commit adultery.*

8. *'You shall not steal.*

9. *'You shall not bear false witness against your neighbor.*

10. *'You shall not covet your neighbor's house; you shall not covet your neighbor's wife, nor his male servant, nor his female servant, nor his ox, nor his donkey, nor anything that is your neighbor's.'*

(Excerpts from Exodus 20:2-5,7-8,12-17 NKJV)

"The thunder roared, the horn blared, the lightning flashed, and the mountain smoked. The people stood at a distance, trembling with fear while Moses entered the thick, dark cloud to receive further instructions from God."

Saul sat wide-eyed. He had been leaning forward to catch every word of the story from the Holy Scriptures.

"Now," his teacher said, "it is time for breakfast at my house. All you hungry boys are to follow me home."

The students eagerly crowded through the doorway. The sweet aroma of warm cakes filled their nostrils. Each boy received several small cakes with letters of the Law written on them. They ate with hearty appetites.

When they had finished, their teacher dismissed them with a parting reminder, "I'll expect you boys back in class this afternoon – at three o'clock."

Day after day, with never any holidays, the boys attended school. The students unvaryingly sat in a semi-circle on the floor, facing the teacher. Through repetition and memory work, Saul faithfully learned his letters until he could read aloud.

When asked to write, Saul worked on a wooden tablet covered with a thin layer of wax. He drew letters in the wax with a pointed stick. He had one textbook – the *Tanach* or Holy Scriptures, which included the Law and the Prophets. Saul studied with passion and earned the reputation of being a bright student. Quickly he advanced to the top of his class.

As a teenager, he had the advantage of studying with one of the finest and most reasonable teachers, Gamaliel. This man was a

Pharisee as well as a Council member who leaned toward the more open-minded side of the Pharisees. He allowed Saul to sit at his feet when he attended meetings of the Sanhedrin, the ruling Council of the Jews.

The Pharisees devoted themselves to the Law of their God. Pressure to convert to using the Greek language had started more than two centuries earlier when a king ruling from Syria had tried to make his Jewish subjects embrace Greek culture. Many of the Hebrews, especially those living a great distance from Jerusalem, did adopt the Greek language. Yet the Pharisees held fast to their strong disapproval of Greek language and culture in Jewish life.

Gamaliel, a peace-loving man with a long beard and flowing robes, had a thorough knowledge of the Old Testament Scriptures. Each day he instructed Saul in every detail of Jewish law. He taught him about the coming Messiah and about how the Jews longed to have someone who would liberate them from their Roman rulers.

Saul learned to read and to write with clarity. He progressed to using a reed pen, which was dipped in a wooden inkwell. He grew skilled at speaking both Hebrew and Greek. In daily life he practiced three cultures – Jewish, Greek, and Roman. His superior education and privileged upbringing helped to make up for his small stature and other physical shortcomings.

Most Jewish boys learned a trade from their father as part of their education. Saul was no exception – he learned to make tents skillfully. He would be free to pursue this practical trade as soon as he finished studying. It could be used in the future throughout the Roman Empire.

As Saul was growing up in the city of Jerusalem, another Jewish boy, slightly older, lived in a small town approximately 60 miles to the north. He was no ordinary boy. An angel of the Lord had come to a young virgin named Mary. This angel had told Mary that she would conceive a child by the Holy Spirit and that He was to be called Jesus, for He would save His people from their sins. Though He had come from heaven, Jesus was born as a baby in Bethlehem.

Now, however, Jesus lived in Nazareth, a small town of five hundred people. It was located in a bowl-shaped valley close to the highway that led southwest to Egypt and northeast to Mesopotamia. Jesus lived with His mother Mary and her husband Joseph, a carpenter who trained Jesus, his adopted son, in the same work.

In a future day Jesus would speak to Saul. This meeting would miraculously change Saul's life. But in these early years the self-assured Saul had no idea what the future held. His goal was to follow the Law exactly. He worked hard and with great enthusiasm, wanting to honor God in everything he did. He progressed in the Jewish religion beyond any of his own age and race, and as a Pharisee, he became a member of the Council. He fought fiercely to preserve traditional Jewish values.

*   *   *   *   *   *   *

A.D. 29, Judea

John the Baptist was the son of an elderly priest. He wore clothes made of camel's hair and he preached in the desert of Judea. "Turn from your sins," he announced. "The kingdom of heaven is near. The prophet Isaiah spoke about me when he said, 'A voice is shouting in the desert. Prepare a way for the Lord; make a straight path for him to travel!'"

Many came to hear John preach. Some confessed their sins, and he baptized them. John also baptized Jesus, the sinless Son of God, to carry out all that God required. As Jesus came out of the waters, the heavens opened and a voice said, "This is the Son I love, and I am fully pleased with Him."

"Jesus is the long-awaited Messiah," John told the crowds. "He is the Lamb of God who takes away the sin of the world!"

After this, Jesus taught publicly and called disciples to follow Him. He traveled from town to town healing the sick and teaching that a person needed to be born again to have eternal life.

The Pharisees met to discuss what to do with Him. "There is something suspicious about that Man," one of them complained. "We should keep an eye on Him."

"I agree," another added. "He is not even keeping the Sabbath. His disciples break off heads of wheat to eat on the Sabbath day."

"And He doesn't keep our rules. He healed a man with a deformed hand in the synagogue, right before our eyes."

"You should have seen the reaction at the Temple when He drove out the merchants and knocked over the money tables. He told the moneychangers who were selling cattle, sheep, and pigeons that they had turned a place of prayer into a marketplace! Imagine! Yet He still goes openly to the Temple to teach each day."

"Too many people are listening to His words."

"We must put a stop to His teaching and find a way to kill Him."

*   *   *   *   *   *   *

In spite of their bitter opposition, Jesus continued to tell the Pharisees that they did not meet God's standards. He stated plainly that each person needed a changed heart. He quoted their prophet Isaiah, "These people honor me with their lips, but their hearts are far away from me."

A.D. 33, Jerusalem

Jesus had been preaching in and around Judea for three years. Each spring the Jews held an eight-day festival to remember their deliverance from the Egyptians. In the year A.D. 33, however, two days before observing this annual Passover festival, the chief priests and councilors met in the house of the high priest, Caiaphas. They gathered to plot exactly how to kill Jesus. The timing seemed perfect because Judas, one of Jesus' disciples, had agreed to betray Him.

One evening after spending time in prayer for His disciples, Jesus left Jerusalem with them. Crossing the Kidron Brook, the group came to the Garden of Gethsemane on the western slope of the Mount of Olives.

Nearby, Judas and a band of men along with a detachment of soldiers watched their movements. These men, from among the chief priests and Pharisees, followed Jesus into the olive grove, taking with them blazing torches, lanterns, and weapons. Here the men arrested Jesus and took Him first to Caiaphas, then to Pilate, the Roman governor of Judea. Though Pilate tried Jesus, he could only give one conclusion to the leading priests and other religious leaders. "I find this man innocent. He has done nothing to deserve the death penalty."

The leaders objected, "We do not want you to free Him. Crucify Him!"

Pilate decided to deliver up Jesus to be killed. So Jesus was led away and crucified. At the very moment of His death, the thick and heavy Temple veil split in two from top to bottom. For three hours from noon until 3:00 p.m., heavy darkness blanketed the earth. People reported the ominous event as far away as Rome and Egypt.

Jesus' death was part of God's plan to redeem man. He was the Deliverer that God had promised to send to save man. God showed He approved of Jesus' death when Jesus rose from the dead after three days. His disciples and hundreds of others saw Jesus before He returned to heaven.

A.D. 34, Jerusalem

Saul boiled with rage every time he thought of Jesus and His disciples. "That Jesus is an impostor," he fumed.

"What do you plan to do about it?" a fellow councilor asked.

"I will increase my efforts to rid the world of any and all who dare to follow Him. Our traditional Jewish religion must be preserved. Surely it will please God if I stop followers of 'the Way.' I plan to personally round them up and throw them into prison."

Chapter
⋐THREE⋑

Voice in the Darkness

Jerusalem, Damascus

A.D. 34, Jerusalem (Roman province of Judea)

Godly men wept loudly over Stephen's body. They had come to prepare his remains for burial. They lovingly washed the body, wrapped it in linen, and carried it away.

On this same day, the crowds that had stoned Stephen turned their attention to other followers of Christ in Jerusalem. Believers ran for their lives to escape cruel persecution. Many fled to the surrounding countryside of Judea or further north to Samaria. But wherever they went they continued to tell others the 'good news' of salvation. However, the apostles stayed in Jerusalem.

A.D. 35, Jerusalem

Saul clenched his fists in determination as he hunted down the followers of Jesus. He forced his way into houses as he went from door to door. At one home, a young mother answered his knock. "Are you a follower of 'the Way'?" he asked in an accusing voice.

She hesitated for a moment too long. Instantly, hot anger flashed across Saul's face. He grabbed her arm, his eyes narrowing in determination. "Come with me," he shouted.

"No!" she gasped. "Let me go!" She struggled to loosen his grip. "Don't take me away from my children!"

"You will pay for your disloyalty," he said, spitting out the words through clenched teeth. With strong arms he wrapped chains around her wrists and pulled her into the street while her young children cried helplessly after her. Saul paid no attention to their cries, as he shoved the young mother toward his companions. "Chain her to the others. I will return with more." He entered house after house, raging like an untamed animal. He dragged men and women out to the street and took them to his waiting friends. After several people had been captured, Saul marched them down the street to the jail. From there the prisoners went on trial, and at each trial Saul voted for the death sentence.

At the synagogue he stood up and proudly delivered fiery messages, threatening any of the Lord's followers who might be attending his lecture. "Renounce your faith or die!"

The thought of men spreading these new teachings in other cities made the blood flow hotly through Saul's veins. He clenched his fists. How could he stop them? He decided to visit the high priest to confirm his plans. "I need letters of introduction to Jewish congregations in the city of Damascus. These new beliefs must not spread."

The ancient Syrian city of Damascus stood several days' journey north of Jerusalem, in the northwest corner of Arabia. It had a large Jewish population and several synagogues, but followers of 'the Way' were still living there at peace among the Jews. "I will find those disciples of 'the Way,'" Saul muttered as he and other like-minded men started their journey. "I will arrest them. I will tie them up and I will personally bring them back to Jerusalem."

He climbed the hills north of the city with determination in his dark eyes and purpose in every step. He had obtained letters from the high priest giving him permission to capture the followers of Jesus and to bring them back to Jerusalem in chains. He tucked the rolled-up letters under his cloak. He would deliver these letters to the synagogues in Damascus when he arrived. The towering city walls of Jerusalem disappeared in the distance behind him. He progressed along the well-traveled Roman road, meeting many people journeying south toward Jerusalem. Some walked. Others rode on horses, donkeys, or camels.

Energized by the fighting spirit common to the tribe of Benjamin, Saul traveled toward Damascus. He followed 'The Way of the Sea,' the direct route along the shores of the Sea of Galilee. At the end of each day he stopped at a rest house. As he drifted off to sleep, his mind constantly rehearsed details of all he planned to do. When morning came, his intense hatred for followers of 'the Way' spurred him on. After several days' travel, Mount Hermon with its three distinct peaks loomed to his left. The mountain rose over 9000 feet above sea level and a bright blue sky stood behind its snow-covered peaks. Melting waters trickled into rocky channels at the base of the mountain and fed the rivers below. Damascus lay ahead, nestled on a plain to the east of the Anti-Lebanon Mountains and west of the Syrian-Arabian desert.

About noon the men were anticipating the end of their journey and talking about their plans for the following day. Suddenly – a light, brighter than the sun, shone around them. All the travelers fell to the ground. Saul lay stunned at the center of the light while the others quickly scrambled away to the side of the road.

Saul's heart pounded in his ears. Above his loud, thumping pulse, a voice from heaven called to him, "Saul, Saul, why are you persecuting Me?"

The hair rose on the back of his neck and color drained from his face. He shook with fear as he looked up and saw the risen Lord. With a mouth so dry he could barely speak he gasped, "Who are you, Lord?"

"I am Jesus, the One you are persecuting. It is hard for you to kick against the goads."

In a flash of understanding, Saul realized that the Lord Jesus had been trying to speak to his conscience just like an owner goads an animal into action with a pointed stick. Saul had not listened, but instead he had thrashed about like a stubborn beast.

Saul had been living in darkness. Satan had blinded his

unbelieving mind. Now the voice from heaven offered to exchange Saul's darkness for light. Jesus was not dead and buried, but very much alive. It was Jesus whom Saul had been persecuting each time he had inflicted pain on followers of 'the Way.' Saul humbly bowed his heart in the presence of Jesus the Nazarene and acknowledged Him as the Messiah, God's promised Deliverer.

"Lord," he said with trembling lips, "what do You want me to do?"

"Get up off the ground," the Lord said with authority. "Stand on your feet. Go into the city of Damascus. There you will be told what you must do."

As Saul stood up, his traveling companions looked on speechlessly, shaking in fear. A voice from the light had spoken with Saul, but none of the others had understood the words.

"You will be My servant and My witness," the Lord continued to Saul. "You will use your voice to tell this world about Me. I will protect you from both Jews and Gentiles, but I am going to send you to the Gentiles. The message I give you will change people. They will turn from spiritual darkness to light, from following the power of Satan to following God's direction. You must go into the city of Damascus. There you will be told what you must do to begin this new life."

As the bright light faded away, Saul stood in the middle of the road. He turned his head to the right and to the left. Which way should he go to travel to Damascus?

"What's the matter, Saul? Can't you see anything?" one of his companions asked.

"No! Nothing!" he replied, as his hands groped to find something familiar. "I need help. I cannot stay on this road by myself."

"Here – let me lend you a hand."

Summer, A.D. 35, Damascus (Roman province of Syria)

Together the travelers moved toward the city of Damascus, a beautiful oasis on the edge of the desert. Here the Abana River flowed east from the mountains and divided into three streams on the wide fertile plain. This was the same river that, centuries earlier, Naaman the Syrian had claimed was 'better than all the waters of Israel.' The middle branch of the Abana River flowed through

Walls of the old city – Damascus, Syria

Damascus. Workers had redirected the waters from each of the other branches to provide streams that ran through many gardens where there were fig orchards and vineyards of purple grapes. Saul, completely blinded, could enjoy none of this beauty. The faint sound of bubbling waters soothed his troubled mind and faltering steps.

As the travelers passed through the city gates of Damascus, Saul remembered the letters under his cloak. He had faithfully guarded these letters to the Jewish congregations in Damascus. Each one of them condemned the followers of Jesus. Now these same writings sentenced him as well to arrest and prison. He, Saul, had now become one of the hated ones described in these letters.

The sound of voices in the streets distracted Saul from his thoughts. Chariot wheels and the clip-clop of hooves down the narrow passageways told him they were inside the city walls. The men found Straight Street, a wider, straighter avenue than the others. It ran through the city from east to west. Saul's companions took him to the home of a man named Judas.

Judas showed his guest to a quiet place. In the stillness of his chamber, Saul sat and waited for God's direction. For three days Saul neither ate nor drank. In spite of his physical blindness, the 'good news' of Christ's glory was shining in his heart.

*   *   *   *   *   *   *

Ananias was a godly man with a good reputation among the Jews of Damascus. One day the Lord spoke to him in a vision. "Get ready and go to Straight Street. Look for the house of Judas. There you will find a man who is waiting for you to arrive – his name is Saul of Tarsus."

Fear gripped Ananias. "But, Lord," he argued, "this man has done terrible things to Your people in Jerusalem. He is in Damascus right now with permission from the chief priests to arrest any who worship You."

"Go anyway!" the Lord responded. "I have chosen this man to serve Me. He will be a witness to make My name known to many nations, to kings, and to the people of Israel. Saul will soon learn how much he must suffer for Me."

Ananias could hardly believe his ears. Did he dare approach Saul? Did this man really have a changed heart?

He left his home and carefully made his way through the narrow streets until he found the house. He hesitated, then nervously cleared his throat and knocked. Judas came to the door. "Is Saul of Tarsus here?" Ananias asked.

"Yes, come in. He's been sitting quietly for three days. I'll show you to his room." Ananias followed Judas through the house to Saul's room.

As Saul sat praying, footsteps came down the hall toward him. A moment later he sensed the rustle of a man's robe in front of him. A pair of gentle hands lightly touched his head.

"Who are you?" Saul asked as he raised his unseeing eyes.

"I am Ananias," the voice responded.

"Why are you here?"

"Brother Saul, the Lord Jesus has sent me to you. He is the One who appeared to you on the road as you traveled. God has chosen you to know His will, to see the Just One, and to hear His voice. You are going to be a witness to the world. The Lord will send you to the Gentiles. They will turn from darkness to light and from the power of Satan to God. Through faith in the Lord Jesus they will receive forgiveness of sins and a place among God's people. But now, Saul, the Lord wants you to see again and to be filled with the Holy Spirit." As Ananias spoke, small scales dropped from Saul's eyes.

Saul blinked. "I can see again!" he said excitedly to Ananias.

"Yes, the Lord has restored your sight," Ananias responded. "Now you must go and be baptized. Don't wait. Do it right away. Baptism with water will tell others that you identify with the Lord Jesus Christ. When you go into the water and come up again, you will be picturing Christ's death, His burial, and His rising again."

*   *   *   *   *   *   *

Saul obeyed and was baptized, being dipped beneath the water. As Saul went under the surface, he was showing that the independent, religious Saul who insisted on his own way had died and been buried. The new Saul would be walking in a relationship with Christ. After his baptism Saul took food, and his strength gradually returned. He stayed for a time with the believers in Damascus.

The large Jewish population in the city had been expecting Saul's arrival. At the first opportunity, Saul went to the synagogues to preach publicly. But he did not teach hatred and death to the followers of Jesus. Instead, he urged them to listen to a new message. He told them that Jesus of Nazareth had come to earth as God's Promised One. The prophets had predicted His coming centuries earlier.

"Who is that man, and where did he get this strange teaching?" one of the listeners asked someone standing nearby.

"Isn't he the man from Jerusalem?" an acquaintance responded. "He was supposed to remind us to keep the traditions of our faith. In fact, I'm sure he's the same man. He came to arrest Jesus' followers – to take them back to the chief priests."

"Yes," added another in shocked surprise, "his plans were well known. He had plans to kill everyone who worshiped Jesus. Why is he now telling us to follow Him?"

Each day Saul's preaching became bolder and more powerful. He claimed that Jesus was the Messiah, the Son of God, and Saul's words carried convincing proof. The Jews in Damascus tried to argue against Saul, but they were not able to prove his claims false.

*   *   *   *   *   *   *

Summer, A.D. 35 to A.D. 37

Soon after his conversion, Saul went out alone into the desert sands of Arabia to be taught by the Lord. When he returned, he preached in the Arabian city of Damascus. After many months the Jews tired of his message. They met to discuss the problems he was creating among them. "We must stop Saul from preaching. He is influencing too many people."

"How do you suggest we stop him?" one of them questioned.

"There is only one way to properly silence him – kill him at the first opportunity."

Chapter
FOUR

Escapes

Damascus, Jerusalem, Caesarea

Spring, A.D. 37, Damascus

"Place armed guards at the city gates," the governor of Damascus ordered. "If anyone sees Saul – kill him! He must not escape!"

High, unbroken walls surrounded the city of Damascus. They rose several times higher than the height of a man. Anyone wanting to leave the city had to pass through the city gates. Saul's enemies watched for him around the clock hoping to catch him. His activities had irritated the Jewish leaders to the point where they were ready to take action against their former champion.

But Saul had new friends who cared for his safety. One of them lived in a house attached to the city wall. "We'll help you escape," the friend offered. "We could arrange to hide you in a large basket and let you down through our window in the wall."

One night Saul left his home and secretly made his way along the city streets. Whenever he neared someone who might recognize him, a warning prickle rose on the back of his neck and he stepped further into the shadows. His heart raced until that person had passed by and he was safely out of danger. At last he reached the home of his friend and fellow-disciple, who lived in the house by the wall. He knocked quietly and sighed in relief when his friend opened the door. Several had come to the house to say their good-byes.

Saul had entered the city in humility as a blind man. At that time he did not know what the future held. Tonight, for the cause of Christ, he had agreed to escape from Damascus in an equally humbling manner.

His friends attached a long rope to a large round basket. "Climb in," one of the men said, motioning to Saul. Then, turning to the others, he admonished, "Quiet everyone! We need to listen for any activity outside the wall." Saul stepped in and got himself settled.

"Do you hear anything?" one of them whispered after a couple of minutes.

"No, it sounds quiet."

"Are you ready, Saul?"

"Yes."

"May God protect you."

Strong arms slowly pushed the basket through the opening as his friends tightly gripped the rope. Saul grasped the sides of the basket with nervous, sweaty palms. It creaked and groaned beneath the weight even of his small frame. The basket inched downwards on the outside of the city wall. The rope above him scraped against the stone windowsill, and he hoped the unusual sound would not attract attention. Each time the basket turned in a semi-circle he felt lightheaded. He reached out toward the wall trying to steady the basket as it swayed back and forth. One final thump told him he had reached the ground. He stood up, steadied himself, and climbed out. With a final wave he disappeared into the night, undetected by his would-be captors.

He hurried away from the city as fast as his feet could carry him. He made his way southwest toward Mount Hermon to return to Jerusalem.

Summer, A.D. 37, Jerusalem

Saul remembered the raging hatred in his heart that had driven him to leave Jerusalem. Many believers had suffered at his hands, and the memory now caused him to burn with shame. His former friends and co-workers would no longer welcome him or even greet him. But Saul had not come to meet his old friends. He wanted to see the apostle Peter.

*   *   *   *   *   *   *

While Saul was settling into his room in Jerusalem, Christ's followers met in the home of one of the believers in another part of the city. They had gathered to discuss how to deal with the man Saul, the persecutor of the church. "What do you think of the fact that Saul now professes to be a follower of Jesus the Messiah? Do you think his faith is genuine?" one of them asked.

"It's probably a trick," another responded. "He will befriend us and then hand us over to the authorities."

"This whole situation makes me uneasy. How can we trust him after all he has done?"

"We can't. I don't believe he is a true disciple."

Their fear grew as they talked. "Let's not have anything to do with him. He was once our enemy and we should treat him as such."

"I agree," Peter added. "I am afraid of Saul."

Barnabas, a Jew from the tribe of Levi and a native of Cyprus, had been a follower of Jesus since the earliest days of the Church. He had remained silent until now, but finally he spoke up. "I disagree with all of you. Saul is genuine, and he must be given a chance to prove himself."

"But – what if he acts like he is one of us – then turns us over to the authorities?"

"I am willing to take that risk," Barnabas said firmly.

*   *   *   *   *   *   *

A short time later Saul paid Barnabas a visit. "Welcome," Barnabas said in a friendly manner as he invited Saul into his home and offered him a place to sit.

"Would you be able to help me?" Saul asked. "Peter has refused to have anything to do with me. He's afraid of me because of my past life."

"You're right. He is afraid of you."

"But all I want to do is to get to know him."

"Saul," Barnabas said, "tell me how the Lord spoke to you."

Saul recounted the story of his conversion and how he had suffered persecution at the hands of the Jews in Damascus.

"I believe you are a true follower of Jesus," Barnabas encouraged. "I'll visit Peter and try to convince him that you are, indeed, a changed man."

*   *   *   *   *   *   *

Barnabas traveled through the streets until he found Peter's house. "I have been talking with Saul. Why don't you give him a chance? The Lord spoke directly to him as he traveled to Damascus, and now the change in his life is dramatic. Consider all the evidence. He no longer hunts down followers of 'the Way' or treats them cruelly. He was baptized in Damascus, and he has since been preaching in the name of Jesus. He has already suffered persecution. Is that not enough to prove that he is genuine? Please try to accept him."

Peter stroked his chin and nodded. "Perhaps you have convinced me. I will at least agree to meet with him."

"Praise God," Barnabas exclaimed. "I will find Saul and tell him the news."

When Saul and Peter finally met, they had many things to talk about, for they now had much in common. For fifteen days Saul stayed with Peter. The two men visited as brothers in the Lord, as equals.

After spending this time with Peter, Saul visited James the

Just, the Lord's half-brother. James' faith was also new, having become a disciple only after the death and resurrection of Jesus.

The followers of Christ watched Saul during his time in Jerusalem. Evidence showed that he had genuinely changed. He preached without fear in the name of the Lord Jesus.

The Hellenists opposed Saul. They were Jews from a local synagogue who had adopted the Greek language, customs, and culture. Whenever Saul spoke, they violently disagreed with him. Their darkened minds had only one aim – to capture and kill Saul. Though they tried to arrest him, Saul always managed to escape.

One day while Saul prayed in the Temple, the Lord spoke to him in a vision. "Hurry! You must escape from Jerusalem! Go immediately. These people will not listen to your voice or receive your words concerning Me."

"But, Lord," Saul replied, "I lived in Jerusalem for years. I traveled from place to place arresting, imprisoning, and beating believers. The people knew that I consented to the death of Stephen."

"Go," the Lord said. "I am sending you far away from Jerusalem to other nations." The Lord had made his instructions clear.

The believers showed great concern for Saul's safety as well. "We will help you escape from Jerusalem," someone offered.

A few hours later Saul and a small group of believers slipped unnoticed through the Damascus Gate. After traveling northward for a time, they took the road that forked to the left, then continued west toward the coast. At nightfall the tired travelers stopped at a resting house.

Autumn, A.D. 37, Caesarea (Roman province of Judea)

The next day they completed their journey to the coastal town of Caesarea. Herod the Great had built this modern city a few decades earlier and named it for the Roman emperor Caesar Augustus.

Saul and his friends traveled through the large, well-planned city. The streets crossed each other at right angles in an orderly way. Attractive buildings of white stone stood along the water's edge. Palms swayed in the sea breezes and whitecaps rolled to shore. Sandy beaches ran parallel to the coast. But Herod the Great had decided that the city should be a great seaport. He built a large harbor with a massive, semi-circular stone wall to protect the harbor at all times. Government buildings stood near the water-front, as did the large amphitheater and a dramatic theater further down the coast. Many people traveled through this busy, commercial center located on the trade routes heading inland. Because of that, Saul would pass through this city several times during his lifetime.

Ancient port of Caesarea

The harbor stood at the heart of the city. Saul breathed deeply of the fresh sea air. Ships from Egypt, Athens, and Cyprus bobbed in the turquoise-blue waters, but no waves entered the protected port. Saul found a ship sailing to Tarsus and paid his fare. He said his good-byes to those who had traveled to the coast with him. As he boarded, water gently lapped against the sides of the ship.

Strong men rowed the vessel out of the harbor into the open sea and hoisted the mainsail. The blowing wind snapped the sail back and forth while the vessel bobbed up and down in the choppy waters. As the hours passed, a glowing sun slipped into the sea, and the sailors looked to the stars for guidance. Saul bedded down on the deck and praised the Lord for His protection. Once again, God had provided a way of escape from enemies who wanted to kill him.

Saul arrived safely in Tarsus, the city of his birth. He would use this opportunity to preach Christ throughout the provinces of Syria and Cilicia. However, he did not personally visit the churches in Judea at this time.

What would the future hold?

Roman Emperors in the First Century

Caesar Augustus
Emperor of Rome
27 B.C. to A.D. 14

Tiberius Caesar
Emperor of Rome
A.D. 14 to 37

Gaius (Caligula)
Emperor of Rome
A.D. 37 to 41

Nero
Emperor of Rome
A.D. 54 to 68

Claudius
Emperor of Rome
A.D. 41 to 54

Chapter
⌒FIVE⌐

The Roman Empire

A.D. 37 to 41

The Roman Empire ruled the entire area surrounding the Mediterranean Sea. No country could wage war on Rome and expect to win. The Empire included most of Europe, the Middle East, and the northern coastal area of Africa. The millions of people who lived in the Empire spoke many languages and worshiped many gods.

The Empire had its beginning in 27 B.C. when the grand-nephew of Julius Caesar was given the title Caesar Augustus. This first emperor had power to direct religious, public, and military life. Since Julius Caesar had called himself a god, Augustus referred to himself as god's son. He allowed a temple to be built in Pergamum, Asia Minor, where a statue of his likeness was worshiped. Augustus ruled the Empire until the time of his death in A.D. 14. Afterwards the people of the Roman Empire worshiped him as 'Divine Augustus.' The practice of emperor worship increased over the years.

Tiberius Caesar, stepson of Augustus, was proclaimed Emperor to replace him. He ruled well – balancing the budget and choosing efficient governors for the provinces. In A.D. 26, Tiberius agreed to have a temple built in Smyrna, Asia Minor, for the people to worship him. That same year he sent Pontius Pilate to rule the Roman province of Judea. Seven years into his term of service (A.D. 33), Pilate left his palace in Caesarea to go to Jerusalem to deal with Jesus, the King of the Jews.

In A.D. 37, four years after Jesus' crucifixion, Tiberius recalled Pontius Pilate to Rome and replaced him with Governor Felix. While Pilate was traveling back to Rome, Emperor Tiberius died. This was the same year that Saul escaped from Jerusalem to go to Caesarea en route to Tarsus.

A popular young prince named Gaius replaced Tiberius. People lined the streets of Rome to catch a glimpse of him. Soldiers saluted with enthusiastic cries of "Hail, Caesar!" He had a childhood nickname, Caligula (Little Boot). His father's soldiers had called him this because he liked to march around in a small soldier's uniform with tiny boots. Gaius (Caligula) was the great-grandson of Caesar Augustus, whose census had sent Mary and Joseph to Bethlehem years earlier.

When Caligula came to power, his sister Agrippina the Younger lived at the palace. While there, she gave birth to Lucius Domitus who was later known as Nero. When the child was three years old, Caligula sent them away. In the days ahead, Nero's life would cast a great and dark shadow across history, which would affect followers of Christ, including Saul.

At first the people liked Caligula. He appeared to be both courteous and generous. After a serious illness, however, he showed signs of being mentally unbalanced. His character became monstrous, and he murdered many people, including one of his sisters. Immorality filled his life and he wasted his money on foolish projects and raised taxes. Some of the richest Romans were condemned to death so he could take all their goods. He demonstrated irrational behavior by appointing his horse to the senate. Caligula believed himself to be all the gods at once, taking his role most seriously by sitting in the temples dressed as one of the gods. Several temples were built with his statue inside.

Caligula was close friends with Herod Agrippa I although

Agrippa was twenty years older. Both men had grown up in Rome. When Caligula came to power, he gave Agrippa the title of 'king' and gave him an area northeast of Palestine to govern. Two years later he also gave him Galilee and Perea. Agrippa was the grandson of Herod the Great (the Herod who had tried to kill Jesus at his birth), and he was also the brother of Herodias, the woman who caused the death of John the Baptist.

One day in A.D. 40, Caligula received a letter concerning the citizens in the town of Jamnia, a town of Palestine located 30 miles west of Jerusalem on the Mediterranean Sea. He read the letter aloud, sharing information as he went. "Listen to this," he proudly exclaimed to an official nearby. "The Greeks have built a brick altar to honor me as a god," he read smiling. But the next sentence brought a scowl. "What is this!" he cried out, glaring at the page. "The Jews tore down the altar – destroyed it! How dare they refuse to worship me as their god! I will show them who their god really is!"

"How do you propose to do that?" the official asked.

"I will order that my statue be erected in the Temple in Jerusalem. My wishes will be fulfilled! I will be their god!"

"Will you be able to carry out such a plan?"

"Yes, of course! The new governor of Syria will have a statue made, have it covered with gold, and arrange for its transport down to Jerusalem. He will then lead two legions of men to Jerusalem. There they will set up my statue in the Holy of Holies. With thousands of soldiers on hand, the Jews will have no choice but to accept their new god."

When the Jews in Palestine learned about Caligula's plans, it caused loud protests. They would rather die than have this happen. Thankfully, before Caligula put this plan into action, his friend Herod Agrippa influenced him to change it. Caligula then sent another command to reverse the earlier one.

About this time someone found two of Caligula's secret notebooks in which he had listed names of Roman Senate members he was planning to kill. And there was no reason to doubt his threats.

Caligula had already forced many top men, and even some of their families, to commit suicide. Senators, palace members, and the military all agreed that it was necessary to kill Caligula before he killed all of them. On a cold January day in A.D. 41, a guard ambushed Caligula in one of the palace's secret passages and ended his life with a sword.

In spite of the personal lives of some of the emperors, the Roman government appeared to run efficiently. This was due to their united military power and the skill of the governors.

Claudius, a man in his early fifties, replaced his nephew Caligula. Claudius was a short man, though solidly built. He had not been a serious candidate for emperor during Caligula's lifetime because he was crippled. Claudius appeared simple because of a stutter, a tendency to drool, and a nervous tic when under pressure. Because of these apparent imperfections, his family had kept him out of public view. Yet Claudius spent much of his time studying and eventually he wrote important works. During his reign he improved conditions in the Roman Empire. He increased Agrippa's kingdom to include Judea and Samaria. He allowed his niece Agrippina and her boy Nero to return to Rome. Within a short time Agrippina married Crispus, a wealthy senator. She was one of the richest and most beautiful women in Rome, but she had a dark and evil heart.

Two years after coming to power, Claudius conquered Britain and made it a Roman province. The people of Rome celebrated the victory and burned incense to their gods. A temple was built in Britain to honor Claudius.

A good number of Jewish people lived in Rome, but at various times laws banished them from the city. Tiberius ordered them to leave during his rule in A.D. 19, and later Claudius would command the same thing. Few people in Rome were aware of a group of people known as followers of 'the Way' who had once worshiped within the Jewish movement but now met separately as the Church.

Chapter
❧SIX❧

Christians

Jerusalem, Antioch of Syria, Jerusalem, Caesarea

Spring, A.D. 41, Jerusalem

"I have recent news from Antioch," one of the believers in Jerusalem said to a leader of the church.

"What is happening in that part of Syria?"

"Do you remember those who fled for their lives when Stephen was stoned?"

"Yes, I recall that persecution as if it happened yesterday."

"Well, the believers who escaped from Jerusalem traveled to distant areas. Some went to Phoenicia, including the ports of Tyre and Sidon. Others traveled to Cyprus, that large island in the Mediterranean, or to Cyrene, the port city on the north coast of Africa. Some time later these same men moved to Antioch where they have been witnessing to a large number of Jews, and now there are many followers of 'the Way.'"

"Wonderful!"

"These men also told the Gentiles that Jesus Christ had come to be their Savior, and many of them responded to the message. Now there are a large number of Gentiles who also follow 'the Way.'"

"Is anyone teaching these new believers?"

"No – once a person is saved, no one gives them further teaching."

"But new believers must be taught from God's Word," the leader said. "I will meet with other believers, and together we will seek the Lord's direction as to what can be done."

Within a short time the leaders of the church at Jerusalem chose someone suitable to go to Antioch. Barnabas was a man full of faith and the Holy Spirit. He would be the right person to teach and to encourage those who had recently made a decision to follow Christ.

A.D. 41, Antioch of Syria

Barnabas agreed to go to Antioch, and after making preparations he traveled north. He arrived tired and dusty, but his heart was full of joy. He looked forward to teaching those who were young in the faith.

Antioch of Syria was the third largest city in the Roman Empire. It was located three hundred miles north of Jerusalem and sixteen miles east of the Mediterranean Sea. It overlooked the Orontes River and stood at the foot of Mount Silpios. Bridges joined the city to a small island in the middle of the Orontes River on which the Royal Palace was located. This city had been founded more than three hundred years earlier by one of the generals of Alexander the Great, and it now held a population of half a million people.

Many Greeks in the city of Antioch followed the Isis cult, a religion that worshiped the Egyptian goddess of fertility. Isis was popular in this city and in other parts of the Roman Empire. Images of her were even imprinted on the floor in mosaics made with small pieces of colored stone.

A temple to Jupiter and a theater stood on the side of Mount Silpios. Four miles west of the city was a temple of the Greek god Apollo, son of Zeus and twin to Artemis. Worshipers believed him to be the god of light, truth, poetry, and music. Daphne was the name given to a park of woods and waters that surrounded this temple. The park was a favorite pleasure resort where people with low moral standards mixed the worship of idols with the practice of immorality.

Barnabas met with the new believers in Antioch and faithfully warned them to stay away from this harmful influence. "Do not give in to the pressures around you," he told them. "Remain faithful to the Lord. He is the True Light who shines into the darkness. Listen to His voice."

Barnabas worked long hours teaching them but was unable to meet all the demands on his time.

Spring, A.D. 43

Since he needed help, Barnabas left Antioch and traveled to Tarsus in search of Saul. When he found him, the two men sat down to talk. "Will you come to Antioch?" Barnabas asked. "There are many Jews and Gentiles who are following Christ, and I don't have time to teach them all."

Saul's intense eyes brightened as he drank in the news. Without hesitation he turned to Barnabas and spoke with a quiver of emotion in his voice, "I have been in this area for several years waiting for God to indicate His future plans to me. Before I left Jerusalem, God said He would send me far away from Jerusalem to other nations. Yes, I will come and help teach Jews and Gentiles in Antioch. I am prepared to leave as soon as possible and to go wherever He leads."

Saul hurriedly packed up the articles and food he needed for the trip. As they traveled back to Antioch together, Saul and Barnabas talked excitedly of the things that God was doing in Syria.

For an entire year Barnabas and Saul met with the church at Antioch and taught them. Believing Jews and Gentiles witnessed to others in the downtown area. The main street was bordered on either side by colonnades. These rows of pillars placed at regular intervals gave the city an attractive appearance. The roadway itself was paved with polished stone. Passersby chattered among themselves or stopped to listen to believers talk about Christ. At times the city people asked questions or had conversations with them. These 'Christ-people' gradually came to be known as 'Christians.' The people of Antioch were the first ones to use this term.

*   *   *   *   *   *   *

A.D. 44, Jerusalem

King Agrippa, ruler of Galilee, Perea, Judea, and Samaria, followed the Law of Moses and liked to please the Jews. He persecuted any who belonged to the Church, hoping to discourage and defeat its leaders. He gave orders to arrest the apostle James and kill him by the sword. At this news, the Jews rejoiced. This James was the brother of John and both were sons of Zebedee and were apostles of the Lord.

"Continue with the arrests!" King Herod Agrippa ordered. "And be sure to find the apostle Peter. He is one of the leaders of the church. Put him in prison and guard him closely."

"Yes, your Excellency."

"And tell the guards to chain him down so he does not escape! I will deal with him as I dealt with James."

"Have you considered, your Excellency, that it is the time of the Jewish Passover celebrations? These festivals often bring disorder and riots."

"Yes, of course," Agrippa agreed, "the Jews' seven-day festival is under way. Travelers have flooded the city. This means more tension for all of us. I will wait until Jerusalem returns to normal."

When Passover ended, the authorities arrested Peter and set the time for his public trial and death. Peter's sandals and coat were tossed in the corner of a prison cell and he was chained between two guards. Every time he moved, heavy chains banged together. Two other soldiers guarded the door of his cell. "You have escaped from prison before," one of them mocked, "but you won't this time."

The night before the trial the Christians gathered to pray for his release. In spite of his surroundings, Peter relaxed and fell into a deep sleep. But in the middle of his sleep an angel of the Lord stood in front of him and a light shone in the cell. The angel tapped him on his side. "Wake up, Peter. Let's go!"

Peter opened his eyes and blinked in surprise. The chains dropped from his wrists without a sound. "Get dressed," the angel urged. "Put on your sandals and your coat. Come with me."

Peter, unsure if he was awake or asleep, stepped from between the sleeping guards and quietly followed the angel through the hallway of the prison. Silently, as if in a dream, he walked undetected past one set of guards, then another. The angel and Peter continued walking until they came to the iron gates that led into the city of Jerusalem. The large gate swung open by itself. Toward the end of the first street the angel disappeared. Peter stood wide-awake and alone on a dark, deserted street. His mind raced back to the night's events, and he shivered. "This is really happening to me!" he gasped in disbelief to no one in particular. "I am a free man. The Lord sent His angel and delivered me from the hands of Herod Agrippa and from certain death."

With eagerness in every step he hurried down the street as quietly as he could to the house of Mary, the mother of John Mark. Peter knocked at her door and waited for an answer. More insistently, he knocked again. No one came. "Where is everyone? Can no one hear me?" he muttered to himself as he banged more loudly.

A servant girl, Rhoda, finally heard his knocking and ran to the entrance of the house. "Who is there?" she called.

"It's Peter," an urgent voice responded from the darkness outside the gate.

With excitement Rhoda ran back into the house. With eyes sparkling she announced to the prayer group, "Peter is at the gate!"

"You're mad!"

"No I'm not. He is here. I recognized his voice."

"It must be his angel."

Peter continued to knock.

Rhoda hurried away from the room full of people and returned to unlock the door. A moment later she re-entered the room with Peter following behind her. Everyone looked up in stunned disbelief. "Peter!" one of the group exclaimed. "We thought you were still in jail!"

Everyone gathered around him and talked excitedly as they welcomed him warmly, reaching out to touch him to be sure he was real. "Our prayers have been answered," one of them said.

Peter held up his hand, motioning for silence. "Listen," he said, "and I will tell you how the Lord sent his angel to deliver me from prison."

He recounted the story and ended with a request. "Would someone go and tell James, the Lord's brother, and the other Christians that I am free? I must not stay here or the authorities will find me. I need to go into hiding for a time."

*   *   *   *   *   *   *

The next morning at dawn, one of the prison guards stirred. He opened his eyes to check on his prisoner. Suddenly he sat bolt upright. He looked down in horror at the chains hanging from his wrist. He reached over and shook the other guard. "Wake up!" he gasped. "Where is Peter? He's not here!" The two men stared in disbelief at the empty spot between them.

The broken chains clattered as the two guards jumped to their feet, fumbling noisily with the door. After leaving the empty cell, the frightened men woke up the whole prison searching for the missing man.

"He is not here," a guard finally conceded. "How could he have escaped?"

"The king will have to be notified of Peter's escape," the prison keeper warned.

*   *   *   *   *   *   *

When Herod received the message, he ordered a search and called the guards to answer for their actions.

"Tell me the events of the night," Herod ordered.

"The prisoner Peter was between us, chained to our wrists. After he fell asleep, we allowed ourselves to sleep as well. Neither of us heard anything. When we awoke this morning, he was gone."

"Do you expect me to believe that a man chained between two strong men escaped while they slept?"

"Yes, your Excellency."

"And you never heard or saw anything?"

"That is exactly what happened."

"Your explanation is not believable," Herod said, as he turned to another set of guards. "Take these men out, and put them to death."

A.D. 44, Caesarea

Soon after this, King Herod Agrippa traveled to Caesarea, the location of the government office under the Romans. This beautiful coastal city boasted a large harbor, as well as a theater and an amphitheater.

Herod Agrippa was angry at this time with the cities of Tyre and Sidon, the two seaports located further north on the Mediterranean Coast. Some of the residents of those cities came down to Caesarea to visit Blastus, the man in charge of the king's business. "Please," one of them pleaded, "will you arrange peace between us and Herod Agrippa? The king is the one who supplies us with our food." The residents pleaded for a peaceful solution and won Blastus over to their side.

"All right, I will arrange a day for you," Blastus told them. "I suggest you present yourselves to the king and make peace with him publicly."

On the chosen day Herod Agrippa awoke before dawn. He put on his royal robes, dressing from head to toe in woven silver. Herod arrived at Caesarea's outdoor amphitheater just as the first rays of sun shone over the horizon. He sat on his throne, to make a public statement to the people of Tyre and Sidon. As the sun reflected from his silver clothing, it shone like a blinding light to those who had gathered.

First one, and then another, and finally the entire crowd shouted, "It is the voice of a god! It is not a man."

A pleased smile played on Herod Agrippa's lips. Proudly he beckoned the crowd to continue their worship. But in that instant an angel of the Lord struck him with a deadly disease, and he was carried out of the theater, a dying man. He had stolen the honor that belongs to God alone. He died at the age of 54, having served four years under the Roman Emperor Caligula (37-41) and three years (41-44) under Emperor Claudius.

A.D. 47

Two or three years earlier, Agabus had warned that there would be a famine in Judea. Just as he had prophesied, there was a lack of rain that resulted in poor harvests. The people of Jerusalem did not have enough to eat. God's provision for the believers there came by the hands of the Christians in Antioch who had saved a large amount of money. The Christians now handed over to Barnabas and Saul what they had set aside. The two men traveled from Antioch to Jerusalem to give this gift to the elders there. It would be used to purchase food for distribution to the hungry. Grain was available from Egypt, as well as figs from Cyprus.

Barnabas and Saul took John Mark with them and returned to Antioch to await further direction from the Lord. Barnabas, once a wealthy landowner who had lived on the island of Cyprus, was related to Mark. Mark's mother Mary, a woman of wealth, is the same Mary who had earlier hosted the prayer meeting in her house when Peter escaped from prison.

Caesarea's outdoor amphitheater located beside the Mediterranean Sea

GALATIA

Antioch of Pisidia

TAURUS MTS

Iconium

PISIDIA

Lystra

Derbe

CILICIA

Perga
Attalia

PAMPHYLIA

Tarsus

Seleucia

Antioch

SYRIA

CYPRUS

Salamis

Damascus

Paphos

Mt. Hermon

Sidon

Tyre

MEDITERRANEAN
SEA

100 miles
(160 km)

Caesarea

Sea of
Galilee

Jordan R.

Jerusalem

Dead
Sea

JUDEA

Alexandria

EGYPT

Paul's First Missionary Journey

Chapter
⋐SEVEN⋑

Voice for God
(1st Missionary Journey)

Antioch of Syria, Cyprus, Perga, Antioch of Pisidia, Iconium, Lystra

April, A.D. 48, Antioch of Syria

"Let's go!" The anticipation in Saul's voice was obvious as he called to Barnabas and John Mark. The two men hurried out of the house and joined Saul in the cool morning air of Antioch. Their bags were packed with provisions for the trip, including an assortment of dried fruit, nuts, and unleavened bread. Skins filled with drinking water would quench their thirst. The rising sun lay hidden behind the mountain to the east. Their quick footsteps echoed through the city streets as they crossed the bridge that spanned the Orontes River.

"Our trip would be easier," John Mark commented, "if ships sailed down this river to the coast."

"You're right," Barnabas responded. "Riding down that twisting waterway would make the trip shorter. The river empties into the Mediterranean Sea at Seleucia near the foot of the mountain. However, the shallow sections make it impossible."

The men moved southwest through the rich, green countryside, thankful that the cool, damp months of winter had passed. Saul's Roman citizenship allowed him freedom to travel anywhere throughout the great Empire that reached west to the country of Spain, east to the Euphrates River, south to Egypt, and north to the recently acquired Britain.

Saul's heart was full of gratitude to the Lord as he recalled the recent autumn and winter months. The Holy Spirit had directed them to make this trip. Saul and several others had spent the winter in Antioch teaching spiritual truths to new Christians. While the prophets and teachers of the church had fasted and prayed, the Holy Spirit spoke to them. "Set apart to Me Barnabas and Saul. I have called them to a special work." The leaders had continued to fast and pray. Then, laying their hands on Barnabas and Saul, they released them from their regular duties and entrusted them to the Lord's work.

A gust of wind blew up the valley, tugging at Saul's coat and bringing him back to the present. For several hours the three men talked about the coming work as they traveled southwest. Near the end of their fifteen-mile journey, the road sloped downwards toward Seleucia and curved in front of low hills. Wisps of white cloud floated across the bright sky as the harbor came into view. The gentle pulse of waves washed ashore.

Saul and Barnabas soon boarded a ship. Land breezes and the flow of the current moved the ship and its passengers out of the harbor toward Cyprus, one hundred thirty miles away. Saul breathed deeply of the fresh, salty air as he stood on deck, thinking and praying. The ship glided on the rippling waters into a seemingly endless blue sea.

At the end of the first day the sinking sun danced on the surface of the water until it shone like shimmering diamonds. A low bank of clouds on the horizon alternated shades of yellow, pink, and gray until the sun faded into the sea. In the twilight the shadowy figures of the crew bustled about preparing for the night. Finally, as darkness rested on the water, the stars began to shine. Passengers bedded down on the deck. Saul shivered, pulling his cloak up to his chin to block out the cool spring wind. The waves and water splashing against the ship finally lulled him to sleep.

The ship continued to progress across the open stretch of water until signs of land appeared. Barnabas stood on deck with Saul and Mark. "Do you see those islands?" he asked, pointing into the distance.

"The small rocky ones?" Saul asked, as spray from the sea dampened his skin.

"Yes. Only a few birds live there. But these islands tell us that the eastern tip of the Karpass Peninsula on Cyprus will soon come into view."

Within a short time the ship sailed south of the peninsula. A thin strip of land stretched into the sea like the tail of a giant stingray. To their right, turquoise waves crashed ashore on a golden beach. Gently sloping hills rose behind the shoreline.

The ship moved west for a few hours until it arrived at the well-kept harbor of Salamis. The crew shouted orders as pulleys and ropes creaked from strain, and the ship came to a standstill in the crystal waters. The three walked ashore, passing dockworkers busily loading copper and fruit onto ships destined for countries such as Syria, Phoenicia, and Cilicia.

The eastern tip of the Karpass Peninsula, Cyprus

April, A.D. 48, Cyprus

Salamis, the main commercial city of the island of Cyprus, stood in a level spot by a small river at the eastern end of the great plain. "Saul," Barnabas said with excitement, "this is it! This is the island where I was raised. To the north is a mountain range, and another to the south – with a fertile plain in between."

Saul, Barnabas, and John Mark walked through the gate of the walled city in the warm spring sunshine. The aroma of a home cooked meal occasionally drifted from open windows out into the street.

"This city appears to be like many others, dominated by idolatry," Saul commented, as his voice choked with emotion.

"Yes," Barnabas agreed. "There are many temples dedicated to Zeus. But the people of Salamis are preoccupied with more than their gods; entertainment is also a priority. The stadium is located at the north end of town, and there are also public baths, an amphitheater, a gymnasium, and a theater decorated with columns and marble statues."

Saul drank in the details as Barnabas described the city.

"Isn't there a large Jewish population as well?" Saul asked, as their sandals beat out a steady rhythm on the stone roadway.

"Yes, there are several synagogues."

"More than anything I have a deep desire to preach Christ. Where are the synagogues located – and the forum for public meetings?"

Barnabas supplied the information for Saul.

At the first opportunity, the three men visited the synagogues. Saul preached that the Messiah, the Lord Jesus Christ, had come to save His people from their sins. God-fearing Jews paid attention to his message.

After a time in Salamis the men traveled west visiting fishing villages on the southern coast of Cyprus and preaching in towns with Jewish communities. The island road took them up hills, down into winding valleys, and past groves of fig trees and fields of newly planted corn. A large, shallow salt lake lay near the western coast, a place where thousands of flamingos spent the winter. Mount Olympus stood majestically to the north. Clouds floating across the sky painted dark patches on the mountain. Melting snow trickled down the slopes. Small, yellow wild flowers poked their heads through the grass. The travelers continued west to a low plateau. At this point the men followed a straight, paved road leading down into the port city of Paphos on the western tip of the island. This was the capital, the seat of the Roman government on Cyprus. The men walked through the main gates and into a city of villas, palaces, and fortresses. A theater was set into the hillside. Palm trees waved in the evening breeze, and the red sky promised another warm day.

Barnabas, Saul, and Mark found a place to stay for the night. During the following days, they searched for the synagogue and preached the 'good news' in the streets. Many worshipers of false gods stopped to pay attention as Saul spoke. Paphos was the center for the worship of Aphrodite, the Greek goddess of love.

Before long, the town was talking about these three strangers who had come to teach new ideas. One day a messenger came to the men, "I work for Sergius Paulus, the Roman Governor of Cyprus. He requests that you come to his palace."

"Where is he located?"

"Follow me and I will lead you to him."

The messenger led Barnabas and Saul down the street and through courtyards. Together they entered the palace of the Roman Governor, an educated man who showed an interest in science and new ideas.

"What is your name?" the governor asked.

"My name is Paul," responded Saul, switching to his Roman name.

"Where are you from?"

"I am a Roman citizen from Tarsus in Cilicia."

"Is it true that you are a teacher of the Jews at the synagogue, and yet you are a freeborn Roman?" the governor asked with a twinge of curiosity. "Tell me what brings you to our city? Are you teaching a new way of thinking?"

"Yes, God brought me here to tell you about the true God – the One who created the world . . . ."

The governor listened carefully to the message about the God who sent His Son, the Lord Jesus Christ, to this world. He learned that Christ had died and had risen again and that God now wanted humans to pay attention to the voice of God, to repent of their sin, and to believe the message.

Without warning, Elymas, the governor's hired magician, interrupted, "Don't pay attention to these men."

Startled, Sergius Paulus glanced over at his magician, "Why not?"

"I don't like their message. Their teachings are worthless."

"But I invited them here so I could learn more about God's message," Sergius Paulus said firmly. Turning to the visitors he said, "Please continue to explain about your God."

Elymas, afraid that Paul would convert the governor and that he would lose his job as a magician, shouted angrily at Sergius Paulus. "Don't involve yourself with these men or their message. It is a useless, foreign message and their god has no power!"

But Saul, whose name had been changed to Paul, stared Elymas in the eye. Filled with the Holy Spirit, Paul stated, "You troublemaker and follower of the devil! You are distorting the truth! Stop plotting against God's saving ways. The Lord will lay his hand of punishment on you, and for a time you will be blind."

Even as the words fell from Paul's mouth, Elymas' eyes grew misty. He groped with outstretched arms, suddenly needing someone to lead him. "Help me," he begged, "I am in darkness. Please, someone, guide me."

The teaching about the Lord greatly impressed the governor and he believed in Christ.

By mid-summer, rainfall on Cyprus had stopped and temperatures soared. Paul, Barnabas, and Mark made plans to leave Paphos. Paul would continue to use his Roman name rather than Saul, his Jewish name, making it easier for him to travel freely within the Empire.

The three men walked down to the circular, rocky harbor below the city. Here they located and boarded a ship traveling to the mainland.

The crew lifted the anchor, allowing the ship to move gently forward along the west coast of Cyprus, passing low hills and stately palms. As the square sail billowed above their heads, the vessel cleared the tip of the island. The turquoise hue of the coastal waters deepened in color until only a cold, dark blue remained.

The ship continued through swelling waves as it headed northwest into the open sea. Pirates were a constant danger in coastal regions. Two days later the ship glided into the gulf at Attalia. Mountains, both to the left and to the right, stood guard over a large plain. The tall, hazy Taurus Mountains rose in the distance.

July, A.D. 48, Perga

After landing at Attalia, the men traveled seven miles inland to the Greek-speaking city of Perga. It was the capital city of the Roman province of Pamphylia in Asia, located on a hill by the Cestrus River. The men entered the city and walked through the wide streets, passing beautiful buildings with columns and porches. A temple to their local goddess stood on the Acropolis, a flat-topped hill overlooking the city. The three men discussed the coming work. "There will be many opportunities to preach God's Word to the Gentiles in this region," Barnabas observed.

The hot, humid coastal weather made work difficult. Among other problems, it created a welcoming atmosphere for buzzing flies and humming, malaria-infected mosquitoes. Traveling to higher ground would take them to a healthier climate in which to work.

"Are you ready to tackle the dangerous mountain ranges with their narrow passages?" Barnabas asked.

"I am anxious to go," Paul said enthusiastically. "The Lord will protect us from danger, even from roving bands of robbers. I am hoping for an early start in the morning."

While Paul and Barnabas prepared for the upcoming trip, John Mark waited for the right opportunity to speak. "I have recently had a change of mind."

"What is it?" Paul questioned.

"I will not be going across the mountains with you or finishing the trip."

"What? Are you going to desert us?"

"I have made plans to return to Jerusalem," Mark said quietly.

"How can you quit when the work is so great?" Paul responded, his temper flaring at the idea of anyone quitting the Lord's work.

The next morning Mark turned back. Paul and Barnabas climbed the foothills alone and headed toward the steep mountain passes. The cool air added color to their cheeks and brought physical refreshment, but the danger from enemies was constant.

July, A.D. 48, Antioch of Pisidia

The two traveled north for one hundred miles through bandit-infested mountains. Paul breathed heavily of the cooler air as they climbed narrow passes. Every muscle in his body ached. Day after day he pushed himself to complete the physically exhausting journey. At last they arrived at the rolling, grassy hills of the interior plateau.

Antioch of Pisidia, in the district of Phrygia, was located on the western bank of the river Anthios. It was an important commercial city that linked Ephesus, on the west coast, with Syria and Mesopotamia, far to the east. Phrygians, Greeks, and Jews all lived in the city, but years earlier Caesar Augustus had made it a Roman colony. The pagan Phrygian religion rejected marriage and preferred freedom. Greek and Roman law required its citizens to be born from a legally married couple. The city also had a synagogue for the Jews.

On the Sabbath day Paul and Barnabas found a seat in the synagogue. As usual, those in charge read from the Book of Moses and from the Prophets. When these readings were done, the leaders sent Paul and Barnabas a message. "Brethren, if you have any helpful words for the people, you are welcome to speak."

Paul stood up and lifted his sun-tanned hand to silence the crowd. "Men of Israel, and all who fear God, listen to what I have to say. God led you out of slavery...gave you land...and a king. He sent Jesus, the promised Savior of Israel, a descendant of King

David. The people of Jerusalem did not recognize who He was and demanded that Pilate have Him killed. His death was the fulfillment of prophecy. Faithful followers of Jesus placed Him in a tomb. However, God raised Him from the dead . . . and now . . ." he said as he glanced at Barnabas, "God has sent us to tell you 'good news!' In Jesus there is forgiveness of sin. Anyone who believes in Him is put right with God – and that is something that the Law of Moses could never do for you."

As Paul and Barnabas left the synagogue, people crowded around them. "Please come back next week," different ones begged. "Tell us more about this teaching."

"Lord willing, we will return and further explain the message," Paul responded.

During the week, Jews and Jewish converts who had attended the synagogue followed Paul around. He taught them and urged them to remain faithful to God.

The next week almost the entire city came to hear the men preach. How Paul longed for these people to respond to God's message. "God's love is great," Paul taught. "He invites all people to hear His voice. God is the one who told the light to shine in darkness. He is the same God who will shine light into your hearts."

Jewish leaders reacted with jealousy to his message. No matter what Paul said, the leaders argued against him. Paul's heart raced as his accusers continuously shouted loud insults. Finally, he responded boldly, "The 'good news' belongs first to the Jewish people. But...since you insist on rejecting the voice of God, His message will be offered to the nations, who until now have walked in darkness. God has appointed me to announce light to the Gentiles, so that those who live in the farthest parts of the earth can know His voice and be saved."

Paul's words delighted the Gentiles. "Paul, thank you for offering God's salvation to us," one of them commented.

"Do not thank me," Paul reminded them. "It is God's plan.

From the time of Abraham, God promised to send His Servant to bring salvation to the ends of the earth."

Some Gentiles had attended the synagogue, but others knew only the darkness of their pagan goddess Cybele. She was known as Mother Earth or the Great Mother. Devoted men who followed her became eunuchs. They dressed as women and behaved as though they were female. Followers of this religion were also associated with wild drinking parties, music, drumming, dancing, and immorality.

The light of Christ that Paul preached contrasted to the darkness of this religion. Thankfully, many received new life in Christ and were filled with joy and with the Holy Spirit. The Lord's message spread in this region.

While Paul preached, Jewish leaders met secretly in another part of the city to discuss Paul's preaching. "Can any of you suggest a way to force Paul and Barnabas to leave town?"

"What would be most effective?"

"There are women who worship at the synagogue who are married to high ranking Roman officials. Stir up these women as well as the city officials, and together they will run them out of town."

"Yes, that should work."

*   *   *   *   *   *   *

One day as Paul and Barnabas spoke in the streets, a mob surrounded them. "Leave our town," different ones yelled. "You are not welcome here." Several people grabbed the two men, pushing, pulling, and beating them as they shoved them along the streets toward the city gate.

The mob roughly tossed them outside the city. As the two preachers retreated, they shook the dust from their feet in protest – the unbelievers would be left to their own fate.

October, A.D. 48, Iconium

Paul and Barnabas traveled southeast for more than eighty miles along a military highway, the Imperial Road. Fifty years earlier slaves and convicts had constructed this road with its carefully fitted stones. The dry, dusty trip in the cool autumn air was made more bearable by inns where they could rest at night.

As they neared the city, Paul squinted into the distance, "Is that Iconium up ahead?"

"Yes, the city is set on a plateau with the Taurus Mountains off in the distance behind it."

"Finally – we are nearing our destination," Paul said with anticipation. He drank in the scenery – a river surrounding the city, the orchards, and the gardens. All were a welcome sight.

Upon arrival the men found the synagogue of the Jews and were invited to speak. Week after week the Spirit of God worked in the hearts of the people. Many believed, both Jews and Greeks. But the unbelieving Jews spoke angrily among themselves. "How dare these men!" one of the leaders said voicing his fury. "Their stories about a Christ who died on a Roman cross are irritating."

"Yes, and they say that their Christ rose from the dead."

"What blasphemy!"

"It is up to us to protect our people from believing anything so meaningless."

The Jewish leaders criticized Paul and Barnabas and caused many of the people to turn away from believing the message. However, because of concern for the people, the two men stayed in the city for several months and continued to speak boldly. The Lord gave them power to do miracles, but the people remained divided: some followed the Jews, and others believed the teaching of the two men of God.

By springtime the fever of hate had grown strong. The leaders of the town, along with the Jewish leaders and the crowds, shouted insults and made plans to stone them.

"Our lives are in danger," Paul said, as fear stirred in his stomach. "It is time to leave town."

"I agree," Barnabas responded. "Iconium has no Roman governor, so we will receive no protection from the Empire."

March, A.D. 49, Lystra

The men made a hurried escape toward the town of Lystra, eighteen miles southwest of Iconium. After hours of travel Paul and Barnabas crossed a ridge and entered a valley. Lystra was built on a low hill within this valley, while the Taurus Mountains stood off in the distance. A stream ran by the city and flowed to the east. Lystra was a Roman colony and had a base for soldiers who dealt with robbers and other raiders who roamed the Taurus Mountains, threatening the peace of Rome. Because the town was away from the main roads, the people spoke the Lycaonian language as well as the usual Greek.

Paul and Barnabas walked past a temple dedicated to Zeus, located outside the main gate of the city. Again, the men took the first opportunity to preach the gospel. Through their message, Lois and her daughter Eunice, practicing Jews, came to faith in Christ. Eunice had a son named Timothy.

One day as Paul preached in the street, a crippled man hung onto every word that he spoke.

"How long have you been crippled?" Paul asked.

"From birth," he said. "I have no strength in my feet. I have never walked."

"Do you have faith?"

"Yes, I do."

"Stand on your feet!" Paul commanded in a loud voice.

The man obeyed and jumped to his feet. His eyes widened in excitement as he put one foot in front of another to take his first step.

Nearby crowds stood amazed at the sight of this man jumping to his feet. Several gasped in surprise – this man had never walked before. Abandoning the Greek language, the bystanders shouted back and forth to one another in the Lycaonian language.

"The gods have come down to us and are like men!" one of

them cried. He motioned toward Barnabas. "This one must be Zeus. He is king of the gods."

Another pointed at Paul. "He is the one who is doing all the speaking. He must be Hermes, the messenger of the gods."

A priest of Zeus, standing nearby, added his comments in a most serious tone, "As gods, these men must be honored."

Paul threw a questioning glance at Barnabas and, standing on his tiptoes, shouted above the crowd. "What is happening? What are these people saying?"

"I cannot understand a word," Barnabas shouted back.

When the excitement settled down, Paul and Barnabas continued their preaching. Within minutes the lowing of oxen distracted them. A priest was guiding oxen up the street from the temple of Zeus. He had decked them with garlands and prepared them for sacrifice.

"Barnabas!" Paul said sharply, as his heart pounded in alarm and hot color poured into his cheeks. "The people are worshiping us as gods. These animals will be killed as a sacrifice to us."

"No," Barnabas objected. "Stop them!"

Both men reacted quickly by tearing their clothes from the neck to the hem to express their sorrow and protest. Waving his arms, Paul shouted, "This is blasphemy against God! Stop the sacrifice! Why are you doing these things? We are ordinary human beings like you. We have come to tell you to turn from these lifeless idols and serve the true and living God. He is the Creator of heaven and earth, of the sea and all the creatures. He is the One who gives us rain and good crops. He provides food for us and fills our hearts with gladness."

The crowd quieted down at Paul's words. Reluctantly, the priest removed the garlands from the oxen and led them away.

Before long, Jews from the neighboring towns of Iconium and Antioch of Pisidia arrived at Lystra to spy on Paul. One of them spoke to the crowds, "Don't pay attention to these men. Paul and Barnabas are troublemakers. We had to run them out of town.

Have nothing to do with them."

Paul continued to preach in the streets, but the mood had visibly changed. "Stone him!" a man from the crowd yelled as he picked up a few pebbles and threw them at Paul. Others joined in and showered Paul with stones. His heart thumped in his chest like a trapped bird. He scrambled to escape, but one of the stones knocked him senseless, and he collapsed to the ground.

"That's it," someone yelled in celebration. "He isn't moving!"

Someone leaned forward to check on him. "He isn't breathing. I think he is dead."

"Good. Let's throw his body outside the city."

Men grasped his arms and dragged him along the roadway. "And we thought he was a spokesman for Zeus," one of the men sneered.

"What a mistake!" another responded.

"He'll never use his voice to speak for the gods again."

Men continued to haul him past the temple of Zeus and dropped him in a heap outside the city gates in the warm spring sunshine. Dusting off their hands, the men of the town walked away, leaving this voice for God silent.

Chapter
⁐EIGHT⁐

Defender of Truth
(1st Missionary Journey continued)

Lystra, Derbe, Lystra, Iconium, Antioch of Pisidia, Antioch of Syria, Jerusalem, Antioch of Syria

June, A.D. 49, Lystra

P aul lay motionless on the ground. Disciples hurried over to his pale, lifeless body. Tears spilled down their cheeks. Barnabas knelt beside him and with quivering voice asked, "Paul, what have the people done to you?"

As Barnabas spoke, Paul's chest heaved and he tried to move. Stars floated around inside his aching head. His swollen eyes flickered as he forced them open. He glimpsed a sea of faces staring down at him before his eyes fell shut again. Every bone in his body ached.

"Paul, can you hear me?" Barnabas asked.

Slowly, Paul turned his throbbing head toward the familiar voice. "Barnabas," he whispered.

"Here, let me help," Barnabas said. Slowly he lifted Paul into a sitting position and brushed the pebbles from his back.

Welts and bruises covered Paul's body, but he was able to steady himself. "I'm going to be all right," he said, managing a faint smile. After a few minutes he stood up. In spite of his injuries, no bones appeared to be broken. "The people of this town may have rejected

God's truth by trying to kill me," he said in a faltering voice as he brushed the dust from his clothing, "but God still has work for me to do."

"What do you plan to do now?" a disciple asked.

"I must go back into Lystra."

"That sounds too dangerous," the disciple said with a worried look on his face.

"I have little choice. It is too late in the day to leave town. After the sun goes down, Barnabas and I will quietly re-enter the city. We will stay with one of the disciples for the night."

June, A.D. 49, Derbe

Paul and Barnabas left for Derbe early the next morning. Each carried a cloak and a supply of water and food as they traveled southeast across the plain. Near the end of their 60-mile trip, tall, scenic mountains rose in the distance. "Derbe is up ahead," Barnabas said, pointing at a low hill surrounded by the plain.

"Good. I can hardly wait to get there. The town looks isolated, right on the eastern edge of Galatia. Maybe that will be to our advantage."

Upon arrival Paul preached the 'good news.' Many chose to follow Christ. One of these was a man named Gaius.

It had now been over a year since Paul and Barnabas had set out on their missionary trip. Paul had no plans to go beyond the borders of Galatia. "It is time to return to the church in Antioch of Syria," Paul suggested to Barnabas.

"By now the church will be expecting a report of the Lord's work in Asia Minor."

"The shortest route home is through the Cilician Gates to Tarsus, but instead of doing that, I prefer to use the longer route so we can retrace our steps. I want to seize every opportunity to strengthen and encourage the new disciples in all the cities."

Summer, A.D. 49, Lystra, Iconium, Antioch of Pisidia

Paul and Barnabas stayed with the Christians at Lystra, the

town of Paul's stoning. From there the two men returned to Iconium and Antioch of Pisidia where churches had been established. Paul and Barnabas prayed and fasted for the newly founded churches and appointed godly men as elders. Paul encouraged the believers to continue in the faith. He reminded them that the Christian life would be full of hardships, and he urged them to respect the godly men who had been appointed as elders.

Paul and Barnabas traveled back through Pisidia, through Pamphylia, and south to the coastal city of Perga, where Mark had deserted them a year earlier. Paul preached before going down to the seaport of Attalia at the mouth of the Cataractes River. There these two tireless workers boarded a ship and sailed east toward Seleucia.

September, A.D. 49, Antioch of Syria

After leaving the ship the two men retraced their steps from the coast to the inland city of Antioch of Syria. This time the sea breezes that blew up through the valley came from behind them, making the trip easier. Trees, permanently bent by the wind, pointed them eastward up the valley toward the city.

City of Antioch, Syria

During the past year and a half the two missionaries had traveled about 1,250 miles. The cooler days of September had arrived when the weary travelers crossed the Orontes River. Their footsteps echoed along the cobblestone streets of Antioch, announcing their arrival.

News of their return traveled quickly, and the church gathered eagerly for their missionary report. Paul stood before the expectant group. "Barnabas, John Mark, and I visited cities on the island of Cyprus. After spending three months there, we traveled to Perga. From that city, Barnabas and I journeyed inland to the interior cities. God worked in each place and opened the door of faith to the Gentiles."

Paul gave a detailed account of their trip and reported that many had turned to Christ. Those gathered had varied reactions. "What a thrill to learn that the people of Asia Minor have responded to the gospel," one of the Christians exclaimed. "God is doing great things!"

But some questioned, "Won't all those converts cause future problems? Jewish Christians at Jerusalem are nervous about the increasing number of Gentile converts who have no connection to the synagogue."

"Why is that?" Paul asked.

"The lower moral standards of the Gentiles will change the structure of the church."

*   *   *   *   *   *   *

Although autumn days brought cooler temperatures, the apostle Peter made the trip from Jerusalem to Antioch to visit Paul, Barnabas, and others. This friendly ex-fisherman visited the Christians and happily ate meals with both Jewish and Gentile believers.

Shortly after Peter's arrival, co-workers of James the Just, the half-brother of Jesus, came from Jerusalem to Antioch. James was one of the leaders of the church at Jerusalem, and he would one day write the Epistle of James. These travelers contacted the elders of the church at Antioch and asked, "Why is Peter eating with Gentiles? He is making it more difficult for James and others in Jerusalem to work with their Jewish neighbors."

Upon hearing these remarks Peter changed his eating habits and refused to eat with Gentiles. Before long other Jewish

Christians, including Barnabas, copied Peter.

A short time later Paul visited Peter. Paul's dark eyes flashed in exasperation. "Peter, what are you doing? Why are you eating only with Jews? Do you not remember how you ate with Gentiles at Caesarea and even here at Antioch! Are you saying that Gentiles are second-class Christians?"

"I wanted to help the Jewish situation in Jerusalem," Peter said, defending himself.

"Peter," Paul said, as he looked straight into Peter's eyes, "you are a Jew by birth. You have been freed from the Jewish law and have been mixing with the Gentiles. Why are you trying to make these Gentiles obey the Law that you have abandoned? Jewish Christians are made right with God, not by doing what the Law commands but by faith in Christ alone. No one will ever be saved by obeying the Law. If salvation comes by keeping the Law, then Christ did not need to die!"

"You are right," Peter responded, hanging his head. "My decision was made in fear and does not help the cause of Christ."

About this time false brethren from Judea came secretly to observe the activity of the believers in Antioch. Before long, these brethren introduced new teaching. One of them stood up and taught, "A person cannot be saved unless he keeps the Jewish custom of circumcision taught by Moses."

Paul jumped to his feet, his heart pounding. "I object. No one can earn salvation by obeying the Law of Moses. That is twisting the truth!"

"It is necessary to keep Jewish traditions."

"No," Paul responded forcefully. "As a young man I followed the traditions of my Jewish faith. As a result, I participated in killing Christ's followers. But no more! I do not follow tradition – I follow only the Son of God!"

"Following God's Son is a good way to start, but that is only the beginning. From there a person must keep the Law of Moses."

"What? Have you lost your senses? Did God give His Holy

Spirit to people who obey the Law of Moses? No! The Spirit is promised to those who believe."

"I disagree. A person needs more than faith – he must do good works and keep the Law."

"Anyone who depends on the Law to become right with God is one who is under a curse. If a person keeps the whole Law but breaks one commandment, he is guilty of breaking them all."

The Judean disagreed and shook his head vigorously. "But people who are not required to obey God's Law will use their freedom to do whatever they want."

"A person either obeys 'all' of God's commands," Paul replied, "or he is cursed. Since no one can obey all of God's laws, that person needs outside help. Only Christ lived a perfect life. Because of that, He was able to carry the curse for our wrongdoing when He hung on the cross."

"Well, why did God give the Law in the first place?"

"He gave it to show people their guilt."

One of the elders had been listening to the discussion and made a suggestion. "Paul, this question must be settled. The elders will make a decision about what should be done."

After the elders met to discuss the situation, one of them spoke to Paul. "The elders plan to send you and Barnabas and a few of the local Christians to Jerusalem. There you can visit the apostles and elders to talk about this issue. Titus should go along with you. He is an uncircumcised Greek believer, and he will serve as a good example for their consideration."

The group set out, traveling south through Phoenicia and Samaria. Along the way, Paul gave missionary reports, telling groups of Jewish believers about the conversion of the Gentiles. This caused much joy among the brethren in these places.

Autumn, A.D. 49, Jerusalem

When the group arrived at Jerusalem, the church, apostles, and elders all welcomed them. Paul, the spokesman, stood before the group. "I would like to give a report of all the things that God has done through our ministry...."

He had hardly finished speaking when a man of faith who belonged to the sect of the Pharisees stood up. "Paul, I don't agree with your teaching. It is important and necessary to circumcise Gentiles who have faith in Christ."

"Yes," another added, "Gentiles must keep the Law of Moses."

"That's impossible!" Paul replied, as a hot rush swept through his blood. "There are large numbers of Gentiles in Caesarea, in Antioch, and in far away places. Many have already been received into Christian fellowship without these requirements."

    *   *   *   *   *   *   *

The apostles and elders in Jerusalem called a council meeting to talk about the issues presented. After a lengthy discussion the apostle Peter stood up. "Brothers, you no doubt remember that God chose me to preach to the Gentiles. God confirmed that He accepts Gentiles by giving them the Holy Spirit, just as He gave Him to us. He makes no distinction between believing Jews and believing Gentiles. All of us have had our hearts cleansed through faith. Why are you now questioning God's way by adding a burden that neither our ancestors nor we could bear? All are saved in the same way, by the grace of the Lord Jesus Christ."

Paul added to Peter's statement. He shared news of their missionary trip and told how God had done wonderful things among the Gentiles.

James the Just responded. "These Gentile conversions are in agreement with what the prophets predicted centuries ago," he said excitedly. "Stop troubling the Gentiles by telling them to be circumcised or to follow the Law of Moses. Neither is necessary. The Council will write a letter to clarify the situation and make known our conclusions. In regards to Titus: he does not need to be circumcised."

After writing the letter the apostles and elders of the church in Jerusalem entrusted it to Judas and Silas. These two men had been chosen to travel to Antioch of Syria with Paul and Barnabas to give a report on the elders' decision.

Autumn, A.D. 49, Antioch of Syria

Upon arrival in Antioch a general meeting of the Christians was called. Judas and Silas delivered the letter to them.

One of the brethren stood before the group and read it aloud.

> *From: The apostles and elders, your brothers in Jerusalem,*
>
> *To: The Gentile believers in Antioch, Syria, and Cilicia:*
>
> *Greetings!*
>
> *We understand that some men from here have troubled you and upset you with their teaching, but we did not send them! So we decided, having come to complete agreement, to send you official representatives, along with our beloved Barnabas and Paul, who risked their lives for the name of our Lord Jesus Christ. We are sending Judas and Silas to confirm what we have decided concerning your question.*
>
> *For it seemed good to the Holy Spirit and to us to lay no greater burden on you than these few requirements.*
>
> *You must abstain:*
>
> - *from eating food offered to idols,*
> - *from consuming blood or the meat of strangled animals, and*
> - *from sexual immorality.*
>
> *If you do this, you will do well.*
>
> *Farewell.*

(Acts 15:23-29 NLT)

As the brother finished reading the letter, happy faces smiled in agreement. "What a relief," one of the Gentiles said.

It had been fourteen years since Paul's conversion, and God had taught him many things. Now he sensed the voice of God speaking to his heart. He longed to protect the babes in Christ who were surrounded by law-keeping teachers in far-away Galatia.

Those teachers had turned away many from believing the 'good news.'

Paul went in search of one of his co-workers and asked a favor. "God has spoken to me," he said. "I must write a letter to the churches of Galatia to explain to them that the Law cannot save. I need someone to record the letter as I speak."

"I will gladly help," his co-worker said. When Paul's helper had prepared papers made of papyrus, he dipped his pen into the black ink. "I'm ready," he nodded, holding his pen above the paper.

From Paul, an apostle: I was not appointed by any group of people or any human authority, but by Jesus Christ himself and by God the Father, who raised Jesus from the dead....

To: the churches of Galatia....

I am shocked that you are turning away so soon from God, who called you to himself through the loving mercy of Christ. You are following a different way that pretends to be the Good News but is not the Good News at all. You are being fooled by those who deliberately twist the truth concerning Christ. Let God's curse fall on anyone, including us or even an angel from heaven, who preaches a different kind of Good News than the one we preached to you....

I received my message from no human source, and no one taught me. Instead, I received it by direct revelation from Jesus Christ....I did not rush out to consult with any human being. Nor did I go up to Jerusalem to consult with those who were apostles before I was. Instead, I went away into Arabia, and later I returned to the city of Damascus....

Fourteen years later, I went back to Jerusalem again... and shared with them the message I had been preaching to the Gentiles....They supported me....In fact, James, Peter, and John, who were known as pillars of the church, recognized the gift God had given me, and they accepted Barnabas and me as their co-workers....

But when Peter came to Antioch, I had to oppose him to his face....When he first arrived, he ate with the Gentile Christians, who were not circumcised. But afterward, when some friends of James came, Peter wouldn't eat with the Gentiles anymore....

Oh, foolish Galatians!....After starting your Christian lives in the Spirit, why are you now trying to become perfect by your own human effort?..."Abraham believed God and God counted him as righteous because of his faith."...But those who depend on the law to make them right with God are under his curse, for the Scriptures say, "Cursed is everyone who does not observe and obey all the commands that are written in God's Book of the Law."...But Christ has rescued us from the curse pronounced by the law. When he was hung on the cross, he took upon himself the curse for our wrongdoing....Why, then, was the law given? It was given alongside the promise to show people their sins....The law was our guardian until Christ came....For you are all children of God through faith in Christ Jesus....There is no longer Jew or Gentile, slave or free, male and female. For you are all one in Christ Jesus....

When I first preached to you...you took me in and cared for me....I am sure you would have taken out your own eyes and given them to me if it had been possible. Have I now become your enemy because I am telling you the truth?...

Oh, my dear children! I feel as if I'm going through labor pains for you again, and they will continue until Christ is fully developed in your lives. I wish I were with you right now so I could change my tone. But at this distance I don't know how else to help you....

Abraham had two sons....The son of the slave-wife was born in a human attempt to bring about the fulfillment of God's promise. But the son of the freeborn wife was born as God's own fulfillment of his promise....So, dear brothers and sisters, we are not children of the slave woman; we are children of the free woman. So Christ has truly set us free. Now make sure that you stay free, and don't get tied up again in slavery to the law....Let the Holy Spirit guide your lives. Then you won't be doing what your sinful nature craves....

If another believer is overcome by some sin, you who are godly should gently and humbly help that person back onto the right path....

Notice what large letters I use as I write these closing words in my own handwriting.

Those who are trying to force you to be circumcised want to look good to others. They don't want to be persecuted for teaching that the cross of Christ alone can save....

May the grace of our Lord Jesus Christ be with your spirit. Amen.

(Excerpts from Galatians: Chapter 1:1-2,6-8,12,16-17; Chapter 2:1-3,9,11-12; Chapter 3:1,3,6,10,13,19,24,26,28; Chapter 4:12,14-16,19-20,22-23,31; Chapter 5:1,16; Chapter 6:1,11-12,18 NLT)

When the letter was finished, Paul prepared to send it to Galatia.

*   *   *   *   *   *   *

Paul and Barnabas stayed in Antioch of Syria for the remainder of the winter to teach and preach God's Word alongside their fellow laborers.

Winter, A.D. 49-50

In A.D. 49, Emperor Claudius of Rome married for a fourth time. His new wife was his beautiful niece, Agrippina. She was the younger sister of Caligula.

Emperor Claudius had come to power in Rome eight years earlier. Before that time he had divorced his first two wives because of their adultery. Yet his marriage troubles continued when he married Messalina Valeria. Claudius doted on her and she bore him a son, Britannicus, named in honor of the conquest of Britain.

However, she planned with her lover to seize power during one of Claudius' absences. Informants warned Claudius of her intentions, and he had Messalina Valeria and her lover executed.

Shortly after Claudius married Agrippina, she set out to dominate him. She had him adopt her 12-year-old son, Lucius, under the name of Nero. She then insisted that Claudius designate him as his eldest son. Agrippina chose Seneca, the philosopher, and Burrus, a military officer, to be Nero's teachers. In this way the boy would be sure to be raised in the palace and would pursue studies under Greek teachers who would influence his tastes in music, poetry, and sports.

Both Claudius' marriage to Agrippina and his adoption of Nero would affect the future of Rome and the future of the apostle Paul.

Winter, A.D. 49-50, Antioch of Syria

Winter in Antioch was windy, rainy, and cold. During these damp, dark months Paul prayed for direction. God's voice spoke to him, and as spring approached, he planned another trip.

He found Barnabas and shared his ideas. "God is leading me to return to each of the cities we visited on our last journey."

"Great," Barnabas responded. "I would like John Mark to accompany us."

"No! He musn't go. He's a quitter. He deserted us in Pamphylia."

"Let's give him another chance," Barnabas said in his most persuasive tone.

"He left when the team needed him most. Will he repeat the same weakness of character? I suspect he will. He is unsuited for the trip, and I am not willing to risk taking him again!" Paul said forcefully. Color crept up his neck and into his face as he spoke. "He did not share in the hard work the first time, so why would it be different the second time?"

"He needs encouragement."

"The work ahead will be difficult – steep mountains to climb, sickness, persecution, beatings, and prison. The last thing we need is someone who wants to turn around and go home when trouble comes."

Silence hung between them as each one pondered the situation. Paul had concerns about Barnabas as well. He had recently displayed weakness in following Peter's example of refusing to eat with the Gentiles. Paul needed a co-worker who would stand for the truth. "I will not change my mind," Paul said firmly. "John Mark must not go with us!"

"Well then," Barnabas concluded, "neither will it work for us to travel together!"

Paul's Second Missionary Journey

Chapter
⟨NINE⟩

Team Leader
(2nd Missionary Journey)

Antioch of Syria, Derbe, Lystra, Troas, Philippi, Thessalonica

April, A.D. 50, Antioch of Syria

"Silas, you are not afraid of difficult situations," Paul said. "You proved yourself trustworthy a few months ago when you carried the letter from Jerusalem to Antioch. Will you travel with me from town to town, preaching the 'good news' and encouraging new believers?"

"With God's help I will accompany you. It is something the Lord has been leading me to consider," Silas responded.

"Good – but you must expect physical hardship and persecution."

"I am prepared for that."

"You have the advantage of Roman citizenship," Paul added, "which could be a benefit in the future. Yet I like the fact that you are a Jerusalem Jew and have gained the confidence of Peter, James, John, and the church there."

"This is true. But being Jewish in the Roman Empire has its disadvantages as well."

"You're right. The idea of 'one true God' is not popular in Rome. Emperor Claudius recently made that clear when he expelled the

Jews from Rome as troublemakers."

"Yes, it is common knowledge that Emperor Claudius expelled the Jews about the same time he married Agrippina, his niece. He even had the laws in the Roman Empire changed so that he could marry her legally. She is about half his age and has a thirteen-year-old son, Nero, from her first marriage."

While Paul and Silas made plans for their trip, Barnabas and John Mark sailed to Cyprus to evangelize. During this crucial time Barnabas would guide his young relative toward spiritual maturity. John Mark's father was no longer alive and Mark needed encouragement.

Paul and Silas completed their preparations, and the believers at Antioch entrusted them to God's grace.

With their backs to the sunrise and the fertile valleys below, Paul and Silas climbed the mountains. The bright sun cast shadows on the crevices of rugged slopes. Paul breathed heavily as he climbed. Cool, clean air spurred them on until they reached the narrow pass that would take them through the hostile mountains ahead. This was the most important route from Antioch to Cilicia. After crossing the forested mountain range, the road descended rapidly to a flat coastal plain beside the Mediterranean Sea. Fruit groves and stately palms welcomed them to the town of Issus in Cilicia.

With the hard climb behind them, the men rounded the Gulf of Issus and headed west toward the plains of Cilicia. There they strengthened the faith of new believers in the churches of Syria and Cilicia. In each place Silas read the decree from the church at Jerusalem to the Gentile flock:

> *For it seemed good to the Holy Spirit and to us to lay no greater burden on you than these few requirements.*
> *You must abstain:*
> - *from eating food offered to idols,*
> - *from consuming blood or the meat of strangled animals, and*
> - *from sexual immorality.*

If you do this, you will do well.

(Acts 15:28-29 NLT)

The two men traveled from city to city, passing lush green fields until Paul's hometown Tarsus came into view. The hardest part of the journey lay ahead of them. The two missionaries turned north toward the steep and jagged Taurus Mountains where they climbed 4000 feet to the Cilician Gates. This narrow gorge was the only crack in the continuous mountain range that led to the plateau of Asia Minor. At times a mountain loomed large in front of them; at other times row upon row of mountains faded into the distance. High, snow-capped peaks and fresh mountain streams provided breathtaking scenery during their many days of hard climbing. Pine trees, firs, and an assortment of bushes grew by the side of the road wherever soil could support life. Thieves often hid in these mountains, hoping to spring out and surprise unsuspecting travelers. Each rolling pebble or snapping twig caused Paul's pulse to quicken as he scanned the hillside for hidden danger.

After crossing a series of ranges, the men made their way carefully down the slopes following the Roman road westward across seemingly endless plains. Occasional mud houses dotted the landscape, along with a stone well here and there in the middle of a field. Although it was springtime, the red soil appeared dry, and dust rose in a cloud behind anyone who might be walking through the fields.

May, A.D. 50, Derbe and Lystra

Paul and Silas visited Derbe and then Lystra. Both of these cities lay in the southeast region of the province of Galatia. At Lystra, Paul pointed out the temple of Zeus near the place where he had been left for dead. His heart quickened as the memory of that day flooded back. "This is the city where the people treated Barnabas and me as gods. A priest tried to sacrifice oxen to us. We begged them to stop and told them about the living God."

"If the people wanted to worship you, why did they end up stoning you? How did the mood change so quickly?"

"Jews from Iconium came to town and turned everyone against

us. The crowd stoned me and dragged me out of the city, leaving me for dead. But," he said brightening, "it is the place where I led a young man, Timothy, and his mother Eunice to Christ."

Since Paul's last visit to Lystra, Timothy had grown well in his Christian faith. He worked actively in his hometown as well as in Iconium, 18 miles away. The believers at both places spoke highly of him. It was helpful that Timothy already knew the Scripture – his mother had taught it to him when he was a child.

During a visit Paul spoke privately to Timothy. "You would make a valuable addition to our team. I have appreciated your self-less devotion. However, there is one problem that needs to be addressed."

"What is that?" Timothy inquired.

"Your mother is Jewish and your father is Greek. Because of your parents' mixed marriage, you are considered an apostate Jew, one who has rebelled against the faith. If you join us in the work as things stand now, Silas and I would be considered apostates as well. This problem could be solved if you were circumcised."

"I do not want to hinder the Lord's work in any way," Timothy replied.

"Good," answered Paul, "for I would not even be allowed to speak in a synagogue ever again."

"That settles it," Timothy resolved. "My father didn't allow this operation when I was an infant, but I will be circumcised now."

Paul performed the minor surgery. This opened the door for Timothy to be a useful worker in the future ministry of the gospel both among Jews and Gentiles. Earlier Paul had been forceful in insisting that Gentiles did not need to be circumcised to be accepted by God. But this situation was different and his foresight allowed the work to continue.

Before the three men left town, Paul and the elders at Lystra laid their hands on Timothy and commissioned him to the Lord's work. Paul, Silas, and Timothy traveled across many miles of tree-less grasslands in order to strengthen the existing churches. In each town Silas read the Jerusalem letter to the churches.

The three workers passed through southern Galatia and Phrygia with plans to continue westward along the road to Ephesus. But Paul's plans changed when the Holy Spirit instructed them to stop preaching the word in Asia. God's voice was unmistakable – but where was He directing them to go? Uneasily, Paul and his companions turned northwest into the district of Mysia, but the Spirit forbade them to preach there. They tried to go northeast into Bithynia along the coast of the Black Sea, but the Spirit again had a different plan. They turned northwest and passed through Mysia toward the coastal city of Troas, a main seaport on the Aegean Sea. Since leaving home Paul and Silas had already traveled 500 miles along Roman roads.

Paul had commenced this trip with many plans. Now the voice of God was guiding him in a different direction. God had told Paul where he was not to preach and had provided brief snatches of light. But the immediate future appeared dark, perplexing, and uncertain.

July, A.D. 50, Troas

Rocky scenery dotted the landscape as the group approached Troas, a town where workers at local quarries produced columns for the finest buildings in Roman cities.

The three travelers entered the city and found other like-minded Christians. One of these was Luke, a physician, a man of culture with a good education. Although he practiced medicine, he had a flair for writing Greek, and he had a fascination with the sea. Dr. Luke was a Gentile with connections to Philippi in Macedonia.

One evening Paul headed to bed at the close of the day. While he slept, God spoke to him in a vision. A man from Macedonia stood before him and pleaded, "Come over to Macedonia and help us!"

Paul awoke with his heart thumping. God had spoken! The darkness and uncertainty about future plans had lifted. Paul would be a voice for God in Macedonia.

With renewed energy and a heart full of gratitude he found his companions and shared the news. "This is why God has forbidden us to preach in Asia and Bithynia. He has called us to preach the gospel in Europe." The men talked eagerly about the new possibilities and made immediate plans to leave.

Paul, Silas, Timothy, and Luke hurried down to the harbor, a busy, but well-kept area sheltering many cargo ships. Upon finding one that suited their needs, they boarded the vessel for the 120-mile crossing. A warm, favorable breeze blew, and the ship quickly sailed out into the Aegean Sea. At sunset the dark waters glistened as the ship docked at the mountainous island of Samothrace. The following morning their journey continued toward the hilly coast of Macedonia.

Excitedly Paul stepped off the ship and into his first European city, Neapolis. An east-west Roman military road, the Egnatian Way, ran from Neapolis to Philippi. If a person wanted to continue traveling to Rome, he could follow the Egnatian Way across the peninsula to Apollonia or Dyrrhachium on the coast of the Adriatic Sea. From there ships could link him to the Appian Way in "the heel of the boot" in southern Italy.

August, A.D. 50, Philippi

The travelers walked ten miles to Philippi on the stone-paved Egnatian Way. Roman chariots clattered by, their wheels following deep ruts already carved by others. The heat of the summer sun beat down on their heads, but occasional shade from surrounding trees provided welcome relief. The Egnatian Way ran through the center of Philippi, dividing the city into northern and southern sectors. A military stronghold stood at the northern end of town on the Acropolis, a hill one thousand feet high. It overlooked the city that had been named for Philip II, father of Alexander the Great.

This Macedonian city was home to a famous school of medicine. For Luke it was like coming home, and he would remain in Philippi when the others left.

The city did not have a synagogue because fewer than ten Jewish men lived in that area. Yet Paul still hoped to find a group of worshipers. On the Sabbath day Paul, Silas, Timothy, and Luke followed the Egnatian Way northwest through a large archway. Once outside the city, they walked a mile to the Gangites River. Bushes and trees hugged the banks of the gentle waterway where a group of women recited a Jewish service of prayer and thanksgiving. The waters murmured soothingly as the men sat down on the grass beside them. Paul introduced himself and spoke to the little group. Lydia seemed to be the leader. She was a hard-working businesswoman, a Gentile of high society from Thyatira in Asia, who had converted to the Jewish faith. Her home town was famous for making purple dye from the juice of the madder root, and Lydia had come to Philippi to market this excellent non-fading dye.

"God sent His Son," Paul explained to the group, "a Savior named Jesus. He came to save mankind from their sin. The only way to become right with God is to trust Him to save you." As Paul continued to speak, the Lord opened Lydia's heart to understand the message. She became Paul's first convert to Christ in Europe. She and her household believed and were baptized. This would be the beginning of a church at Philippi. Clement, Euodia, Syntyche, and others would later be added to their number.

"If you agree that I am faithful to the Lord, come and stay at my home," Lydia said.

"But there are four of us."

"I insist! Come and stay for the remainder of your time in Philippi."

"We are grateful for your hospitality and we gladly accept," Paul responded.

Later, as Paul and his companions walked to the place of prayer, a slave-girl who practiced fortune telling passed them. She made a large amount of money for her masters. As she passed Paul, she began to follow him through the streets shouting, "These men are servants of the Most High God. They have come to tell you how to be saved." Day after day she followed them and kept shouting,

"These men are servants of the Most High God. They have come to tell you how to be saved." She had a spirit of python, a demon power attributed to Apollo, the Greek god. The girl's strange sounding voice indicated she was possessed by a demon.

Every time she spoke, Paul tensed up. Her persistent announcement grated on his nerves and disturbed his opportunities to tell others of Christ. Waves of emotion beat in his chest until he felt as if he would burst. He had to stop this girl. He turned and spoke to the demon, "I command you in the name of Jesus Christ: Come out of her!" Instantly the demon left her and the girl stopped shouting. But she had also lost her ability to tell fortunes.

"What's going on?" one of her masters yelled angrily at Paul. "You have ruined everything. We charge a fee for her advice. How are we supposed to make money?" Severely annoyed, the girl's owners grabbed Paul and Silas. "You are going to the authorities at the south end of town."

Paul struggled to escape, but too many hands held him. Luke and Timothy were left standing on their own while the entire crowd followed Paul and Silas to the public square. The crowd pulled them over to the speaker's platform on the north side of the forum opposite the marketplace.

"These two traveling Jews are disturbing the peace," one of the girl's owners told the Roman military governors. "Their religious teachings are against the laws of the Empire. We are Roman citizens and cannot accept or practice their ideas. Their visit to Philippi has created confusion in the whole city."

The crowds shouted in agreement. The governors reached forward and attacked Paul and Silas, roughly tearing off their clothing. A governor turned to a police attendant and commanded, "Beat these two rebellious drifters!"

As the strongly built police lifted their rods, Paul's muscles tensed in preparation. The bundled branches, tied together with leather, slammed against his body. An axe, tied into the branches, made it a weapon that could kill. Paul winced as searing pain shot through his rib cage. Stroke after stroke crashed down causing him to cry out in pain and stumble forward. His heart pounded like a giant hammer in his chest. He regained his balance only to be struck again with another dizzying blow. Finally, a governor motioned to the police. "Take them to jail."

The police took hold of the two dazed men and pulled them down the streets toward the prison. As Paul limped along, huge welts rose on his back and limbs.

At the jail the police handed the bloodied men over to the jailer. "This way," the jailer ordered. The police roughly pushed their two captives toward the lower dungeon. The jailer lifted a flickering torch from its mount on the wall. It would provide enough light for the group to make their way to the inner prison. Rough stone walls encircled the dirt floor of the dungeon. The men were shoved to their knees and ordered to put their feet into a wooden frame.

As the police attendants left, one of them spoke to the jailer. "Keep an eye on those troublemakers. Don't let them escape."

The jailer grunted in agreement. "Those two won't be going anywhere with their feet in stocks."

The door of the cell slammed shut, and the jailer slipped the bar into position. His footsteps retreated as he carried away the flaming torch. Paul and Silas sat uncomfortably in the dark, damp cell.

Prisoners in other cells spoke back and forth to one another, cursing their situation. Every time Paul moved, he winced in pain. Blood oozed from his unwashed wounds. Sleep was impossible. In the darkness the two men spoke to God in prayer and sang hymns of praise. The unusual sound of singing stilled the other prisoners, and they listened intently to the words.

About midnight, as the two continued to sing, a grating rumble shook the ground beneath the prison. "Earthquake!" Paul exclaimed to Silas. Goose bumps rose on his flesh as the building creaked and groaned, cracking the foundation. Doorposts broke apart and bars slipped from their holds. Doors danced to the swaying motion of the quake. Spaces opened up between the stones in the wall, freeing their chains. Stocks broke away from the walls, releasing all the prisoners.

The startled jailer awoke with a jolt as the building shook and pieces dropped from the ceiling. "My prisoners!" he cried, jumping up in panic. "They have escaped." Suicide would be better than being tortured and executed by the authorities when they discovered the men were missing. Faint starlight outlined the prison keeper as he stood near the outer doorway with his sword raised to his chest.

"Wait!" Paul shouted. "Don't hurt yourself. Everyone is here."

The jailer turned toward the voice and squinted into the darkness of the inner prison. "What did you say?" he asked, lowering his sword. "Bring me a light."

A servant brought him a flaming torch. It penetrated the thick darkness as the jailer rushed to check on his prisoners. He secured any who might escape. Finding Paul and Silas still in their dungeon, he fell at their feet. His body shook with fear. "I've heard your songs and your prayers," the jailer said, "and I want to talk with you." He led them outside to a safe place where he and his household could speak with these two unusual guests.

"Gentlemen," he asked, as he knelt before them, "what must I do to be saved?"

"Believe on the Lord Jesus Christ, and you will be saved," Paul answered, his face strangely aglow, as he shared this 'good news' with all who lived in the jailer's house. He also taught them the importance of baptism – identifying with Christ in His death, burial, and resurrection.

"Come into the courtyard," the jailer beckoned through the darkness, "and I will wash your sores." The soothing water brought relief as the jailer gently cleansed their wounds.

As the jailer worked, he asked to be baptized. So the jailer and each member of his household were baptized in the name of the Father, the Son, and the Holy Spirit.

"Would you come into my house for a meal?" the jailer asked.

As he spoke, the aroma of cooking filled the air. "Your God has filled our hearts with joy."

After the meal the jailer reluctantly returned the men to their cells. When morning arrived, the Roman governors sent police attendants to the prison with a message. "Tell the two captured men they may go free."

"Wait here," the jailer said. He hurried to tell Paul the news. "The Roman governors sent a message saying that you and Silas are free to leave. May you go in peace."

"Not so fast," Paul said, his eyes flashing with determination. "They beat us in public and put us in jail. We are Roman citizens! As with any Roman citizen, the charges against us should have been investigated before anyone laid a finger on us. If the governors want us to leave secretly, the answer is 'No.' Tell them to come themselves and lead us out." The police returned to the Roman governors to tell them Paul's message.

"They are Romans?" one of the governors inquired nervously. "We thought they were Jews. If news of our rough treatment reaches Rome, there could be trouble."

The governors traveled to the jail to speak with Paul and Silas. "Forgive us for beating you publicly without a trial," one of them said. "We will personally escort you from prison. However, we'd appreciate it if you would leave our city without causing further problems."

Paul and Silas returned to Lydia's house, but they did not leave the city immediately. They taught and encouraged the Philippian believers, who responded by giving money to Paul to help him on his journey.

Paul, Silas, and Timothy said good-bye to Luke and the other Christians and left town to travel 90 miles west along the Egnatian Way. They spent the first night at Amphipolis and the second night at Apollonia.

November, A.D. 50, Thessalonica

On the third day the beautiful coastal city of Thessalonica came into view. The Egnatian Way ran through the city from northwest to southeast. Hills stood on one side of the city and the turquoise-blue waters of the harbor lay on the other. This commercial and military center would be a suitable place to preach the 'good news.'

Paul soon found the synagogue. On the next three Sabbaths he held discussions with the people. "The Scripture plainly teaches," Paul explained, "that the Messiah had to suffer and rise again from the dead. This Jesus I am telling you about is the promised Messiah." Some Jews and a large number of Greeks who joined in the Jewish services believed, along with a number of women from leading families. Idol worshipers turned away from the darkness of man-made gods to serve the living and true God.

January, A.D. 51

During weekdays Paul used his tent-making skills to earn a living. He did not want to be a burden to anyone while he preached to them. Even though he stayed with a man named Jason, he did not accept food from anyone without paying for it.

Gradually, the small group of believers developed into a large, growing congregation. This included God-fearing men such as Aristarchus and Secundus.

Jewish leaders grew jealous of all the converts. Their resentment drove them down to the marketplace to round up gangs of low-class troublemakers from the public square. "Do you fellows want action?" one of the leaders asked. "Call your friends together so you can form a crowd to cause a riot."

A group quickly gathered. Noisy, bad-mannered gangs moved down the street to the home of Jason. One of the ringleaders shouted, "Send out Paul and Silas." The street-gang waited restlessly for the two men to show up. When no one appeared, they banged at the door and pushed until it burst open.

"Where are they?" one of them asked.

"The men have left," Jason replied.

"What!" an annoyed man yelled, his nostrils flaring. "You will pay for allowing them to escape."

Angry men rudely dragged Jason and some of the other believers from the house. "Come with us!" one of them said. "You are going before the city council."

When they arrived in front of the council members, one of the Jewish leaders acted as a spokesman. "This traitor, Jason, has welcomed two troublemakers, Paul and Silas, into his home. These men have upset the whole civilized world. Paul seems to be the leader. He promotes rebellion and causes trouble wherever he goes. He is disturbing our city, and Jason is to blame for protecting him."

"Charge the Christians with treason," a Jewish leader yelled. "They refuse to obey the laws of Claudius Caesar. They claim instead that a man named Jesus is their King!"

Tower of the Winds (right), Athenian marketplace. This 1st century B.C. building served as a water clock, sundial, and weather vane in Paul's day. Ruins of the market can be seen in the foreground.

Discouraged Evangelist
(2nd Missionary Journey continued)

Thessalonica, Berea, Athens, Corinth

January, A.D. 51, Thessalonica

"**A**re these accusations true?" a member of the city council asked. "Do Paul and Silas tell Christians to overthrow the government?"

"Yes," one of the Jews said insistently. "Both men teach that Jesus is King. The Christians are united in their refusal to obey Caesar."

"These are serious charges. Can you prove them?"

"I can present witnesses who will tell you that Paul and Silas teach that Jesus is superior to anyone."

"That kind of teaching certainly challenges the authority of our Emperor."

"Paul even predicts that Jesus will come back to rule as King over all the earth."

"Surely the Christians know that the Roman Empire does not permit anyone to predict such future events."

"That is what I have been trying to tell you," the accuser said. "All the Christians, including Jason, follow this strange teaching and do not obey Caesar."

The city official turned to Jason. "I am going to make you responsible for the conduct of Paul and Silas. If you want your freedom, you must pay bail. This will serve as a guarantee that you will not protect these men and that they will leave town. There must be no more disorder!"

"You have my word," Jason said, as he paid the amount demanded of him. "There will be no more trouble."

Jason left the area and searched for Paul, Silas, and Timothy. When he found them, he guided them to a quiet spot and spoke to them plainly. "You must leave town. I have guaranteed that there will be no more trouble."

"But who will strengthen the new converts?" Paul asked, as sadness crept into his voice. "Many have turned to Christ from a background of idolatry. Who will teach them?"

"With God's help the faith will be maintained, but you must leave. Go quietly – leave tonight. If you don't go, many of the Christians will be sent to prison."

After sunset Paul, Silas, and Timothy traveled a few miles west on the Egnatian Way, then left the main road and turned south. The situation in Thessalonica weighed heavily on Paul's mind. The work was so promising and the new believers so inexperienced. He had not wanted to leave town, but the powers of darkness had opposed the work and he had been forced out.

February, A.D. 51, Berea

Berea, thirty-five miles inland and forty miles southwest of Thessalonica, lay nestled at the foot of Mount Bermios beside a stream of water that flowed into a larger river.

Shortly after entering the town, the men made their way to the Jewish synagogue. When Paul stood up to speak, the open-minded people of Berea listened carefully. Each day they studied the Scriptures to make sure that what Paul had taught them was, indeed, the truth. As a result, many Jewish people, as well as a number of outstanding Greek men and women, turned to Christ. Among them was Sopater, a man who would one day travel to Jerusalem with Paul.

Eventually, Jews in Thessalonica discovered that Paul had moved to Berea to preach. Like hunters seeking their prey, the Jews traveled to Berea. At a public location a large crowd gathered, and one of their men addressed the mob. "Recently a man named Paul came to Berea. Before that, he taught us in Thessalonica. He is a person who causes problems and riots. Why are you listening to him? I am here to tell you to beware of him."

Confused and agitated, the people nervously discussed this new information. The noise level grew as citizens shouted angry threats.

One of the Christians quietly slipped away from the edge of the uncontrollable mob. He searched until he found Paul with a group of Christians. "Men have come from Thessalonica," he told them. "The mob is angry and is coming to search for you. It would be wise to leave town because your life is in danger."

"What is their attitude toward the rest of us?" Silas asked. "Should Timothy and I also leave Berea?"

"That shouldn't be necessary," one of the Christians said. "The crowd appears to be after Paul."

"I have only been here for a short time," Paul lamented. "It would be good for someone to remain and help teach the new converts."

"But who will travel with you?"

"I'll go on alone," Paul stated. "Our team should split up. Timothy, you go back to Thessalonica. The believers there will be going through troubles and will need encouragement. Silas, you could stay here to help the new Christians at Berea. I'll go on to Athens until things are quieter."

With this being settled, a number of the Berean Christians escorted Paul to the coast. Together the group boarded ship and sailed down the eastern coast of the Roman province of Macedonia toward Athens.

March, A.D. 51, Athens

At the harbor in Athens Paul wrote a short message for Silas and Timothy, "Please join me as quickly as you can." He handed the note to the Bereans, who then boarded the ship to return to their homes. "Good-bye, dear brethren," Paul said gratefully, "and thank you for traveling with me."

Alone, Paul headed away from the harbor. Walls 250 feet apart rose on either side of the roadway as he walked several miles into the city. Altars along the side of the road were dedicated to unknown gods. His heart sank every time he passed one. Athenians worshiped many gods and they did not want to leave any out.

Hills surrounded the walled city of Athens. The Parthenon, a place of worship, stood majestically on the Acropolis, a high rocky plateau. It had been built entirely of white marble more than four hundred years earlier. The Parthenon's tall columns gleamed in the sun. But its outward beauty did not fool Paul. It was a place filled with intense spiritual darkness. Inside this mag-

The Parthenon, Athens

nificent building the citizens worshiped an enormous gold and ivory statue of the goddess Athena Parthenos. Athens, a city of culture and art, had been named for this supposed goddess of wisdom.

As a university city, Athens encouraged higher education. The world's best orators, writers, and philosphers once lived in Athens. It was the native city of Socrates and Plato and the adopted home of Aristotle, Epicurus, and Zeno.

Athenians enjoyed sunshine and believed the sun god was gracious in answering their prayers. They also loved entertainment. The Theater of Dionysus seated fifteen thousand on simple stone benches. Here the people listened to plays. The seats partly surrounded an area of packed earth which served as a platform for orchestra and dancers. And in its center stood the altar of Dionysus, god of wine.

As Paul walked along the main street, narrow alleys angled off to the side, showing rows of houses with red tiled roofs. Occasionally a door would open, and a bucket of dirty water would be thrown into the street.

Wherever he walked there were idols. He felt sick at heart. "Idols, idols, idols," he mused, "hundreds of idols – and people worshiping demons." He had never witnessed such religious zeal. The city held more decorated idols than people.

Paul soon located the synagogue. After listening to the readings from the Law and the Prophets, he held discussions with the Jews and the God-fearing Gentiles. "Oh, to be a voice for God," he thought with passion, "to make known the light of salvation to those in spiritual darkness!"

Each day Paul walked to an area north of the Acropolis. He could find plenty of people at the *agora*, the marketplace. He paused, glancing at the forty-foot Tower of the Winds, the market's timepiece. Even here the people paid tribute to their gods. Above eight sundials were sculptures of eight wind gods. The tower was topped with a weather-vane figure of the god Triton.

Shoppers crowded the large public square and visited stores located around the outer edges of the market's permanent buildings. Farmers sold their vegetables, wheat, and barley in temporary market stalls. Caged birds squawked, and the clink of moneychangers added to the din of vendors selling their wares. The wheezing, whistling sound of a braying donkey interrupted the chatter of human voices.

Paul passed a makeshift stall offering hot drinks, but these he ignored for he was in search of someone to talk with. He caught a glimpse of the place where the philosophers of Athens met to talk, and walked over to join them. He approached a follower of the philosopher Epicurus.

"Are you interested in learning where you have come from?" Paul asked.

"We already know," the Epicurean responded. "Matter always existed, and it was a rotating motion that brought the worlds together."

"That is a popular theory," Paul answered, "but there is a God who lives and cares about people. He is the Creator who made the world."

"I agree that the gods exist," the Epicurean stated, "but none of them created the world. The gods are not interested in the problems of human beings. They are all too busy."

"But the God of heaven is interested. Because of His great love for mankind, He sent His Son, the Lord Jesus Christ, to die as a substitute. Jesus was buried in a tomb, but after three days God raised Him from the dead. Anyone who believes can receive Him. A person will have new life from God and will not be judged, but forgiven."

"I'm not interested in learning more about the gods. I'll deal with death when it comes. Besides, there is no life after death, so why should I spend my time gaining more knowledge? All I care about is having a good time and living a happy life. Nothing else matters."

"Knowledge is important," another man said, interrupting the conversation. "Man should live in harmony with nature and with the universe. I follow the teachings of Zeno. He taught that Stoics should feel no emotion, so we must avoid both grief and joy. We consider that anyone who gives in to emotions shows an error in judgment."

"It is not necessary to live without emotion," responded Paul. "The living God, the God of heaven, is compassionate. He sent His only Son to earth. He was the perfect God-Man. He felt many emotions, including joy and sorrow. He even wept. God created man to have a meaningful life. Those who choose to follow God's Son, the Lord Jesus Christ, experience joy in their hearts. After death these followers will live with God in heaven."

"There is no life after death," the Stoic scoffed. "The god you talk about is strange."

A man of authority came up to Paul and grabbed hold of his arm, "You are obviously an educated man. Come with us."

"Why?" Paul asked as he tried to free his arm.

"We are going to the place of our great god of war, Ares."

"Where?" Paul questioned.

"To the council of the Areopagus; the philosophers like to be familiar with visitors who come to teach."

When Paul arrived, members of the court surrounded him. "Paul, tell us about this teaching of yours. Our people like to hear orators and we like to discuss the latest ideas, but nothing has ever sounded as strange as your teaching. Who is this new god? Tell us about him. When you are done, we'll evaluate what it means."

Paul stood before this group of philosophers and thinkers and raised his voice:

"Men of Athens, I notice that you are very religious in every way, for as I was walking along I saw your many shrines. And one of your altars had this inscription on it: 'To an Unknown God.'

"This God, whom you worship without knowing, is the one I'm telling you about. He is the God who made the world and everything in it. Since he is Lord of heaven and earth, he doesn't live in man-made temples, and human hands can't serve his needs—for he has no needs. He himself gives life and breath to everything, and he satisfies every need. From one man he created all the nations throughout the whole earth. He decided beforehand when they should rise and fall and he determined their boundaries.

"His purpose was for the nations to seek after God and perhaps feel their way toward him and find him—though he is not far from any one of us. For in him we live and move and exist. As some of your own poets have said, 'We are his off- spring.' And since this is true, we shouldn't think of God as an idol designed by craftsmen from gold or silver or stone.

"God overlooked people's ignorance about these things in earlier times, but now he commands everyone everywhere to repent of their sins and turn to him. For he has set a day for judging the world with justice by the man he has ap- pointed, and he proved to everyone who this is by raising him from the dead."

(Acts17:22-31 NLT)

Men nodded in approval as Paul quoted their poets, but the mood soon changed when he mentioned resurrection. "Dead men do not come back to life!" a court member said mockingly. "Where did you learn to reason? When our goddess Athena founded this court, the god Apollo announced:

'When the dust drinks up a man's blood,
Once he has died, there is no resurrection.'"

"Apollo's words are right," a bystander shouted. "Paul is full of empty words. He doesn't know what he is talking about."

"He's not very bright," someone added. "He is like those low-class worthless fellows who hang around the marketplace waiting for food. When scraps fall to the ground, they rush over to eat them."

"Like a bird, he has only picked up a few crumbs of learning!" another insulted with a slang expression. The crowd burst into laughter.

As the insults continued, Paul's shoulders drooped and sadness filled his eyes. Everyone seemed to be making fun of the living God and of the message to repent. Paul had tried to preach the gospel in a way they could understand, but these men were treating him like a peddler of an offbeat cult.

Finally, the informal court session ended. "We have reached a conclusion," a spokesman said. "There is no sense to anything you are saying. Your teachings are worthless."

As Paul turned to leave, a few men came up to him, "We will consider your words," one of them said. "Perhaps you could tell us more at a later date."

At that moment Paul sensed a stirring behind him. He turned quickly, unsure what to expect. Dionysius, one of the members of the court, pushed his way through the crowd until he caught up to him. "Paul, I believe what you said about the God of heaven. Please tell me more about this Man of God's choosing. I want to be a follower." A bystander, a woman named Damaris, also believed, along with several others.

But the philosophers and "thinkers" of Athens had rejected the message. The streets of Athens would continue as before, a city of religious people who worshiped false gods. With sagging spirits, Paul longed for a fellow-worker to share the burden. If Silas and Timothy could join him, they would provide encouragement. He hoped to receive news that it was now safe for him to return to Thessalonica.

When Paul didn't hear from his fellow workers, he tired of waiting for them. He wanted to continue preaching rather than wasting time. So he left Athens. The early morning sun warmed his back as he headed west. Farmers traveling in the opposite direction hauled goods, poultry, and livestock to the city's market. Donkeys pulled clumsy carts with solid wheels. As the carts creaked by, objecting hens cackled in chorus.

Paul passed farms with stone or brick houses. Stone walls kept animals inside the farmyards. When needed, sheds protected them from the cold. Recently planted fields of barley and wheat poked through the earth. Pasturelands, orchards, vineyards, and dark green olive groves lay on every side. The countryside displayed the fresh green of spring, and Paul breathed deeply of the clean country air.

As he neared Corinth, Paul traveled across the isthmus, a narrow strip of land connecting two larger pieces of land. He followed a high ledge on the north shore. Thieves hid in this area, ready to rob travelers and throw them to the swirling green waters below.

March, A.D. 51, Corinth

Paul had no home, no money, and no friends nearby, but he breathed a prayer of thanksgiving when God brought him safely through the city gates.

Corinth, a wealthy city of 200,000 inhabitants, stood on a four-mile-wide strip of land between a peninsula and the mainland. Built on a plateau, it was the capital city of Achaia. Corinth controlled two deep-water seaports: Cenchrea to the east on the Aegean Sea and Lechaeum to the west on a gulf that led to the Adriatic Sea. Because of this, the city was heavily involved with commercial trading.

Julius Caesar had rebuilt the city a hundred years earlier and had given it a new look. Corinth now had wide streets, market-

Map of Corinth with seaports

places, temples, theaters, statues, and fountains. A white and blue marble *bema* seat rested on a raised platform. The Roman governor would sit there to hand out his judgments. Corinth, a sports city, hosted the Isthmian Games. Every second year Greek city-states participated in the games that honored the sea-god Poseidon. Competitors entered wrestling matches, chariot races, musical events, and poetical contests.

A steep, rocky hill, the Acrocorinthus, rose 1900 feet at the south end of the city. This hill had its own water supply and a fortress that provided protection for Corinth. A temple stood at the top of the hill, as did a statue of Aphrodite, the goddess of love. The temple housed one thousand prostitutes. People often came to town to 'play the Corinthian,' but a number of them left town with syphilis, also known as the Corinthian Disease.

When Paul first arrived in Corinth, he felt weak and full of fear. His style of preaching was not with the persuasive language of man's wisdom. Would these people who lived in spiritual darkness listen to the message about the God of heaven? Pagan temples and false gods dotted the landscape. The city had a mixed population of Romans, Greeks, and Jews, each of whom brought with them their varied religious beliefs. These factors all worked together to give Paul a sense of unrest.

Paul made his way through the busy streets. Local residents gathered at the marketplace, mixing with the travelers who spoke in various languages. At the south end of the city, noisy voices drifted into the streets from the pubs. After several hours customers staggered out with reddened eyes and slurred speech.

One day Paul met a man and his wife from Italy. Paul discovered they were Christians and quickly formed a friendship with them.

"I understand you are a tentmaker as I am," Paul commented.

"Yes," Aquila replied. "I was born in Pontus. My wife's name is Priscilla. We left Rome two years ago when Emperor Claudius ordered all Jews to leave. If you need a place to stay, we'll be happy to have you. We could work together in the tent business for a time."

Gateway to the marketplace in Corinth

"I definitely need a place to stay. I am waiting for my co-workers, Silas and Timothy, to come from the north."

Each week Paul attended a Jewish synagogue. The building's stone doorframe carried a Greek inscription announcing "Synagogue of the Hebrews." Paul hoped to convince his hearers, from Scripture, that Jesus was the promised Messiah.

*   *   *   *   *   *   *

Late spring to early summer, A.D. 51

When Silas and Timothy arrived from Macedonia, Timothy eagerly shared the latest news. "The Christians at Thessalonica have remained faithful to the Lord, but they miss you and would like to see you again."

"I long to be with them," Paul responded, "but Satan has put difficulties in the way. Because I could no longer bear the suspense, I sent you up to Thessalonica to find out if their faith was still strong. I was afraid that the Devil had tempted them and that all our work had been for nothing. I am pleased that their faith and love are strong. It brings me great comfort. How I miss them, but I cannot return. However, the Lord is leading me to communicate with them. As soon as the papyrus is ready, I will write a letter."

From: Paul, Silas, and Timothy....

To: the church in Thessalonica, to you who belong to God the Father and the Lord Jesus Christ. May God give you grace and peace.

We always thank God for all of you....We think of your faithful work, your loving deeds, and the enduring hope you have because of our Lord Jesus Christ....

You received the message with joy from the Holy Spirit in spite of the severe suffering it brought you....You have become an example to all the believers in Greece—throughout both Macedonia and Achaia....For they keep talking about the wonderful welcome you gave us and how you turned away from idols to serve the living and true God....

You know how badly we had been treated at Philippi just before we came to you and how much we suffered there. Yet our God gave us the courage to declare his Good News to you boldly, in spite of great opposition. Don't you remember...how hard we worked among you? Night and day we toiled to earn a living so that we would not be a burden to any of you as we preached God's Good News to you....We never stop thanking God that when you received his message from us, you didn't think of our words as mere human ideas. You accepted what we said as the very word of God—which, of course, it is....

Dear brothers and sisters, after we were separated from you for a little while (though our hearts never left you), we tried very hard to come back because of our intense longing to see you again. We wanted very much to come to you, and I, Paul, tried again and again, but Satan prevented us. When we could stand it no longer, we decided to stay alone in Athens, and we sent Timothy to visit you....I was afraid that the tempter had gotten the best of you and that our work had been useless. But now Timothy has just returned, bringing us good news about your faith and love....

We urge you in the name of the Lord Jesus to live in a way that pleases God....God's will is for you to be holy, so stay away from all sexual sin....

God himself has taught you to love one another....Live a quiet life, minding your own business and working with your hands....Then people who are not Christians will respect the way you live, and you will not need to depend on others.

And now, dear brothers and sisters, we want you to know what will happen to the believers who have died so you will not grieve like people who have no hope. For since we believe that Jesus died and was raised to life again, we also believe that when Jesus returns, God will bring back with him the believers who have died....First, the Christians who have died will rise from their graves. Then, together with them, we who are still alive and remain on the earth will be caught up in the clouds to meet the Lord in the air. Then we will be with the Lord forever....

For you know quite well that the day of the Lord's return will come unexpectedly, like a thief in the night. When people are saying, "Everything is peaceful and secure," then disaster will fall on them....But you aren't in the dark about these things, dear brothers and sisters, and you won't be surprised when the day of the Lord comes like a thief. You are all children of the light and of the day; we don't belong to darkness and night....God chose to save us through our Lord Jesus Christ, not to pour out his anger on us....

Honor those who are your leaders in the Lord's work.... And live peacefully with each other....We urge you to:

- *Warn those who are lazy.*
- *Encourage those who are timid.*
- *Take tender care of those who are weak.*
- *Be patient with everyone.*
- *See that no one pays back evil for evil, but always try to do good to each other and to all people.*
- *Always be joyful.*
- *Never stop praying.*
- *Be thankful in all circumstances....*

Now may the God of peace make you holy in every way, and may your whole spirit and soul and body be kept blameless until our Lord Jesus Christ comes again....

I command you in the name of the Lord to read this

letter to all the brothers and sisters. May the grace of our Lord Jesus Christ be with you.

(Excerpts from 1 Thessalonians: Chapter 1:1-3,6-7,9; Chapter 2:2,9,13,17-18; Chapter 3:1-2,5-6; Chapter 4:1,3,9,11-14,16-17; Chapter 5:2-5,9,12-18,23,27-28 NLT)

*   *   *   *   *   *   *

When Silas and Timothy arrived in Corinth, they carried with them a gift of money from co-workers in Philippi. This gift allowed Paul to leave his tent-making for a time and to give himself entirely to preaching the gospel to the Jews. The Spirit compelled him to tell the same message he had preached in other towns, "Jesus has fulfilled the Hebrew prophecies. He is the long-awaited Messiah."

But the Jews reacted with intense opposition, insulting both Paul and the Messiah about whom he spoke.

"My conscience is clear," Paul said, as he shook his clothing in protest. "The responsibility for your future is in your own hands. From now on I'll go to the Gentiles." He turned his back and walked away.

Yet one by one, some did turn to Christ. Stephanas and his household were among the first. Justus was a man who worshiped God and lived next door to the synagogue. "Feel free to stay with me," he told Paul. "Use my house as needed." It would be the first meeting-place of the Corinthian church.

Paul praised God for Crispus, the ruler of the synagogue, for he and his household believed on the Lord. Paul personally baptized Crispus, Gaius, and the household of Stephanas. Through Paul's preaching, Fortunatus and Achaicus believed, as did many others.

However, weakness and fear crept back into Paul's heart again. Everywhere he traveled, he created enemies. His scars reminded him of earlier beatings. Would he be beaten again? He trembled at the thought.

That night the Lord spoke to him in a vision, "Don't be afraid! Keep preaching! Don't give up, because I am with you. No one will attack you or hurt you while you are here in

Corinth. Many people in this city belong to Me."

God's voice had greatly encouraged and comforted him. Paul returned to the work with new enthusiasm. But God continued to burden Paul's heart for the converts in Thessalonica. He dictated a second letter to them.

From: Paul, Silas, and Timothy....

To: the church in Thessalonica....

May God our Father and the Lord Jesus Christ give you grace and peace....

We can't help but thank God for you, because your faith is flourishing and your love for one another is growing. We proudly tell God's other churches about your endurance and faithfulness in all the persecutions and hardships you are suffering. And God will use this persecution to show his justice and...he will pay back those who persecute you. He will come with his mighty angels, in flaming fire, bringing judgment on those who don't know God and on those who refuse to obey the Good News of our Lord Jesus....

Now, dear brothers and sisters, let us clarify some things about the coming of our Lord Jesus Christ and how we will be gathered to meet him. Don't be so easily shaken or alarmed by those who say that the day of the Lord has already begun. Don't believe them, even if they claim to have had a spiritual vision, a revelation, or a letter supposedly from us....For that day will not come until there is a great rebellion against God and the man of lawlessness is revealed...He will exalt himself and defy everything that people call god and every object of worship. He will even sit in the temple of God, claiming that he himself is God....For this lawlessness is already at work secretly, and it will remain secret until the one who is holding it back steps out of the way. Then the man of lawlessness will be revealed, but the Lord Jesus will kill him with the breath of his mouth and destroy him by the splendor of his coming.

This man will come to do the work of Satan with counterfeit power and signs and miracles. He will use every kind of evil deception to fool those on their way to destruction, because they refuse to love and accept the truth that would save them....

With all these things in mind....stand firm and keep a strong grip on the teaching we passed on to you both in person and by letter....

Pray for us. Pray that the Lord's message will spread rapidly and be honored wherever it goes...Pray, too, that we will be rescued from wicked and evil people....

We hear that some of you are living idle lives, refusing to work and meddling in other people's business. We command such people and urge them in the name of the Lord Jesus Christ to settle down and work to earn their own living....

Here is my greeting in my own handwriting – Paul. I do this in all my letters to prove they are from me.

May the grace of our Lord Jesus Christ be with you all.

(Excerpts from 2 Thessalonians: Chapter 1:1-8; Chapter 2:1-4,7-10,15; Chapter 3:1-2,11-12,17-18 NLT)

      *   *   *   *   *   *   *

A short time later opposition arose once more. Members of the Jewish community dragged Paul down to the market to be tried at the *bema* seat, the place of judgment.

Gallio, a pleasant man, was the new governor of Achaia. He belonged to a respected Roman family of Spanish origin. Emperor Claudius Caesar had appointed him in July, A.D. 51. Gallio's younger brother Seneca was also influential. He worked in Rome as a tutor to the teenaged prince Nero.

"What is the accusation against this man?" Gallio asked as he called the court to order.

"He is persuading people to worship God in a way that is forbidden by the Law. He is not preaching a true form of Judaism."

Paul took a deep breath and opened his mouth to defend himself. Before he could say a word, Gallio turned to Paul's accusers and said, "Listen, you Jews. If you have evidence of an actual offence or if there is a case involving a serious crime, I will listen to you. But if it is a simple question of words and people and your Jewish law, deal with the matter yourselves. I refuse to be a judge of such small things. I want you to leave this court now!"

As the crowd moved outside, bystanders took advantage of Gallio's rebuke to the Jews by taking matters into their own hands. They captured Sosthenes, the ruler of the synagogue, and beat him on the pavement right in front of the courthouse. Gallio seemed aware of the beating but chose to do nothing about it.

Gallio's response had given Paul new liberty to preach. People paid more attention to the message he spoke, and a good number decided to follow Christ. Drunkards, thieves, and the immoral turned from their sin to the true and living God.

Paul stayed at Corinth, preaching and teaching for one and a half years. During that time both Jews and Greeks believed, and the church grew.

"If I am going to return to Antioch of Syria before winter," Paul said to Aquila, "it is time for me to travel."

"We'll accompany you as far as Ephesus," Aquila responded. "Priscilla and I plan to resettle there and continue with our tent-making business."

September, A.D. 52

As soon as things were packed up, the little group traveled to the seaport of Cenchrea. There, as the eastern sun rose above the waters, the travelers boarded a ship to cross the Aegean Sea. The land of Achaia disappeared into the distance behind them. Splashing waves washed against the front of the ship as the salty breezes beckoned them over to Asia.

God had encouraged Paul's heart. Many had come to Christ. What lay ahead?

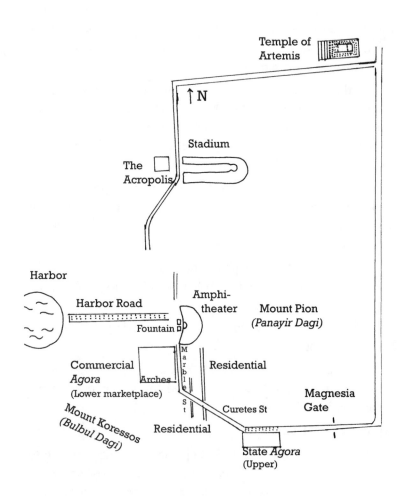

City of Ephesus

Capable Co-workers
(2nd Missionary Journey continued)
(3rd Missionary Journey)

Ephesus, Antioch of Syria, Asia Minor, Ephesus

A s the ship neared Ephesus, it stopped at the customs' house near the head of the Cayster River and then proceeded inland toward the port. Paul, Aquila, and Priscilla stood on deck, anticipating their arrival in this Asian city. A few minutes later Ephesus came into view. A high hill rose to the west of the city and two lower hills to the east, with the city of Ephesus in the valley between. Paul breathed a prayer that many in this place would one day know Christ.

The ship eased its way toward land, gently nudging against the dock. The harbor bed was a mixture of sandy-clay that had drifted down to the coast from further upstream. This made the harbor increasingly shallow. Roman engineers had cleaned out the waterfront and widened it into a shipping basin, but still it needed constant care.

September, A.D. 52, Ephesus

Tanned dockworkers carrying grain, ceramics, wine, and other goods hurried to and from vessels while supervisors shouted orders in various languages. Wagons waited on shore to receive incoming goods.

Paul, Priscilla, and Aquila made their way down the gangplank. Vendors crowded around, anxious to make a sale, but Paul paid no attention. "Before we go into the city," he said, "I need to find out when the next ship leaves for Caesarea."

Once Paul had arranged for his trip, the three co-workers walked up the stone-paved Harbor Street. Columns supporting covered walkways lined both sides of the street. The walkways led into busy stores filled with merchants and customers. The little group pushed past the haggling shoppers and continued up the street.

Harbor Street, Ephesus, leading from the amphitheater to the harbor

Upon reaching the large amphitheater built into the hill, the company turned right and made their way into the city.

Although Paul didn't have much time, he walked to the synagogue to speak with the Jews and to tell them about the Messiah.

"We are interested in what you're telling us," one of them responded. "Would you stay and explain this to us more thoroughly?"

"I can't stay now," Paul replied. "I want to keep one of the feasts in Jerusalem. A ship is about to leave the harbor and it will take me to Caesarea. But I'll return later, God willing."

Paul boarded the ship and sailed from Ephesus to the coastal city of Caesarea. From there he traveled inland and visited the church at Jerusalem. By November he had headed north to Antioch where he would spend the winter months.

Spring, A.D. 53, Antioch of Syria

Falling rain and occasional windstorms swept up the valley from the Mediterranean Sea bringing dampness and a biting chill. But as the winter months ended, Paul was ready to set out on another missionary journey – his third.

He traveled northwest from Antioch up a steep climb, until he reached the pass over the mountains known as the Syrian Gates. This mountain pass separated Antioch from Issus to the north. From there he journeyed around the bay and across the plain to the base of the mountains, near Tarsus in Cilicia. The steep slopes of the Taurus Mountains again lay before him. This was the same route he and Silas had traveled three years earlier on their second journey. As he hiked up yet another mountain, the spring sun warmed his face. Melting snow running down the mountain broke the quiet solitude. At last he reached the narrow pass, the Cilician Gates. The thawing snow had caused the stream on the valley floor to become a raging torrent.

After many days of hard climbing he reached the interior plateau. There he re-visited the Christians in Derbe, Lystra, Iconium, and Antioch of Pisidia. He encouraged them and taught them more about the Lord. While Paul worked and traveled in Asia Minor, Aquila and Priscilla continued with their tent-making business in Ephesus, a city Paul hoped to visit soon.

*   *   *   *   *   *   *

Summer, A.D. 53, Asia Minor

Apollos, a Jewish traveling merchant, had recently come to Ephesus from Alexandria, Egypt, to do business. While there, he eloquently taught the way of the Lord at the synagogue. Afterwards Priscilla and Aquila befriended him and invited him to their home. "We are followers of the Lord Jesus," Aquila said. "Your enthusiasm and accuracy when you speak of Him is much appreciated. However, when you speak of baptism, a Christian should be baptized in the name of the Lord."

"I have only been taught about the baptism of John the Baptist," Apollos admitted.

"After Christ's death and resurrection, on the Day of Pentecost the Holy Spirit came upon all the believers gathered in Jerusalem. On that day the apostle Peter preached to a large crowd and taught that each person should turn away from his own personal sins to the Lord Jesus Christ and that each one should be baptized in His name."

Apollos received the new teaching and stayed at Ephesus until he had completed his business commitments. He then boarded a ship and sailed across the Aegean Sea to Cenchrea, the harbor of Corinth. When he arrived in the city, he located the Christians and showed them a letter of introduction written on his behalf by the church at Ephesus. They welcomed him warmly and responded to his clear teaching and sound doctrine.

But within a short time arguments developed among the Corinthians. "Apollos is best because he speaks more fluently than any of the others. I am a follower of Apollos."

"I disagree," someone answered. "I choose to follow Paul."

"But Paul doesn't speak as eloquently in public as Apollos. Besides, look at Paul. He looks, well...weak!"

"Peter is the true leader," said another.

The arguing continued. While some remained loyal to Paul, others preferred Apollos and still others favored Peter.

In spite of the controversy surrounding him, however, Apollos continued to strengthen the Christians. He visited the synagogue and used powerful arguments from Scripture to prove to the Jews that Jesus was the Messiah.

*   *   *   *   *   *   *

September, A.D. 53, Ephesus

By the end of the summer Paul was ready to leave Antioch of Pisidia and travel to Ephesus. He had the choice of taking either of two major highways. If he traveled south, he would go along a trade route through Laodicea. However, Paul preferred the more direct northern route.

Leaving the highlands behind him, he traveled west through the upper country and then turned south toward Ephesus. As he neared the city, the sun glistened on the elaborate marble temple, located one mile northeast of the city at the base of a hill. The temple had been there for centuries and was dedicated to Artemis, the goddess of the Ephesians. It was one of the largest temples in the world. More than 100 pillars, each about 60 feet tall, lined all four sides of the building. A broad set of steps led to the front entrance. Inside, priests offered sacrifices to their goddess on behalf of the people. It was also a place where people performed acts of immorality and considered it a form of worship. People milled around the entrance of the temple. Idol-makers mixed with the crowd, making money by selling images of their lifeless goddess. Dozens were going inside to worship. The sight oppressed Paul's spirit.

Ephesus was built at the mouth of the Cayster River, a few miles inland from the Aegean Sea. It was a large and important city, the capital of the Roman province of Asia, with a population of a quarter of a million people. Mountains and high city walls provided protection for the inhabitants. Ephesus lay tucked in a valley with the twin peaks of Mount Pion and Mount Lepre to the east and Mount Koressos to the west. For a time Mount Pion blocked Paul's view as he approached the city. He followed the base of the mountain along a covered walkway until he arrived at the city gates. Two tall rectangular towers stood on each side of the Magnesia Gate. Paul carefully avoided the deeply carved ruts made by the wheels of Roman carriages in the large, gray blocks of stone pavement.

Curetes Street, Ephesus, sloping down toward the Commercial *Agora*, the amphitheater, and the harbor

The State *Agora* at the upper end of the city lay straight ahead. A few people discussed the day's events as they left the *agora*, a building used for state-supervised political and religious meetings. Curetes Street carried him downhill toward the busier section of town. Buildings with red-tiled roofs dotted the valley. Larger structures proudly displayed ornate pillars at their entrance. The wealthy Ephesians lived in houses clustered densely together up the hillside. The spacious homes were decorated inside in several ways – with frescos (wall paintings on fresh plaster) or with mosaics (small pieces of colored tile set in mortar to form pictures or patterns). The buildings boasted luxurious bedrooms, bathrooms, and a kitchen. The dining room was furnished with a triclinium, a table with a couch surrounding it on three sides, where the family reclined for their meals. Narrow alleys separated groups of houses.

The Commercial *Agora* (marketplace) stood at the lower end of the city beside the marble-paved street. From his last visit Paul remembered that the city gradually sloped downhill toward the protected harbor. Beyond that, the Cayster River flowed toward the sea through a broad coastal plain. Distant mountains, like guards watching over the city, stood on the far side of the river.

Paul made his way past wine shops and the tantalizing aroma of bakeries to reach Priscilla and Aquila's house. He knew a welcome awaited him there.

One day Paul found a group of a dozen men claiming to be disciples of Jesus. He asked them, "Did you receive the Holy Spirit when you believed?"

"No," one of the men answered. "Who is this Holy Spirit? We did not realize that He existed."

Paul questioned them more closely, "How were you baptized?"

"We were baptized with the baptism of John."

"John's baptism was intended to show only a change of heart," Paul explained. "It prepared people for the One who would come after him – Jesus, the Messiah."

As soon as the men learned this, each of them believed and then was baptized in the name of the Lord Jesus. Paul placed his hands on them, and the Holy Spirit came upon them. They spoke in foreign tongues and preached God's Word in languages that others could understand.

Paul had made a promise a year earlier, when traveling through Ephesus on his way from Corinth to Jerusalem, that he would return and explain the way of the Lord more clearly. For that reason he went to the synagogue to keep that promise. For three months he enjoyed the freedom of preaching and discussing ideas there. But slowly opposition arose. Many refused to accept what Paul taught and they criticized the way of the Lord in front of the entire group.

Finally, Paul could no longer use the synagogue as his teaching center, so he left and invited the Christians to meet with him at a separate location.

Triple arch entrance to the Commercial *Agora*, the main marketplace in Ephesus

He settled into a regular routine. Each morning he rose before sunrise and traveled down the sloping street in the cool morning air to the city's main shopping area. The Commercial *Agora* was located southwest of the amphitheater.

He didn't pause to read the decorated band above the triple-arched entrance because he had read the idolatrous words before: 'To the Emperor Caesar Augustus, Son of God, the High Priest, twelve times Consul, twenty times Tribune.' The lengthy inscription finished with the names of Caesar's family members.

Paul passed under one of the arches and into the large square. It was surrounded on all sides by shops, also arched; each shop was about 40 feet deep. He squinted in the pre-dawn light at the water clock next to the sundial and then joined the vendors preparing for their day's work. Vendors selling brightly colored fruit and vegetables stacked their produce in an attractive way to tempt customers. Paul spent the morning hours working as a tent-maker. When the sundial indicated 11 a.m., many of the people made their way home to rest during the heat of the day. Some, however, remained in town. Paul seized this opportunity to use the unoccupied lecture room of Tyrannus to teach the Word of God each day between 11:00 a.m. and 4:00 p.m. He continued to do this for two full years.

During the cooler months of November through March, temperatures dipped as low as forty degrees Fahrenheit. Thunderstorms rolled over the city at regular intervals. Warning cracks in the distance reminded Paul to head for shelter. Once the storm had arrived, lightning flashed continuously. Loud explosions sounded and resounded from mountain to mountain.

Springtime brought warmer weather, but summer months grew hot. The temperature climbed to ninety degrees Fahrenheit and heat rose in waves from the stone roads and walls. On those days Paul could not get cool; perspiration dripped from his forehead.

In spite of the heat, Paul worked tirelessly in Ephesus while other workers evangelized outlying towns. Epaphras was one of his co-workers who preached in the Lycus Valley, an area 100 miles east of Ephesus. He witnessed to the people of his home town of Colosse and traveled to Laodicea and Hierapolis. Through this joint effort, the people who lived in the province of Asia heard the Word of the Lord Jesus.

Ephesus was famous for its practice of magic and fortune-telling. People, empowered by the forces of darkness, used charms and spells to attempt to cure diseases and to remove evil spirits. The Ephesians had learned from books that certain words or letters needed to be spoken in a particular order to bring results. Volumes of books throughout the city carried recipes for love potions and charms.

Paul taught that a Christian should listen only to the Holy Spirit. All other spirit guides are demons and are deceiving people by acting as angels of light.

Since Paul was a public figure, a group of traveling Jewish exorcists tried to copy him. These idle Jews wanted to use the name of the Lord Jesus as a magic phrase to cast out demons. Seven brothers, sons of a Jewish priest named Sceva, were among those who did this. Imitating Paul, they walked up to a demon-possessed man and commanded in a voice of authority, "Come out – by the Jesus whom Paul preaches."

"I have knowledge of Jesus, and I understand who Paul is," one of the demons replied in an unnatural voice, "but who are you?"

At that moment the demon-possessed man jumped on the sons of Sceva and attacked them like a wild animal. He overpowered them and tore the clothes from their backs. The seven wounded men escaped by running out of the building.

These events filled the bystanders with awe. Many confessed their occult practices and turned their lives over to the living God. "The power of our magic did not come from God!" some admitted.

"You are right," Paul agreed. "The Scripture forbids fortune-telling, palm-reading, and astrology. Neither should a person try to communicate through mediums with those who have died. These powers come from the devil and his demons. All your books with their mystic spells must be destroyed."

"Let's build a fire," someone suggested. "If we burn the books in public, it will show that we no longer follow these practices."

Word spread and many people brought their books. One by one, individuals piled the scrolls together. When there was a great heap, one of them set it on fire. The blaze grew hot and snapping sparks flew into the air drawing attention from passersby. Faces glowed from the rising heat and from the joy that sprang from their hearts as they destroyed the books that had kept them in darkness. The flames quickly reduced the books to ashes before the eyes of the watching crowd.

"Can you imagine how expensive those books must have been?" a bystander asked.

"Yes, their total value is at least fifty thousand pieces of silver," another responded.

"What a waste of money! How can anyone burn all those books when many of us earn only one piece of silver for a day's wage?"

*   *   *   *   *   *   *

From time to time visitors came from Corinth to Ephesus, bringing with them news of the believers. Stephanas, Fortunatus, and Achaicus visited Paul to help and encourage him. Members of Chloe's household, however, brought disturbing news to Paul. "People in the church at Corinth are arguing about which leader to follow."

"What do you mean?" Paul asked.

"Some Christians are following you. Others are devoted to Apollos or Peter."

"And," one of the men added, "Christians are suing each other."

"Oh, no!" Paul replied, as his heart tightened.

But before he could respond, more news spilled out. "There are even cases of drunken and disorderly conduct at the Lord's Supper. The people are filled with pride. One group claims to be more spiritual because they speak in tongues."

Deep concern crossed Paul's face. His eyes blurred and tears spilled down his cheeks. When he tried to speak his voice choked up. "How I love the Christians at Corinth. But," he said as he covered his face with one hand and struggled to control his voice, "I grieve for the poor choices they have made."

Later, when alone, Paul prayed for wisdom and guidance. The Lord directed him to write the following letter to the Corinthians.

Early spring, A.D. 56

> *From: Paul, chosen by the will of God to be an apostle of Christ Jesus, and from our brother Sosthenes....*
>
> *To: God's church in Corinth, to you who have been called by God to be his own holy people....*
>
> *I appeal to you, dear brothers and sisters, by the authority of our Lord Jesus Christ, to live in harmony with each other....For some members of Chloe's household have told me about your quarrels....Some of you are saying, "I am a follower of Paul." Others are saying, "I follow Apollos," or "I follow Peter," or "I follow only Christ." Has Christ been divided into factions? Was I, Paul, crucified for you? Were any of you baptized in the name of Paul? Of course not!...*
>
> *After all, who is Apollos? Who is Paul? We are only God's servants through whom you believed the Good News. Each of us did the work the Lord gave us. I planted the seed in your hearts, and Apollos watered it, but it was God who made it grow....*

You are God's building....For no one can lay any foundation other than the one we already have—Jesus Christ.... Anyone who builds on that foundation may use a variety of materials—gold, silver, jewels, wood, hay, or straw. But, on the judgment day, fire will reveal what kind of work each builder has done. The fire will show if a person's work has any value....So don't boast about following a particular human leader....

Our dedication to Christ makes us look like fools....Even now we go hungry and thirsty, and we don't have enough clothes to keep warm. We are often beaten and have no home. We work wearily with our own hands to earn our living....

I can hardly believe the report about the sexual immorality going on among you—something that even pagans don't do. I am told that a man in your church is living in sin with his stepmother....You should remove this man from your fellowship....

When one of you has a dispute with another believer, how dare you file a lawsuit and ask a secular court to decide the matter instead of taking it to other believers!...Isn't there anyone in all the church who is wise enough to decide these issues?...

Now regarding the questions you asked in your letter. Yes, it is good to live a celibate life. But because there is so much sexual immorality, each man should have his own wife, and each woman should have her own husband....So I say to those who aren't married and to widows—it's better to stay unmarried, just as I am. But if they can't control themselves, they should go ahead and marry....

My dear friends, flee from the worship of idols....Am I saying that food offered to idols has some significance, or that idols are real gods? No, not at all. I am saying that these sacrifices are offered to demons, not to God....So you may eat any meat that is sold in the marketplace without raising questions of conscience....But suppose someone tells you, "This meat was offered to an idol." Don't eat it, out of consideration for the conscience of the one who told you....

There is one thing I want you to know: The head of

every man is Christ, the head of woman is man, and the head of Christ is God....A man should not wear anything on his head when worshiping, for man is made in God's image and reflects God's glory....Because the angels are watching, a woman should wear a covering on her head to show she is under authority....

But in the following instructions, I cannot praise you....When you meet together, you are not really interested in the Lord's Supper. For some of you hurry to eat your own meal without sharing with others. As a result, some go hungry while others get drunk. What? Don't you have your own homes for eating and drinking?...On the night when he was betrayed, the Lord Jesus took some bread and gave thanks to God for it. Then he broke it in pieces and said, "This is my body, which is given for you. Do this to remember me." In the same way, he took the cup of wine after supper, saying, "This cup is the new covenant between God and his people—an agreement confirmed with my blood. Do this to remember me as often as you drink it." For every time you eat this bread and drink this cup, you are announcing the Lord's death until he comes again....

Regarding your question about the special abilities the Spirit gives us....There are different kinds of spiritual gifts, but the same Spirit is the source of them all....A spiritual gift is given to each of us so we can help each other.... Earnestly desire the most helpful gifts. But now let me show you a way of life that is best of all....Let love be your highest goal!...

Since we preach that Christ rose from the dead, why are some of you saying there will be no resurrection of the dead?... Christ was raised as the first of the harvest; then all who belong to Christ will be raised when he comes back....And why should we ourselves risk our lives hour by hour....if there will be no resurrection from the dead?...But let me reveal to you a wonderful secret. We will not all die!...For when the trumpet sounds, those who have died will be raised to live forever. And we who are living will also be transformed....

Now regarding your question about the money being collected for God's people in Jerusalem....On the first day of each week, you should each put aside a portion of the money you have earned. Don't wait until I get there and then try to collect it all at once....

The churches here in the province of Asia send greetings in the Lord, as do Aquila and Priscilla and all the others who gather in their home for church meetings....

Here is my greeting in my own handwriting—Paul. ...

My love to all of you in Christ Jesus.

(Excerpts from 1 Corinthians: Chapter 1:1-2,10-13; Chapter 3:5-6, 9,11-13,21; Chapter 4:10-12; Chapter 5:1-2; Chapter 6:1,5; Chapter 7:1-2,8-9; Chapter 10:14,19-20,28; Chapter 11:3,7, 10,17,20-22,24; Chapter 12:1,4,7,31; Chapter 14:1; Chapter 15:12,23,30,32,51-52; Chapter 16:1-2,19,21,24 NLT)

*   *   *   *   *   *   *

Springtime brought red poppies, nodding their heads in the gentle breezes. Long-legged storks built their grassy nests on top of the tall pillars. For Paul, springtime brought compulsion to travel once again. He spoke with his co-workers Timothy and Erastus. "There are great opportunities here in Ephesus, but I have many enemies. God is leading me by His Spirit to go through Macedonia and Achaia before returning to Jerusalem."

"How much longer will you stay here?" Timothy asked.

"I plan to remain in Ephesus until late spring, after Pentecost. Then I hope to travel to Philippi in Macedonia and to stay there for the summer and fall. Afterwards I would like to visit with the Corinthians, perhaps for the winter, if the Lord permits."

"Then you will return to Jerusalem?"

"Yes, Lord willing, I will go in the spring of next year. I want to be there in person, along with church delegates from the areas around the Aegean Sea. If it seems right for me to go, we will deliver the money collected from the various churches to help the poor in Jerusalem."

"Do you have plans after Jerusalem?" Timothy asked.

"After that, I must travel to Rome. However, right now it would help if you and Erastus would go ahead of me to Macedonia, and I will ask Titus to go to Corinth. I want to stay here in Asia a little longer."

Early May, A.D. 56, Ephesus

Shortly after Paul had talked about his travel plans, trouble developed in Ephesus. Demetrius, an Ephesian silversmith, had a large business making silver shrines of the Greek goddess Artemis. The people of Asia believed that she protected wildlife and nature. She was considered such an important goddess that the cities' coins bore her image. Hundreds of priests and priestesses worked at the magnificent temple, and the deeply religious Ephesians treated their place of worship as the most important building in the city.

Demetrius was president of the guild of silversmiths. One day, as his employees were busily working, tapping gently on the silver images with their tools, he called them together. "Gentlemen, this business requires a good deal of money for the raw materials, but it makes a decent profit. However, sales are down because this man Paul has convinced many of our people that they should no longer worship our gods. He says that gods made with hands are not gods at all. This is happening both here in Ephesus and throughout the whole province of Asia. If we allow him to continue, people will refuse to buy our products. The temple of the great goddess may lose its influence, and our magnificent Artemis will be robbed of worship from the people in the province of Asia and perhaps throughout the whole Roman Empire."

Demetrius' words stirred up feelings of anger. The smiths talked loudly among themselves and ran into the open street, shouting in protest, "Our goddess is in danger. Great is Artemis of the Ephesians!"

A crowd gathered and a wave of people pushed their way down Curetes Street, turned right near the marketplace, and moved toward the theater. The noise and confusion grew as the group traveled through the city, passing the shops and marketplace. Suddenly, someone in the crowd recognized Aristarchus, a Macedonian, and Gaius from Derbe. "You are friends of Paul, aren't you?" he shouted.

"Admit it," another yelled more loudly. "You came to Ephesus to help Paul."

Without waiting for an answer, several men grabbed hold of them and dragged them along the stone road into the theater that had been built into the western slope of Mount Pion. Claudius Caesar had built this 25,000 seat structure a few years earlier.

The amphitheater of Ephesus looking toward the harbor

Hundreds now hurried up the stone steps. Some crowded onto the hard benches near the stage; others climbed twenty, forty, or fifty steps toward the top to find a vantage point. The theater, larger than a semi-circle, was designed so everyone could easily see the stage and the three-leveled front of the stage building.

Although the crowd had captured Paul's co-workers Gaius and Aristarchus, Paul was not with them. He learned of the protest when several believers burst through his door exclaiming, "The silversmiths are after you!"

"Where?"

"Down at the theater. A large crowd has gathered there."

"What an opportunity!" Paul said with enthusiasm. "I'll go to the theater and speak with them."

At that moment a messenger arrived from a sympathetic provincial official. "Do not risk your life by going into the theater."

"I agree," one of the believers added. "It is far too dangerous. The mob is angry with YOU."

"But what about those who live in the darkness of idolatry?" Paul questioned. "Some may hear God's voice for the first time!"

"Do not go to the theater!" the messenger from the provincial officials ordered firmly. "The crowd will kill you!"

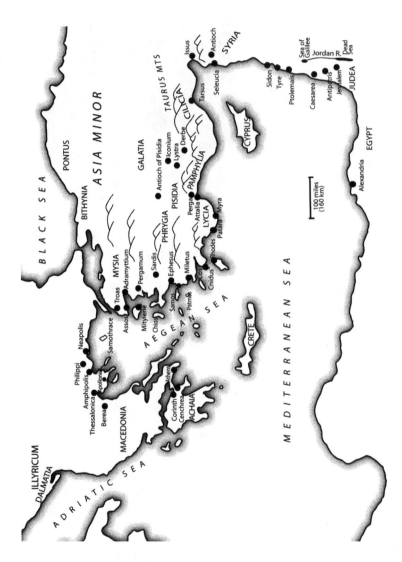

Paul's Third Missionary Journey

Chapter
⌒TWELVE⌒

Enemies Everywhere
(3rd Missionary Journey continued)

*Ephesus, Troas, Macedonia, Illyricum, Corinth, Philippi, Troas,
Miletus, Cos, Rhodes, Patara, Tyre, Caesarea*

Early May, A.D. 56, Ephesus

The crowd shouted and milled about the theater. Demetrius, who had started the confusion, did not come forward to give a public explanation for the gathering. Eventually people shrugged their shoulders, threw up their hands, and asked, "Why are we here?"

Not far from the theater a group of Jewish leaders huddled nervously. "The officials will probably accuse us of starting this riot," one of them worried.

"You're right," another responded. "As Jews, we oppose idols so the officials will accuse us of this unrest."

"Alexander, you are the kind of person who could defend our position. Explain to the people what is happening." With these words the Jews pushed Alexander to the front of the crowd.

He stepped onto the stage, lifted his hand, and motioned for silence. As the noise level dropped, an individual shouted, "You don't worship Artemis."

A second person cupped his hands to his mouth and yelled, "You Jews have caused all this trouble."

Before Alexander could say anything, a chant rose from the thousands jamming the theater, "Great is Artemis of Ephesus! Great is Artemis of Ephesus! Great is Artemis of Ephesus!" The shouting continued non-stop for two hours.

The town clerk finally quieted the crowd. "Residents of Ephesus," he said, facing the sea of faces as the sound of his voice traveled clearly throughout the entire theater. "The whole world recognizes that Ephesus is the guardian of the temple of the great goddess Artemis. Her image fell from Zeus in the sky."

Thousands of voices cheered their approval.

"These facts," the clerk stated firmly, "cannot be denied. Keep calm. Do not act so recklessly. You have brought these men here, but they have not stolen anything from the temple. They have said nothing to insult our goddess. The courts are open if Demetrius and his fellow craftsmen want to press charges. A judge will hear their case at once if that is what Demetrius chooses. If there are other complaints, deal with them in a lawful assembly. There is no reason for this disorderly riot. If the Roman government hears about it, there will be trouble. I suggest you go home." A hush fell over the group as the crowd left the theater and walked back to their homes and places of work.

Within a short time, word spread that Paul wanted to visit with the Christians at his home. "I have many enemies here. Those who care about my safety have advised me to leave Ephesus as soon as possible." His voice choked with emotion, and he fought to keep it steady. "Over the past two and a half years I have made many friends and I have grown to love you. I will miss you, and I hope you will keep following Christ in my absence." Blinding tears burned his eyes as he hugged each of them affectionately and tried to comfort them.

Paul's friends and fellow-workers, Priscilla and Aquila, would also be leaving Ephesus in the near future to return to Rome. But a growing church with recognized elders was emerging in Ephesus.

Paul and the believers walked down the wide marble road to Harbor Street. Paul fought with feelings of discouragement at having to leave Ephesus before he had planned. He paid his passage and boarded a ship that sailed close to the coast on its journey northward to Troas.

Troas

At Troas the vessel glided into the protected harbor. Paul entered the walled city with its stone archways. Though he had opportunities to preach the gospel, he felt restless in his spirit. He wanted to find Titus, his brother in the Lord, to ask him how the Corinthians had reacted to the letter he had sent. After searching for him without success, Paul paid the boat fare and left Troas for Macedonia.

Early June, A.D. 56, Macedonia

Macedonia included the cities of Neapolis, Philippi, Amphipolis, Apollonia, Berea, and Thessalonica. Paul traveled from place to place, encouraging the Christians, but he found no time to rest. Each day seemed more difficult and more exhausting than the one before. No matter which town he visited, he found trouble and opposition. Pressures and problems produced an agitated, heavy feeling in his heart. And where was Titus?

Then when he least expected it, God provided the comfort he needed for his discouraged heart and weary body. Titus arrived in town! Paul greeted him warmly and asked about the work in Corinth.

"Everything is well," Titus reported. "I had a wonderful time with the Corinthians."

"What was their reaction to the letter I wrote a few months ago?"

"Grief filled their hearts when they read it."

"That news alone revives me. But has the letter made a difference in their conduct?"

"Yes, in many ways. The Corinthians mourned over their careless attitudes and willingly made the changes you suggested. Among other things, they now realize the importance of living with one wife and avoiding sexual immorality."

"I'm delighted to hear the news," Paul said, breathing a sigh of relief. "Is there still disorder at the Lord's Supper?"

"They have made changes there as well."

"What about the false teachers? I'm referring to the ones who tried to make me look bad in the eyes of the Corinthian church."

"Their schemes didn't work. The Christians are eager to visit with you again," Titus added. "They feel a sense of loyalty to you and love you dearly."

Paul felt blessed and encouraged by the news. He would write them a second letter and send it with Titus, this beloved friend who had proved he could handle difficult situations.

September – October, A.D. 56

From: Paul...an apostle of Jesus Christ, and...Timothy....

To: God's church in Corinth and all his people throughout Greece.

May God our Father and the Lord Jesus Christ give you grace and peace.

All praise to God, the Father of our Lord Jesus Christ. God is our merciful Father and the source of all comfort. He comforts us in all our troubles so that we can comfort others....

The reason I didn't return to Corinth was to spare you from a severe rebuke....I wrote that letter in great anguish, with a troubled heart and many tears. I didn't want to grieve you, but I wanted to let you know how much love I have for you. I am not overstating it when I say that the man who caused all the trouble hurt all of you more than he hurt me. Most of you opposed him, and that was punishment enough. Now, however, it is time to forgive and comfort him. Otherwise he may be overcome by discouragement. So I urge you now to reaffirm your love for him....

If the Good News we preach is hidden behind a veil, it is hidden only from people who are perishing. Satan, who is the god of this world, has blinded the minds of those who don't believe. They are unable to see the glorious light of the Good News. They don't understand this message about the

*glory of Christ, who is the exact likeness of God. You see, we
don't go around preaching about ourselves. We preach that
Jesus Christ is Lord, and we ourselves are your servants for
Jesus' sake. For God, who said, "Let there be light in the
darkness," has made this light shine in our hearts so we could
know the glory of God that is seen in the face of Jesus Christ.
We now have this light shining in our hearts, but we ourselves are like fragile clay jars containing this great treasure.
This makes it clear that our great power is from God, not
from ourselves....*

*Though our bodies are dying, our spirits are being re-
newed every day....For we know that when this earthly
tent we live in is taken down (that is, when we die and
leave this earthly body), we will have a house in heaven, an
eternal body made for us by God himself and not by human
hands....For we must all stand before Christ to be judged.
We will each receive whatever we deserve for the good or
evil we have done in this earthly body....*

*God was in Christ, reconciling the world to himself, no
longer counting people's sins against them. And he gave us
this wonderful message of reconciliation. So we are Christ's
ambassadors....We speak for Christ when we plead, "Come
back to God!" For God made Christ, who never sinned, to
be the offering for our sin, so that we could be made right
with God through Christ....*

*Don't team up with those who are unbelievers. How
can righteousness be a partner with wickedness? How can
light live with darkness? What harmony can there be between Christ and the devil? How can a believer be a partner with an unbeliever? And what union can there be
between God's temple and idols? For we are the temple of
the living God....Therefore, come out from among unbelievers, and separate yourselves from them, says the Lord.*

*When we arrived in Macedonia, there was no rest for
us. We faced conflict from every direction, with battles on*

the outside and fear on the inside. But God, who encourages those who are discouraged, encouraged us by the arrival of Titus....When he told us how much you long to see me, and how sorry you are for what happened, I was filled with joy!...

So we have urged Titus, who encouraged your giving in the first place, to return to you and encourage you to finish this ministry of giving. Since you excel in so many ways... I want you to excel also in this gracious act of giving....Last year you were the first who wanted to give....Let the eagerness you showed in the beginning be matched now by your giving. Give in proportion to what you have....

I am jealous for you with the jealousy of God himself.... You happily put up with whatever anyone tells you, even if they preach...a different kind of gospel than the one you believed....These people are false apostles. They are deceitful workers who disguise themselves as apostles of Christ. But I am not surprised! Even Satan disguises himself as an angel of light....

I have received...wonderful revelations from God. So to keep me from becoming proud, I was given a thorn in my flesh, a messenger from Satan to torment me and keep me from becoming proud....

I close my letter with these last words: Be joyful. Grow to maturity. Encourage each other. Live in harmony and peace. Then the God of love and peace will be with you. Greet each other with Christian love. All of God's people here send you their greetings. May the grace of the Lord Jesus Christ, the love of God, and the fellowship of the Holy Spirit be with you all.

(Excerpts from 2 Corinthians: Chapter 1:1-4,23; Chapter 2:4-8; Chapter 4:3-6,16; Chapter 5:1,10,19-21; Chapter 6:14-17; Chapter 7:5-7; Chapter 8:6-7,10; Chapter 11:2,4,13-14; Chapter 12:7; Chapter 13:11-14 NLT)

Illyricum

After writing this letter Paul left with his companions to travel northwest through Macedonia to preach the gospel in Illyricum, a large and mountainous region. While Paul worked there, Titus carried Paul's completed letter down to Corinth.

Late November, A.D. 56, to February, A.D. 57, Corinth

Paul and his company journeyed to Corinth for the winter months. Here Paul visited the home of Gaius, now one of the leaders of the church. Gaius welcomed him warmly. "Will you stay here with me during your time in the city?"

"Gladly," Paul responded, "if it isn't too much to have a houseguest as well as having the church meet in your home."

"I owe you much," Gaius replied. "It was through your preaching that I turned to the Lord."

"Yes, I remember. You are one of the few people I baptized personally."

*   *   *   *   *   *   *

Paul's desire to visit Rome increased, and he felt compelled to write them a letter. He wanted to give them a thorough statement of the gospel message and to prepare them for the visit he hoped to make on his way to Spain.

Tertius agreed to act as secretary while Paul dictated the letter.

From: Paul, a slave of Christ Jesus....

To: all of you in Rome who are loved by God and are called to be his own holy people. May God our Father and the Lord Jesus Christ give you grace and peace....

I planned many times to visit you, but I was prevented until now....So I am eager to come to you in Rome...to preach the Good News. For I am not ashamed of this Good News about Christ. It is the power of God at work, saving everyone who believes—the Jew first and also the Gentile....

But God shows his anger from heaven against all sinful, wicked people who suppress the truth by their wickedness....

Their minds became dark and confused....

You may think you can condemn such people, but you are just as bad, and you have no excuse! When you say they are wicked and should be punished, you are condemning yourself....

You who call yourselves Jews are relying on God's law, and you boast about your special relationship with him.... You are convinced that you are a guide for the blind and a light for people who are lost in darkness....

All people, whether Jews or Gentiles, are under the power of sin....As the Scriptures say, "No one is righteous— not even one."...No one can ever be made right with God by doing what the law commands. The law simply shows us how sinful we are.

But now God has shown us a way to be made right with him...by placing our faith in Jesus Christ. And this is true for everyone who believes, no matter who we are. For everyone has sinned; we all fall short of God's glorious standard. Yet God, with undeserved kindness, declares that we are righteous. He did this through Christ Jesus when he freed us from the penalty for our sins. For God presented Jesus as the sacrifice for sin. People are made right with God when they believe that Jesus sacrificed his life, shedding his blood....Can we boast, then, that we have done anything to be accepted by God? No, because our acquittal is not based on obeying the law. It is based on faith....

Well then, should we keep on sinning so that God can show us more and more of his wonderful grace? Of course not! Since we have died to sin, how can we continue to live in it?...Don't you realize that you become the slave of whatever you choose to obey? You can be a slave to sin, which leads to death, or you can choose to obey God, which leads to righteous living....For the wages of sin is death, but the free gift of God is eternal life through Christ Jesus our Lord....

Now we can serve God, not in the old way of obeying

the letter of the law, but in the new way of living in the Spirit....

You have no obligation to do what your sinful nature urges you to do....You have not received a spirit that makes you fearful slaves. Instead, you received God's Spirit when he adopted you as his own children....

My heart is filled with bitter sorrow and unending grief for my people, my Jewish brothers and sisters....They are...chosen to be God's adopted children. God...made covenants with them and gave them his law....

The longing of my heart and my prayer to God is for the people of Israel to be saved. I know what enthusiasm they have for God, but it is misdirected zeal....Refusing to accept God's way, they cling to their own way of getting right with God by trying to keep the law....

For since their rejection meant that God offered salvation to the rest of the world, their acceptance will be even more wonderful....

And so, dear brothers and sisters, I plead with you to give your bodies to God because of all he has done for you.... Don't copy the behavior and customs of this world, but let God transform you into a new person by changing the way you think....

Just as our bodies have many parts and each part has a special function, so it is with Christ's body. We are many parts of one body, and we all belong to each other. In his grace, God has given us different gifts for doing certain things well....

Everyone must submit to governing authorities. For all authority comes from God....Accept other believers who are weak in faith...for God has accepted them....

I have fully presented the Good News of Christ from Jerusalem all the way to Illyricum....I have finished my work in these regions, and after all these long years of waiting, I am eager to visit you. I am planning to go to Spain, and when I do, I will stop off in Rome...But before I come, I must go to Jerusalem to take a gift to the believers there...

Give my greetings to Priscilla and Aquila, my co-workers in the ministry of Christ Jesus. In fact, they once risked their lives for me...Also give my greetings to the church that meets in their home...Timothy, my fellow worker, sends you his greetings, as do Lucius, Jason, and Sosipater, my fellow Jews. I, Tertius, the one writing this letter for Paul, send my greetings, too, as one of the Lord's followers. Gaius says hello to you. He is my host and also serves as host to the whole church. Erastus, the city treasurer, sends you his greetings....

All glory to the only wise God, through Jesus Christ, forever. Amen.

(Excerpts from Romans: Chapter 1:1,7,13,15-16,18; Chapter 2:1,17,19; Chapter 3:9-10,20-25,27; Chapter 6:1-2,16,23; Chapter 7:6; Chapter 8:12; Chapter 9:2-4; Chapter 10:1-3; Chapter 11:15; Chapter 12:1-2,4-6; Chapter 13:1; Chapter 14:1,3; Chapter 15:19,23-25; Chapter 16:3-5,21-23,27 NLT)

"This letter must be delivered to Phoebe," Paul said to his companions. "She will soon be leaving for Rome." Phoebe was a very kind woman who helped Christians in whatever way she could. She lived east of Corinth in the port city of Cenchrea.

By late February of A.D. 57, Paul again felt anxious to travel. "It is time to return to Jerusalem," he told his companions. "Let's plan to sail from Cenchrea across the Aegean Sea. The winter is almost over. By early March it is usually possible to travel on the open seas of the Mediterranean."

Seven of Paul's fellow-workers from various churches in Macedonia, Asia, and Galatia planned to accompany him on this journey. The travelers included his trusted friend Timothy; Aristarchus, who nearly lost his life in the riot at Ephesus; and Trophimus, a Gentile from Ephesus. Within a few months time Trophimus would unintentionally cause Paul's arrest.

As the ship prepared to leave the port, a believer ran up to them with disturbing news. The messenger panted as he tried to catch his breath long enough to deliver the details. "Paul, you are in serious danger from your enemies! There are Jews who plan to travel on the same ship. These evil men intend to kill you."

"Did this information come from a reliable source?" Paul asked.

"Yes!"

"In that case, I must change my plans. If this ship is carrying enemies who hope to kill me, I will have no chance to escape. Instead of sailing, Luke and I will travel by land through Macedonia and meet you at Troas. The rest of you can go ahead and take the ship as planned. It is important that the large gift of money arrive safely in Jerusalem."

April 7 to 14, A.D. 57, Philippi

Luke and Paul journeyed north and reached Philippi for Passover (the Feast of Unleavened Bread). Afterwards, they traveled east to the port of Neapolis and found a ship sailing to Troas, the main seaport in the northwest corner of Asia Minor. The voyage across the open water lasted five days, twice as long as an earlier trip when Paul had taken the ship in the opposite direction.

April 15 to 25, A.D. 57, Troas

In Troas, Paul and Luke rejoined the other seven who had sailed from Cenchrea. Together the men spent a week visiting and sharing with the Christians. On the first day of the week the nine men attended meetings in an upper room to break bread. This would be the travelers' last full day in Troas, since Paul and his companions planned to leave the next day. The Christians held a meeting in the evening, a convenient time for slaves and servants who worked all day. Burning torches glowed as Paul preached until midnight. Stale air refused to circulate in the cramped and stuffy room. One young man, Eutychus, fought sleep, but his eyelids grew heavy, his head nodded, and his body slumped. Suddenly, he lost his balance and fell backwards from the third story window.

"He's fallen," one of the men whispered loudly. A few people raced downstairs to check on him. Luke, being a physician, followed them.

"He's not breathing!" a panicky voice gasped. Eutychus lay limp and lifeless.

"He's dead! He's dead!" another wailed.

Luke checked the man and did not dispute their conclusion. "Go quickly!" he ordered. "Ask Paul to come down to the street."

One of the men rushed upstairs and a moment later returned with Paul, who hurried over to Eutychus' motionless body. Paul fell on him and wrapped his arms around him. "Don't worry. He's alive."

A moment later Eutychus opened his eyes and slowly sat up. A sigh of relief and awe rippled through the crowd as he gingerly stood to his feet. He had no serious injuries and was able to rejoin Paul and the others as they went back upstairs to eat the Lord's Supper together. Paul continued speaking for the rest of the night – right up until the streaks of dawn lit the eastern sky.

Because Paul wanted to be in Jerusalem before the end of May, the group could not spend any more time at Troas. Paul arranged for his companions to travel by boat to the coastal city of Assos on Monday morning, April 25. Each day, from early morning until late afternoon, the north wind blew, making the morning the best time to travel. Paul, however, wanted to remain in Troas until the last possible moment and then to take a shortcut on foot.

After the ship left, Paul visited with the Christians for a short while. Then he walked through the city gates and headed 20 miles south by land to the city of Assos. It stood on a high rock 750 feet above sea level. Short bushes dotted the hillside as Paul made his way down the path that led to the

The eastern gate and wall of Troas, facing away from the harbor and the shoreline

sheltered south shore. An enormous stone wall encircled the man-made harbor and protected it from incoming waves.

When his companions sailed into port, Paul joined them, and together the group sailed further south to the city of Mitylene where the captain stopped for the night. This port, on the island of Lesbos, was a favorite holiday resort for the Romans.

The next night the captain traveled to a port on the mainland opposite the island of Chios. From there the ship sailed across the mouth of the Ephesian Gulf, continuing southward between the island of Samos and the coastline of Asia. The crew and passengers spent the night at Trogyllium, a high ridge that juts out into the sea from the mainland. The narrow strait between Trogyllium and Samos would not be safe to negotiate after dark.

April 29 to May 2, A.D. 57, Miletus

On April 29, Paul stood on deck soaking in the beauty of the scenery to the east as the ship approached the great harbor at Miletus. This city was built on a peninsula and stood at the mouth of the Meander River. It boasted several harbors, marketplaces, and an amphitheater that seated 15,000.

Paul and the travelers left the ship. It would be docked for a few days, so Paul would have time to visit with the Christians at Miletus. He also wanted to see the leaders of the Ephesian church once again. Paul had sailed past Ephesus, hoping to arrive in Jerusalem by the Day of Pentecost, May 29. From Miletus, Paul scribbled a quick message to the church elders at Ephesus, "Could you meet me at Miletus? My ship is in port, but only for a few days." He handed the note to a messenger who traveled the 30 miles north to Ephesus.

As Paul had hoped, the Ephesian elders made the trip down to Miletus. Upon their arrival Paul spoke to the group. "From the first day that I came to Asia until now, I have served the Lord with humility and often in tears. Though the Jews plotted against me, this did not stop me from telling you the truth both publicly in the lecture hall of Tyrannus and in your private homes. I have preached the same message to Jew and Gentile alike: that is, the need to turn from sin to God through faith in our Lord Jesus.

"Now I am drawn by the Spirit to go to Jerusalem. I don't know what is waiting for me there except that in every city the Holy Spirit has been telling me that prison and suffering lay ahead. These things don't bother me. My life is worthless if I do not use it for the work the Lord Jesus has given me to do – and that is to tell others the 'good news' of God's wonderful grace.

"None of you who have heard my preaching will see my face again. But my conscience is clear. I have faithfully declared the Word to all, and no one can blame me if God condemns them.

"Be on guard as elders. Tend and feed God's flock, His church, which He purchased with His own blood.

"When I am gone, cruel wolves will attack you and do much damage to the flock. Even some of you here today will distort the truth in order to have followers. Remember that for three years I worked with you, warning you often and weeping over you. Now I give you into God's care and to His gracious Word. His Word will build you up and give you an inheritance with all those that He has set apart for himself.

"I never wanted anyone's gold or silver or clothing for myself. You know that I have worked for what I needed," Paul said, holding up his tent-making hands, "and for the needs of those who are with me. I have been an example of how to help the poor by working hard. Remember the words of the Lord Jesus Himself when He said, 'It is more blessed to give than to receive.'"

Paul finished speaking and dropped to his knees on the shore. One by one the others did the same. In a voice breaking with emotion, he prayed aloud as tears rolled down his cheeks. A few of the elders stifled sobs while Paul prayed. When he had finished, they wept loudly, threw their arms around his neck, and kissed him. The Ephesians grieved over his words that they would not see his face again.

Paul glanced toward the harbor, aware that his time with them was slipping away. The ship would soon be ready to leave. Together the group walked down to the dock. With churning emotions Paul tore himself away from the grieving Ephesians and boarded the vessel with his traveling companions.

May 2 to 9, A.D. 57, Cos, Rhodes, Patara

The captain sailed straight for Cos, a mountainous island and the home of the medical school founded by Hippocrates several centuries earlier. The next day the passengers were ready to sail before sunrise. Prevailing winds sent the ship on a straight course to the city of Rhodes on the island by the same name. By sunset the winds had died down and the sea had calmed. Beside the harbor lay the ruins of the gigantic Colossus of Rhodes, built more than 300 years earlier for the people's patron god Helios. An earthquake had destroyed it fifty-six years after workers had built it.

From there the ship turned east and sailed along the southern coast of Asia Minor until it arrived at Patara. "Our little group needs a larger merchant ship," Paul told his traveling companions. The men walked about the harbor and found one that would travel to the Syrian province of Phoenicia in record time – five days at sea. Besides cargo, the ship had room for several dozen passengers.

On May 5 a favorable wind blew. The passengers boarded and the crew raised the sail. Leaving the coastline of Asia the ship ventured across the open waters of the Mediterranean Sea. It then sailed south of Cyprus and continued toward the coast of Phoenicia.

As Paul's eyes scanned the eastern horizon, the city of Tyre came into view. Buildings hugged the shoreline of the blue Mediterranean waters. Palm trees waved in the breeze, and gently sloping mountains protruded along the north shore of the city. An officer informed the passengers of coming plans. "Workers will need several days to unload the cargo and prepare the ship to sail again. Those planning to sail to Caesarea should return in one week's time."

May 10 to 16, A.D. 57, Tyre, Ptolemais

Warm sunshine beat down on Paul and the other travelers as they stepped ashore. Several years earlier many from Tyre had traveled to hear Jesus speak, and He had healed some of them. Now Paul and his companions found local Christians and settled in for a seven-day visit.

While there, one of Christ's followers prophesied to Paul through the Spirit, "You should not go up to Jerusalem." Various believers repeated the same warning to him several times over. However, the prophecy did not change Paul's mind.

"I must continue the trip," he told them. "I cannot quit! Even though enemies are everywhere, I must safely deliver the funds to Jerusalem."

At the end of the seven days in Tyre, the men, their wives, and their children accompanied Paul to the seashore where all knelt together in the soft sand to pray. Paul and his companions said their good-byes, boarded ship, and sailed 25 miles south to Ptolemais. Again they sought out local Christians but were able to stay for only one day.

May 17 to 25, A.D. 57, Caesarea

The next day, May 17, Paul's ship sailed 30 miles down the coast to the city of Caesarea. As the ship pulled into the harbor, whitecaps broke against the shore. Government buildings stood boldly near the waterfront, and the large theater faced proudly toward the sea. An aqueduct provided a good supply of water to the city, and a large underground plumbing system allowed for proper drainage.

Philip the evangelist invited Paul and his friends to stay at his home.

"How long have you been a believer?" Paul asked.

"More than twenty years. I served as a deacon in the church at Jerusalem. I worked with Stephen and six others to distribute daily food to the widows there."

Paul burned with shame as his mind flashed back more than twenty years. With racing heart he remembered his own involvement with the Council that had sentenced Stephen to death.

"When the persecution came," Philip continued, "I preached the gospel in Samaria. I also had the opportunity to lead an Ethiopian eunuch to Christ on the road to Gaza. After I traveled and preached for a time, I settled here in Caesarea. Now I have four unmarried daughters who prophesy."

During Paul's stay in Caesarea a man named Agabus, who had the gift of prophecy, arrived from Judea. While visiting Paul and the Christians, he picked up Paul's belt and tied his own hands and feet with it. "The Holy Spirit says," Agabus stated, "that the owner of this belt will be tied up by the Jewish leaders in Jerusalem and turned over to the Romans!"

"Oh, Paul," one of the believers urged, "if your enemies are going to capture you, you mustn't go up to Jerusalem."

"My mind is made up," Paul stated firmly.

Several began to weep. Through tears one of them pleaded, "Paul, you have many enemies in Jerusalem. Please be careful."

"I understand what is waiting for me in Jerusalem," Paul responded.

"Please, don't go!"

"This is not the first time people have urged me to stay away from Jerusalem," Paul said as he remembered his farewell in Tyre.

The little group continued to plead tearfully with him. "Why won't you pay attention to our suggestions? You will probably be thrown into jail or killed."

Caesarea

Chapter
THIRTEEN

Courageous Servant

Caesarea, Jerusalem

May, A.D. 57, Caesarea

"Why are you weeping?" Paul asked with a catch in his voice. "You are breaking my heart. Do you not understand that I am ready to be jailed or even to die for the Lord Jesus?"

"Please, Paul...don't go to Jerusalem!"

"Nothing you say will change my mind."

"All right," one of the Christians said with resignation. "May the Lord's will be done."

Paul busied himself preparing his baggage for the upcoming trip. One of the believers entered the room and spoke to him. "A few of us will travel with you. You do not have much time if you still hope to arrive in Jerusalem by Pentecost. The 60-mile trip into the hill country will be much faster with horses. Mnason will be returning to his home. It should be easy to make it to his house by evening."

When it was time to leave, Paul, Luke, and the travelers mounted horses for the trip to Jerusalem. The rhythmic clattering of the horses' hooves echoed through the streets of Caesarea. The group left the city, traveled across a fertile plain, and turned southeast.

As their first day drew to a close, they reined in at Mnason's house. This Jewish man with a Greek name was a native of Cyprus, and he had been one of the first converts to Christianity. He provided an overnight place for Paul and his Gentile companions to stay.

Jerusalem

The next day the travelers continued their trip through pine forests as the roads wound upwards toward Jerusalem. At the top of the last ridge the stone walls of the city appeared before them. The group entered through one of the gates at the north end of the city. The Temple in the northeast corner covered almost a quarter of Jerusalem's land.

As he had hoped, Paul arrived fifty days after the Passover, just in time for the one-day festival of Pentecost on May 29, A.D. 57. This feast marked the end of the harvest and the beginning of firstfruits, a time when people remembered the needy – the orphans, the widows, and the poor. The travelers delivered the gifts they had brought from the churches in Macedonia and Greece for the destitute believers in Jerusalem.

James, a half-brother of the Lord, was a leading elder in the church of Jerusalem. He sent word to the other elders to meet with the travelers at his place. As the men arrived, various ones entered the room and exchanged greetings. "Welcome back, Paul. It's great to have you here again."

"I am thankful that the Lord has kept me and brought me back safely."

"When did you last visit Jerusalem?"

"I made a short visit almost five years ago, but I spent the winter in Antioch. I left the following spring on my most recent journey."

"Tell us about your trip."

"God did wonderful things among the Gentiles. The churches are growing in many cities of Asia, Macedonia, and Greece." Paul continued to describe in detail what God had done.

"Praise God," one of the elders said. "May the Lord be glorified for His great grace to the Gentiles. Here in Jerusalem many thousands of Jews follow Christ. And all of them have great respect for the Law of Moses. A group of these Jewish Christians are concerned that you are teaching the Jews who are living among the Gentiles that they should no longer follow the Law of Moses. When these individuals learn that you have come to town, they will not be pleased. They say that you teach people not to circumcise their children or to follow traditional customs. Such teachings could potentially touch off an explosive situation."

"But," Paul reminded them, "I already made clear my position regarding circumcision when I wrote the letter to the Galatians. I have no objection to circumcision, but insisting it is necessary in order to be right with God is going too far."

"I have an idea," an elder suggested. "Four of us have vowed to purify ourselves. We are about to shave our heads and go to the Temple as part of the purification ceremony. Why don't you join us? You can pay for us to have our heads shaved. The people will realize that the rumors are false and that you still practice Jewish law. As for the Gentile believers, refer them to the instructions sent from Jerusalem to the Gentile churches several years ago – 'Don't eat food offered to idols, don't eat blood, and don't eat meat from animals killed in such a way that the blood is not completely drained away. And stay away from all sexual immorality.'"

"Fine," Paul agreed. "I will go with you to the Temple tomorrow. It may help the ones who are weak in the faith."

The next day Paul and the men performed the purification ceremony. Paul entered the Temple and announced how many days it would be until the purification would end.

Near the end of the seven days Paul walked through the streets of Jerusalem with Trophimus, a fellow-worker from Ephesus.

Jews from the province of Asia caught sight of Paul and discussed him among themselves. "There goes Paul with one of those Gentiles," one sneered. "He even has the nerve to go into the Temple with that Gentile."

"Are you sure?" his companion asked.

"Yes, he takes Gentiles into the inner court, even though that is expressly forbidden."

Unaware of the conversation taking place nearby, Paul and Trophimus continued through the streets, passing local vendors. As they neared the Temple, Paul turned to Trophimus, "I must go on alone."

"I'll see you later," Trophimus said as the two men parted.

Paul walked through the outer court of the Temple and up to the barrier separating it from the inner court. He glanced at the sign hanging from the barrier: 'No foreigner may enter within the barricade which surrounds the Temple and its enclosure. Anyone who is caught trespassing will bear personal responsibility for his ensuing death.'

The Jews who had seen Paul in the street with Trophimus a few minutes earlier entered the Temple and now found Paul in the inner court. "There he is," one of the men said, pointing across the court toward Paul. "That Gentile must still be with him!"

Men surrounded Paul and grabbed him. With angry eyes one of them shouted, "Look at this man, you Israelites! He causes all kinds of trouble!"

Paul's heart pounded as he struggled to pull himself free. But he could not break away.

"Hold that man down!" someone yelled.

"Don't let him escape! He travels all over, teaching our people to disobey Jewish law."

Steps leading down from the inner court to the outer court of the Temple

"It's worse than that," the leader of the pack said as he spat out the accusations with hatred. "He speaks against the Temple and even brings Gentiles into it. Our holy place has been made unclean by his actions."

Strong men dragged Paul out of the inner court. The Temple police shut the gates tightly behind them. Paul's body bumped heavily from step to step as the men pulled him into the outer court. Curious people ran from all directions toward the disturbance.

"Okay, you troublemaker," one of the attackers muttered. "Let's finish you off!"

Paul's stomach tightened as the men aimed their blows at his body and head. He raised his arms to protect himself. Fists slammed against his flesh until he could hardly breathe. His legs shook and the blood pounded in his head.

"Kill him, kill him!" came the cry from every direction.

A concerned onlooker from the crowd quickly ran into the Antonia Fortress, a prison located outside the northwest corner of the Temple grounds. "Where is Claudius Lysias, the commander of the Roman regiment?"

"Why do you need him?"

"A man is being badly beaten."

Claudius Lysias, who stood nearby, turned and asked, "Where is the trouble?"

"Come quickly! There's a riot at the Temple – a man is being attacked, and things are out of control."

Immediately the commander ordered officers to go with him to the scene of the trouble. The men ran down the two flights of stairs that connected the prison to the outer court of the Temple.

"What's going on?" the Roman commander shouted. At the sound of his voice, many in the crowd turned toward the commander and left Paul lying alone in agony.

"Arrest the accused," the commander ordered his officers. "Bind him with two chains."

'Two chains!' The words thundered in Paul's ears. The prophecy made by Agabus in Caesarea had come true: "The Holy Spirit says that the owner of this belt will be tied up by the Jewish leaders in Jerusalem and turned over to the Romans." It had been fewer than two weeks since Agabus had prophesied these words.

The commander raised his voice and spoke to the crowd, "Who is this man? What has he done?"

One by one, individuals shouted accusations. "He's destroying our laws."

"He is ruining our Temple."

"He's...." The noise and confusion swallowed up the answers. No two people said the same thing. Finally, the commander ordered his officers, "Take him up the steps and into the Fortress."

Officers surrounded Paul and pulled him toward the outside stairs of the Fortress. As the mob pushed and shoved, the crushing throng squeezed against Paul's small frame until he could hardly breathe. Finally, the officers lifted the battered and bruised prisoner above their shoulders to protect him from being mauled by the angry crowd and carried him up the stairs.

"Away with him! Kill him!" the crowd shouted.

"May I have a word with you?" Paul said to the commanding officer at the top of the stairs.

"Do you speak Greek?" the commander asked in surprise. "Aren't you the Egyptian who caused a riot a while ago? Didn't you lead four thousand members of the Assassins out into the desert?"

"No, I am a Jew, a native of the well-known city of Tarsus in Cilica. Please allow me to speak to the people."

"Go ahead," the commander agreed.

Paul stood on the stairs, thankful he could use his voice one more time to tell his fellow Israelites about the Light that shines in darkness. Surrounded by officers he calmly motioned with his chained hands for the people to be quiet. "Brothers and esteemed fathers," Paul said, raising his voice. "Allow me to defend myself." A hush fell over the angry crowd as Paul spoke to them in their own Hebrew language.

"I am a Jew, born in Tarsus, a city in Cilicia, but I was raised and educated here in Jerusalem under Gamaliel. He taught me to follow the details of our Jewish law. I wanted to honor God in all that I did. I attacked followers of 'the Way,' even to the point of death. I chained and imprisoned men and women. The high priest and the whole Council of leaders can tell you that this is true. I had letters of introduction from them to our Jewish brothers in Damascus. These letters gave me permission to arrest Christians and to bring them to Jerusalem for punishment.

"At about noon, as I neared Damascus, a bright light from heaven suddenly shone around me. I fell to the ground, and a voice spoke, 'Saul, Saul, why are you persecuting Me?'

" 'Who are you, Lord?' I asked.

" 'I am Jesus of Nazareth, the One you are persecuting,' He answered.

" 'What must I do, Lord?' I responded.

" 'Stand up,' He said, 'and continue your journey to Damascus. When you arrive, you will be told what to do.'

"I had been blinded by the bright light, and my companions had to lead me into the city. Ananias, a God-fearing man who kept the Law, came to me and helped me regain my sight. He told me that the God of our ancestors had called me to know His will, to hear His voice, and to carry His message everywhere – to the whole world. After that, I was baptized.

"Later I returned to Jerusalem. While praying in the temple I went into a trance, and Jesus told me to leave Jerusalem because the people there would not accept my witness. I argued with the Lord because I cared about my fellow Israelites. 'Surely,' I told Him, 'my fellow-Jews know that I imprisoned and beat any who followed Jesus. I accompanied those who stoned Stephen and his death pleased me. I held the coats while the others killed him.'

"However, the Lord told me, 'Go! I will send you far away to the Gentiles.'"

When the crowd heard the word 'Gentiles,' the protests resumed. "Away, away," the crowd chanted waving their arms wildly.

"Rid the earth of this fellow," an individual shouted above the confusion.

"Such a man is not fit to live."

"Kill him!"

The turmoil of the crowd made it impossible for Paul to continue speaking. His heart sank as he stood helplessly at the top of the steps and watched the reaction of his own people. He wanted to continue telling them the 'good news' about Christ, but the men in the crowd made listening impossible as they tore off their coats, waved them around, and threw handfuls of dust into the air.

Chapter
⁔FOURTEEN⁔

Roman Citizen

Jerusalem, Caesarea

June 3 to 9, A.D. 57, Jerusalem

"Find out what crime this man has committed," the commander ordered his officers. "Lead the criminal inside the Fortress and give him a whipping. He will soon be ready to tell us the truth." Officers guided Paul inside and removed his outer clothing to lay bare his skin. They tied him down with straps, stretching his body over a frame so the pieces of bone on the leather whip would most effectively bite into his flesh.

As the officers were finishing their preparations, Paul turned to one of them and asked, "Are you permitted to whip a Roman citizen who has not been tried or found guilty?"

The officer recoiled in shock, fear clutching his heart. He had been about to commit an illegal act. He quickly left the room in search of his commander. "Do you realize what you have asked me to do? This man says he is a Roman citizen!"

"What? Are you sure?"

"That's what he told me."

"I'll go and ask him myself," the commander said. He hurried into the room where Paul waited. "Tell me, are you a Roman citizen?"

"Yes, I am," Paul replied with calm dignity.

"Well, so am I," the commander responded. "But I had to buy my citizenship for a large sum!"

"I am a citizen by birth."

The commander turned to his men. "Untie him. He will not be whipped or interrogated."

The next day the commander proceeded with the case in a more orderly way since the Roman Empire required that he provide protection for any Roman citizen. "Unchain Paul," he ordered an officer. To another he said, "This case will need a formal inquiry. Go to the leading priests of the Sanhedrin, the Jewish High Council, and tell them to call their members together for a legal session."

Later the court session was held in the open-air Council chamber on the western slope of the Temple hill. As the men arrived, they sat in seats forming a semi-circle. Two clerks took up their positions. One would record the 'not-guilty' votes, and the other, the votes of 'condemnation.' Disciples of the court sat in the front. When everyone had arrived, the commander instructed, "Bring in the prisoner."

"Today's court session is to find the real reason for yesterday's trouble," a Roman officer stated. "Paul, what do you have to say to the Council in your own defense?"

Paul's eyes scanned the Council members. "Fellow Jews, I have listened to God's voice and lived my life with a clear conscience before God up to this day!"

Ananias, the high priest for the last ten years, shouted orders in a heated voice, "Slap that man on the mouth!"

Paul's eyes flashed with anger and his blood boiled as he reacted to this unjust order. He could feel the sting of the hand even before it landed. Without thinking, he snapped back at Ananias, "God will strike you, you whitewashed wall! How dare you judge me by the Law! You are breaking it yourself by ordering an officer to strike me before I have been tried in court!"

Stunned silence hung in the room. A man standing next to

Paul leaned toward him and said in a loud whisper, "Do you realize that you are insulting God's high priest?"

"I could not tell that he was the high priest," Paul replied. "I have been absent from Jerusalem for several years, and he is sitting as an ordinary member of the Council. A Roman officer is presiding today, not the high priest. For that reason, I did not recognize his position."

Paul adjusted his tone of voice and turned to the high priest, "I apologize for my comments. The Scriptures say, 'You must not speak evil of anyone who rules the people.'"

Paul's sharp mind now noted that the Council members consisted of two groups united against him, the Sadducees and the Pharisees. As a Pharisee himself, Paul understood that beneath the surface the two groups disagreed with each other on many important points.

Paul wanted everyone to see the real reason the Jews had brought him to trial. He cleared his throat and spoke in a loud voice, "Brothers, I am a Pharisee and my ancestors were Pharisees. I am on trial today because my hope is in the resurrection of the dead."

"There is no resurrection of the dead," a Sadducee called out.

"Yes, there is!" a Pharisee retorted.

"No, there is not! There is neither resurrection nor angels nor demons!"

"The unseen world exists, even if you say otherwise!" a Pharisee hotly protested. The two groups jumped to their feet and yelled insults at each other.

A spokesman for the Pharisees managed to shout above the confusion. "This man Paul believes in the resurrection of the dead and so do we. He teaches that angels and spirits exist – and that teaching is true. Perhaps a spirit or an angel has spoken to him. It is not right to fight against God."

The Pharisees grabbed Paul and pulled him toward their side. The Sadducees snatched at his clothing and pulled him back. The two groups pulled Paul first in one direction and then in the other.

"Enough!" the commander ordered, as he turned to his soldiers. "Escort this man back to the safety of the Fortress before he is literally torn apart."

The soldiers took Paul from before the Council and walked him back to his cell at the Fortress. As Paul sat alone in the descending darkness, the events of the last two days weighed heavily on his mind. What would happen next? Would there be days of suffering ahead? His heart sank as he realized that his plans to visit Rome and other far away lands might never occur. After praying, he lay down hoping for a good night's rest.

During the night the Lord appeared to him in his dark cell and spoke words of comfort. "Have courage, Paul. You have witnessed for Me here in Jerusalem, but you must yet preach the 'good news' in Rome."

At the first light of day, a group of forty Jews gathered in a secret location. "How could Paul have slipped through our fingers?" one of them asked. "Doesn't anyone have a foolproof plan to capture him? We must not fail this time."

"Let us bind ourselves with this oath: 'None of us will eat or drink anything until Paul has been killed!'"

When the men had taken the oath, some of them hurried over to talk with the leading priests. "Forty of us have sworn to neither eat nor drink until Paul has been killed."

"How can we help with your plan?" a Council member asked.

"This is how it will work. You will send word to the commander, asking him to bring Paul back before the Council. Pretend you want to question him further for information that is more exact. While he is being moved from the Fortress to the Council chambers, our men will be ready to attack and kill him."

As the group plotted how to proceed, Paul's nephew, his sister's son, learned of the planned attack. He belonged to an influential family in Jerusalem and reacted quickly. He hurried to the Fortress. Entering the building, he found Paul and told him what he had discovered.

Paul immediately called to a guard. "Officer, come here for a moment."

"What do you want?"

"Would you show this young man to the commander? He has important information to tell him."

Paul's nephew followed the officer through the dimly lit hallways.

"Commander," the officer said when they arrived, "Paul, the prisoner, called me over to his cell. He asked that I bring this youth to you. He has information for you to consider."

The commander caught hold of the young man's hand and led him to a quiet area. "What is the news you have for me?"

"A number of Jews are planning to ask you…" his voice trailed off as he nervously gulped for air.

"Yes, yes – tell me more."

"The Jews want to ask you to send Paul to the Jewish Council tomorrow."

"Again? Why would they do that?"

"Their plan is to tell you that they need more precise information from him." The youth's voice shook with emotion as he continued, "I beg you, do not do it! More than forty men will be hiding along the way to jump out and kill him. The men have made a vow to neither eat nor drink until they have murdered Paul. Everything is ready to proceed, and they expect you to give your consent."

"Do not mention this information to anyone," the commander warned in a stern voice. "Now you can be on your way."

This 'commander of a thousand' called two of his officers. "Make preparations for two hundred foot soldiers to leave for Caesarea at nine o'clock tonight. Go with seventy horsemen and two hundred men armed with spears. Provide a horse for Paul to ride. Make sure that this prisoner is delivered safely to Felix, the governor of Judea."

When he had finished giving orders, he sat down and wrote a letter to the governor:

Jerusalem

"From Claudius Lysias,

To his Excellency, Governor Felix:

Greetings!

This man was seized by some Jews, and they were about to kill him when I arrived with the troops. When I learned that he was a Roman citizen, I removed him to safety. Then I took him to their high council to try to learn the basis of the accusations against him. I soon discovered the charge was something regarding their religious law – certainly nothing worthy of imprisonment or death. But when I was informed of a plot to kill him, I immediately sent him on to you. I have told his accusers to bring their charges before you."

(Acts 23:26-30 NLT)

That night, three hours after sunset, the troops and their prisoner mounted their horses. The clatter of hooves echoed through the narrow stone streets as they passed through the city gates and into the dark countryside, following the great Roman road that led from Jerusalem to Caesarea. The soldiers and their prisoner traveled north over the rocky hills, aware that, at any moment, the enemy could spring out from the shadows or from behind a large rock. They journeyed through the night until they reached the city of Antipatris, thirty-five miles northwest of Jerusalem. This fertile wooded area lay in the foothills toward the coast. Herod the Great had rebuilt this city several years earlier and named it for his father Antipater.

The traveling party no longer needed the extra protection, so in the morning the two hundred foot soldiers and two hundred men armed with spears returned to the Fortress. Paul and the horsemen resumed their travel north through open country to cover the remaining twenty-seven miles to the coastal city of Caesarea, a city named after the Roman emperor Caesar Augustus.

Caesarea

As they neared the sandy shores of the coast, the horses trotted over a ridge. The city of Caesarea stood before them, complete with theater, stadium, and marble temples. An aqueduct parallel to the beach supported pipes carrying fresh water to the city from a northern spring.

The horses slowed to a walking pace as the group entered the city. This was the official home of the Roman governor Felix, Emperor Nero's representative. Governor Felix lived in a palace built by Herod on a high point of rock that overlooked

Aqueduct beside the Mediterranean Sea at Caesarea

the water. The elegant residence had generous living quarters for Felix, his family, and his servants. A private bathing pool and tropical gardens added a luxurious touch to the mansion. The governor's offices stood at the center of the building. Felix was a man of humble birth, but he had advanced to his current position in A.D. 52 through the influence of his brother Pallas, a freedman, who was a favorite of Emperor Claudius Caesar.

One of Claudius Lysias' men handed the letter to the governor. Felix opened it and quickly read the contents. He glanced at the unimpressive man standing before him, "From which province do you come?"

"Cilicia, your Excellency," Paul responded. "I am a citizen of Tarsus."

"Very well. Since you come from a Roman province, I will deal with your case when your accusers arrive." He turned to his officials, "Keep this man under guard in the prison at Herod's palace."

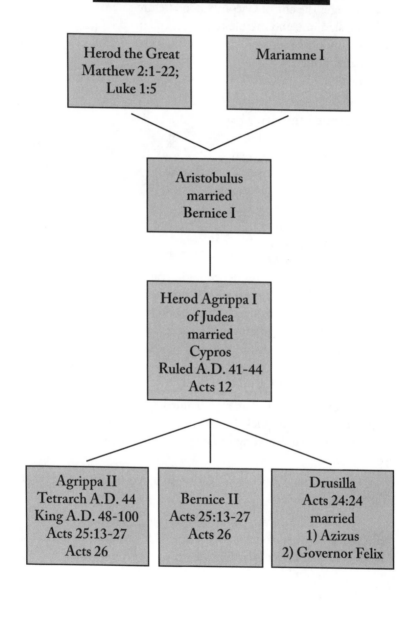

Herod's Family Tree

Herod the Great
Matthew 2:1-22;
Luke 1:5

Mariamne I

Aristobulus
married
Bernice I

Herod Agrippa I
of Judea
married
Cypros
Ruled A.D. 41-44
Acts 12

Agrippa II
Tetrarch A.D. 44
King A.D. 48-100
Acts 25:13-27
Acts 26

Bernice II
Acts 25:13-27
Acts 26

Drusilla
Acts 24:24
married
1) Azizus
2) Governor Felix

Chapter
FIFTEEN

Faithful Witness

Caesarea

Paul waited in one of the prison cells attached to Herod's Palace. Five days later Ananias the high priest and various Jewish leaders arrived in Caesarea. Tertullus, a man skilled in public speaking, had come to act as their lawyer.

June 9, A.D. 57, Caesarea

"Bring in the prisoner," Governor Felix ordered when members of the court had come together.

A guard left the room, and moments later the rattle of chains announced Paul's arrival.

"Are you Paul?" the governor asked from the judge's seat.

"Yes, your Excellency, I am."

Governor Felix nodded at the Jews' lawyer, Tertullus. "You may proceed."

Tertullus rose and spoke directly to Governor Felix. "Your Excellency, your wise leadership has given us peace. You have provided many reforms to our country. In doing that, you planned well for our future, and we are deeply grateful to you. But since I do not want to use too much of your time, I ask that you kindly listen to the case against this man. He is a troublemaker, a real nuisance. He has made a habit of causing riots among the Jews all over the world.

He encourages people to rebel against the Roman government. In fact, he is a ringleader of the sect called the Nazarenes. He recently tried to defile the Temple in Jerusalem – and that is when these men arrested him. If you question him, you will find that our accusations are true."

Having concluded his argument forcefully, Tertullus sat down.

The Jews nodded their heads in agreement, and various ones around the room voiced their approval. "He's right."

"Yes, Tertullus has spoken the absolute truth."

Governor Felix cut off their casual comments. "Order in the court," he instructed as he motioned for the prisoner to speak.

Paul breathed a prayer for God's guidance and then turned his attention to Felix. "Your Excellency, you have had years of experience in judging matters relating to the Jewish nation, so I am pleased to make my defense before you. It has been only twelve days since I traveled to Jerusalem to worship. I did not argue with anyone, nor did I stir up a riot at the Temple or on any of the streets of the city. These men have no evidence. There is no proof to confirm their accusations against me. However, I confess that I do follow 'the Way,' which those who are against me call a sect. In this teaching I worship the God of our fathers and accept as true everything written in the Law and the Prophets. I have hope toward God as they do. I have faith in the fact that there will be a resurrection of the righteous and the wicked. I do my best to have a clear conscience before God and man.

"I left Jerusalem several years ago to travel. I returned a few days ago with money to help my people and to offer sacrifices to God. My accusers, Jews from the province of Asia, found me in the courtyard of the Temple where I had gone to complete a purification ritual. I was not having a heated debate or speaking to a disapproving crowd. Things were quiet. The men who have charged me ought to be here as witnesses, but they have not bothered to come. Of what crime did the Jewish Council find me guilty? Perhaps the real reason I am here today is because I shouted, 'I am being judged today because I believe in the resurrection of the dead!'"

"Enough!" Governor Felix said, cutting him off. "I am familiar with 'the Way.' I will re-examine your case when the garrison commander Claudius Lysias arrives from Jerusalem."

Felix turned to one of the officers. "Keep Paul in custody, but allow him to have a certain amount of freedom. He is a Roman citizen, and no one has proved his crime. He may receive visits from friends to provide for his needs."

Several days later Felix spoke to one of the guards. "Bring Paul from his cell. Perhaps he will entertain us today."

Felix sat with his beautiful teenaged wife Drusilla, who came from a well-known Jewish family. Her father, Herod Agrippa I, had ordered the death of the apostle James and had planned to kill the apostle Peter. But God struck Herod with an illness in A.D. 44 at Caesarea when he encouraged the crowd to worship him as a god. Drusilla was six-years-old when her father died. Drusilla's great-uncle, Herod Antipas, had killed John the Baptist, and her great-grandfather, Herod the Great, had ordered the killing of the babies of Bethlehem.

In recent years Drusilla had caused quite a scandal. Her brother, Herod Agrippa II, had given her in marriage to Azizus, king of an unimportant state in Syria. Shortly afterwards, Governor Felix persuaded the sixteen-year-old to desert her husband by telling her he would give her much 'felicity,' or happiness, if she would agree to be his third wife.

When Paul arrived, Felix asked him, "What do you have to say for yourself today?"

After greeting the governor, Paul seized the opportunity to witness. "Most noble Felix, you are in a position to judge people. You may choose to reward them for their good deeds or punish them for their crimes. In a similar way, God will be the final Judge at the end of each life. God is just, and no one can bribe Him. He gives equal justice to the proud and to the humble person. God's grace brings salvation to all men. I am not ashamed of God's 'good news.' It is God's power to save all who believe. Christ Jesus came into this world to bring light to those who live in darkness. You will answer to God for the way you have lived and for giving in to your passions."

Felix squirmed uncomfortably in his seat and fidgeted with his hands.

"Everyone will be required to give an account of himself to God," Paul said forcefully. "God will judge the secrets of all men. He has a day set to judge the whole world with justice. He will do it through a Man whom He has chosen. He gave proof that He would do this when He raised that very Man from death. God has exalted the Lord Jesus Christ, and one day every knee will bow to Him and every tongue will confess that Jesus is Lord."

Felix swallowed hard and his hands trembled. He did not always rule with justice or show mercy. He did not practice self-control. He had married one wife after another, his first being the granddaughter of Anthony and Cleopatra. He had married a second time, and now he sat before Paul with Drusilla, his third wife.

"Now is a good time to respond to God's salvation," Paul continued. "Every man has an appointment with death, and after that, he will face God's judgment."

Felix shifted his position and avoided eye contact with Paul. "Stop!" Felix ordered, raising his hand. "That's enough for today. I will call for you again at a more convenient time."

The guards entered and escorted Paul back to prison.

*   *   *   *   *   *   *

For Paul one long day blended into the next, but he thanked God for friends who came to visit and to meet his needs. Governor Felix noted that Paul spoke as a man who might have come from a wealthy family. At times he called Paul to talk with him because he secretly hoped that during these talks Paul would offer him a large bribe in return for his freedom.

A.D. 59, Caesarea

As the months passed, Felix worried about unrest in Caesarea. Tension mounted as Jews and Gentiles clashed. Felix sent in troops, and many Jewish leaders died. Because of the unrest, Emperor

Nero recalled Felix as governor and replaced him with Porcius Festus. Felix left Paul in prison even though he had found no evidence of his guilt. He did not want to offend the Jewish leaders by freeing Paul.

Three days after entering the province of Judea as the new governor, Festus left Caesarea and traveled up to Jerusalem. Here the chief priests and the Jewish leaders met with Governor Festus and exchanged greetings. The Jews had been eager to re-open Paul's case. One of the spokesmen addressed Festus. "Would you do us a favor? Could you transfer Paul back to Jerusalem?"

Hushed voices at the back of the group made secret plans. "Paul's trip from Caesarea to Jerusalem will give us another opportunity to kill him."

Though new to the job, Festus answered them matter-of-factly, "No, I will keep Paul in Caesarea. He is safe there. Besides, I don't plan to stay in Jerusalem long. Have your leading men come with me if you would like. In that way you can charge Paul with whatever crime he has committed."

Festus remained in Jerusalem for a week and then returned to Caesarea.

July, A.D. 59

The day after his arrival in Caesarea, Governor Festus sent for Paul. The governor called the court to order. He would also serve as judge.

Turning to the accusers, he nodded, "State your charges."

"This man breaks the Jewish law. He violates the holiness of our Temple." The accusations continued for several minutes.

"Are there witnesses?" the judge asked.

"No, there are no witnesses."

Festus turned toward Paul, "Please state your defense."

"I am not guilty. I deny all the charges. I have committed no crime against the Jewish law, nor have I defiled the Temple in Jerusalem. Neither have I suggested that anyone rebel against the

Roman government. I am being falsely accused!"

Festus noted the lack of evidence against Paul. Yet as a new governor and judge, Festus wanted to gain popularity among the Jews, so he turned to Paul and asked, "Are you prepared to go to Jerusalem and stand trial before me and the Jewish leaders?"

"No! Absolutely not!" Paul said, as his heart pounded wildly. "I am standing in an official Roman court, and this is where I must be tried. I am not guilty. If I had committed a crime that deserved the death penalty, I would not object to dying. But I have done nothing. There are no witnesses here today. No one has a right to turn me over to these bloodthirsty men. They will kill me at the first opportunity. I appeal to Caesar."

Festus consulted for a few minutes with his experienced advisors. Afterwards he turned to Paul, "You have appealed to Caesar – to Caesar you will go."

The current Caesar, Emperor Nero, was a young man in his early twenties. Five years earlier Claudius Caesar had ruled the Empire. But Agrippina, his wife, poisoned him. She set in motion plans to insure that her son Nero would be head of the Roman Empire instead of Claudius' son Britannicus. Nero became Emperor on October 13, A.D. 54, during the time that Paul had been working in Ephesus. Shortly after Nero came to power, he followed his mother's evil example by poisoning Claudius' son Britannicus. He then had him quickly and secretly buried. During the early years of Nero's reign, Seneca, his tutor, and Burrus, a military official, strongly influenced him. As a result, he earned a good reputation as a capable administrator. However, no one could have imagined the evil that lurked in this man's heart.

*   *   *   *   *   *   *

Several days after Paul's appeal to Caesar, King Agrippa II arrived with his sister Julia Bernice. Both in their early thirties, these two were the adult children of the late Herod Agrippa I and were the older siblings of Drusilla. Her father had earlier given Bernice in marriage to his own brother. When her husband died in the year A.D. 48, she chose to live with her brother Agrippa.

Years earlier Emperor Claudius had given Agrippa II the title of King. In addition he gave him the territories northeast of Palestine. Now Agrippa II had come to visit Festus to congratulate him on his recent appointment as governor.

After the visitors had been there several days, Festus asked for Agrippa's help. "You are an expert in Jewish religious questions, are you not? I need your opinion regarding a man that Felix left in prison."

"What crime has he committed?"

"The Jewish leaders informed me of the charges against him during my stay in Jerusalem and asked me to convict him. Of course, I told them that Roman law does not convict people without a trial. An accused man must first have an opportunity to defend himself. When I returned to Caesarea, the accusers followed me back to the coast but did not accuse him of the usual crimes. Their complaint seemed to be centered on a religious dispute about a man named Jesus who died a few years ago. Paul insists that He is still alive.

"I asked Paul if he would return to Jerusalem to face the charges, but he refused and appealed to Caesar. He is here in prison until I can arrange to send him to Rome. Of course, that means that I will have to write a report of the case as it has developed. But first I need to understand the issues."

"I would like to hear this man's case," Agrippa remarked.

"You shall," Festus replied, "tomorrow."

*   *   *   *   *   *   *

A retinue of servants escorted King Agrippa and Bernice to the courtroom. They entered dressed in their royal robes. Military commanders and leading men of the city accompanied them.

"Bring in Paul," Festus ordered. When the invited guests had settled into their seats, officers ushered Paul into the room. Festus addressed them. "King Agrippa and all who are here today, this is the man that the Jews in Jerusalem and Caesarea are saying must not be allowed to live. He appears to have done nothing to deserve the death penalty. He has made an appeal to His Majesty the Emperor, and I will be sending him to Rome. But I have nothing specific to write concerning him to my Imperial master. Today I have brought him before all of you, and especially before you, King Agrippa, that I might find something definite to write. It is ridiculous to send a prisoner to Rome without indicating the charges!"

"Yes, it would be a little embarrassing," Agrippa agreed, as a slight smile played on his lips.

"Agrippa, why don't you take charge of the session?"

Agrippa nodded at Festus and turned to Paul. "You have permission to state your case."

Paul managed to raise his hand in greeting in spite of his chains. "I am happy, King Agrippa, to be able to defend myself before a man of such importance. You are an expert when it comes to the customs and problems of the Jews. I request that you patiently hear me to the end.

"As a youth I received a thorough Jewish training in Jerusalem and belonged to the Pharisees, who taught the resurrection of the dead. Today I am on trial because of the fulfillment of God's promise made to our ancestors. God promised that a Messiah would come, but our ancestors are not here to witness it. The twelve tribes served God in the hope of that promise, but they died without seeing it fulfilled. However, God kept His Word to our ancestors. The Messiah did come."

Paul turned away from Agrippa to face the whole audience. "If God sent the Messiah as He promised, why does it seem incredible to any of you that God can raise the dead?"

Paul turned back to Agrippa and continued, "I once opposed the followers of Jesus of Nazareth. The leading priests authorized me to send them to prison. I voted for their death. I had them whipped in the synagogues, hoping that followers of 'the Way' would curse Christ. Enraged, I hunted them down in distant cities and foreign lands. One day I traveled toward Damascus...."

His audience sat spellbound as Paul communicated in detail his encounter with the Lord and then God's promise to send him to the Gentiles.

"And so, O King Agrippa," Paul concluded, "I am preaching, as God instructed, and the message is that all must turn from their sin to God. After that, they should live in a way that proves their heart has changed. When I preached this message to the Jews, they did not like it, so they arrested me in the Temple and tried to kill me. But I am alive today, and I am teaching exactly what the prophets and Moses said would happen – that the Messiah would have to die and rise again from the dead and that he would be a light in the darkness to both the Jews and the Gentiles."

"Paul!" Festus shouted, jumping to his feet. "You are mad! You have studied too much and are losing your mind."

"I am not out of my mind, most excellent Festus. I am speaking the absolute truth. King Agrippa is familiar with these things. I can speak openly to him because this is common knowledge. King Agrippa, do you believe the prophets?"

Silence hung in the air as the people in the room waited for King Agrippa to answer.

"I know you do," Paul added.

Agrippa cleared his throat and carefully worded his response so he would please both Festus and the Jewish leaders. "Paul, you are trying to persuade me to be a Christian."

"I pray to God that everyone here today might be as I am – except for these chains," Paul said, holding up his shackled and scarred wrists.

"That will be enough for today," Governor Festus announced. "The session is ended. Guards, escort Paul back to his prison cell."

King Agrippa, Bernice, and others stood up to leave. As Festus and King Agrippa walked toward the door, they discussed Paul's case. "What do you think?" Festus asked.

"There is no evidence that this man deserves prison or death," Agrippa observed. "This man might have been set free if he had not appealed to Caesar!"

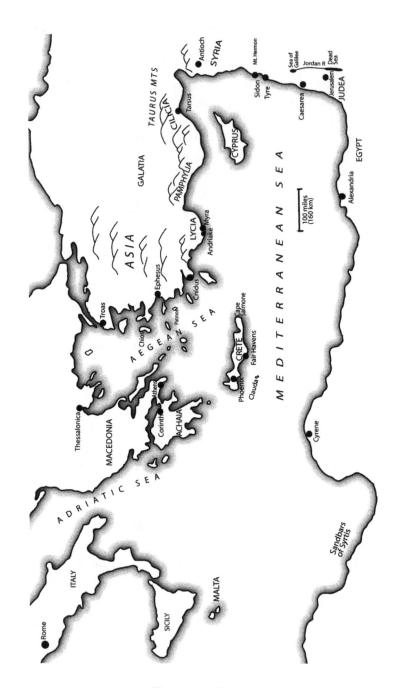

Voyage to Rome

Chapter
⌒SIXTEEN⌒

Voice in the Storm

Caesarea, Crete

August, A.D. 59, Caesarea

"Julius," Governor Festus commanded, "you will be responsible for Paul and the political prisoners. Take them from prison and deliver them to Rome."

"Consider it done, most excellent Festus," the centurion responded.

"Go before the season changes and the climate makes it impossible to travel."

"I will make immediate plans."

Julius, a Roman officer in the Emperor's Division, left the room. Without delay he headed straight for the harbor to find a ship sailing to Italy. Striding through the streets in full dress, he left quite an impression. He wore a leather breastplate, a tall helmet, and had a sharp sword hanging at his side. A wooden staff indicated his rank.

The harbor had been built years earlier by Herod the Great. Boats entered the 200-foot wide harbor from the northwest. Two enormous stone breakwaters stood as an arc in the sea. One of these had towers, a walkway, and houses where seamen could live. The waves of the Mediterranean buffeted the sandy shore along the coast, but the breakwater protected the ships.

Julius spoke to one of the captains, "Are there any large ships heading to Italy by way of Alexandria in Egypt?"

"No, there are none."

Julius hesitated for a moment. "Where is this smaller vessel going?"

"It's sailing up the coast to our home port Adramyttium, a small town located south of Troas on the west coast of Asia Minor, but it will be stopping at various coastal towns along the way."

"That should work. I'll be able to connect with a ship going to Italy from one of the larger ports. Do you have room for extra passengers?"

"Yes, there is enough space for a number of people."

"When will the ship be leaving?"

"As soon as possible."

"Good. I'll be traveling with a group of prisoners."

*   *   *   *   *   *   *

Julius prepared the prisoners for the coming trip. When all were chained and ready to go, he escorted them to the harbor. Paul's loyal friends and co-workers, Luke the physician and Aristarchus of Thessalonica, embarked with him. Aristarchus had suffered earlier with Paul in Ephesus. More recently he had accompanied Paul from Ephesus to Jerusalem at the end of Paul's third missionary trip.

Harbor at Caesarea

The water quietly lapped against the side of the ship as the group boarded the coasting vessel. It loosed anchor. A brisk wind propelled the vessel northward along the coast.

The following day the ship entered one of Sidon's well-protected harbors, 70 miles to the north. The ancient Phoenician city hugged the shoreline on a narrow plain between the Lebanon Mountains and the sea.

"Our ship will be spending a few days in port, off-loading and on-loading cargo," the captain announced.

Julius was a kind officer. He turned to Paul, "I suggest you go ashore and visit with any friends you may have. Perhaps they will be able to meet your needs for the long journey ahead."

"Thank you," Paul replied. Even though he would be chained to a soldier, he appreciated this small measure of freedom after having spent two years in jail. He hoped the Christians in Sidon would welcome him.

Throughout Sidon's history, the people had worshiped demons in the form of many gods. Sidonians had built a temple in town for Eshmun, the god of healing. Years earlier Jesus, the Christ, had come to this area. A Canaanite woman had asked Him to heal her demon-possessed daughter. He had confronted the powers of darkness, and with a voice of compassion had said to her, "O woman, great is your faith. It will be done as you desire."

At the time when Paul had participated in Stephen's stoning and had persecuted the Christians in Jerusalem, many Christians had fled to Sidon in Phoenicia to escape death. But now it was twenty-five years since Stephen had been cruelly killed. Today those who had fled received Paul as a friend and brother in the Lord. They kindly provided supplies for the long and possibly dangerous journey ahead. Paul's heart was warmed as he soaked up the love and devotion shown by these fellow Christians. When their visit was over, Paul and the soldier guarding him returned to the harbor. Luke and Aristarchus followed behind, carrying enough food and supplies for the next few weeks.

The ship sailed out into the Mediterranean. Winds blew violently. Passengers braced themselves against the fierce gusts and tried not to lose their balance. The captain guided the ship close to the east end of the Island of Cyprus, hoping to lessen the impact of the winds. This measure provided temporary relief, but as the vessel moved north past the island, the winds continued to blow salty waves onto the deck. The ship rolled from side to side in the open waters between Cyprus and Asia Minor. Near the southern coast of Asia Minor a series of mountain ranges dropped sharply down to the sea. The waters calmed as the ship neared the shores of Cilicia and Pamphylia. Steadily moving westward, the ship made good progress with the help of the strong current that flowed along the rugged coastline.

Early September, A.D. 59

Passengers perked up as the ship sailed into the smoother waters of the port of Andriake. The harbor was home to a large grain business and lay 3 miles west of Myra, a main city of Lycia. Germanicus, the adopted son of Tiberius, and his wife Agrippina had visited Myra in A.D. 18, and now their statues stood proudly at Andriake.

As soon as the ship docked, Julius left the prisoners in the charge of an officer. His eyes searched the area beyond the masts of the smaller vessels in the harbor. He approached the captain of an Egyptian vessel from Alexandria. "I am hoping to find room on a large ship that will sail west across the open sea toward Rome."

"Our ship is going that way."

"I am taking prisoners to Rome. Do you have room?"

"Yes, we do, and we will sail shortly. The wind has blown us off course, but our plans are to leave for Italy soon. The ship is loaded with wheat but, yes, there is room for passengers."

Julius worked out the details and returned to the smaller coasting vessel. With clattering chains Paul and the other prisoners awkwardly made their way to the larger Alexandrian ship. Paul breathed deeply of the fresh seaside air as he moved up the gangplank. Luke and Aristarchus followed, carrying the supplies. The crew and passengers numbered 276.

The large sail billowed as the ship moved west along the coast of Asia. Passengers brought their own food, and anyone could make use of the ship's kitchen to prepare meals. Wealthy citizens stayed in cabins at the stern of the boat. Each evening they slept comfortably, while the remainder of the passengers set up tents or prepared to bed down on deck. Paul was grateful for a warm blanket that kept out the cold wind.

For several days the ship struggled against the strong northwest wind as it passed through rough waters. At Cnidus, a port on the southwest point of Asia Minor, the captain directed the ship to leave the protection of the coast and turn southwest into the open waters. The strong northwest headwinds prevented the ship from sailing directly west to Italy, so the crew, yelling to one another above the sound of the winds, aimed for the east end of the island of Crete. The tossing ship finally passed Cape Salmone, a high ridge of land on the eastern end of the island, which jutted into the sea. Passengers felt relief as land partially broke the force of the violent wind, but the best the ship could do was to inch along the coastline, making slow progress indeed.

October 5, A.D. 59, Crete

Partway along the island, a small bay opened to the southeast. "This is Fair Havens, near the city of Lasea," the captain announced. "It will provide temporary shelter from the winds until the weather changes."

"I don't like the idea of another long wait," Julius said to the captain. "Since leaving Caesarea there has been one delay after another. I want to reach Italy before winter."

"Yes, I'm sure you do. But it is late in the season. Sailing can be dangerous at this time of year."

Turning to his most notable prisoner, Julius inquired, "Paul, you are an experienced traveler. What do you think?"

"There will be problems up ahead," Paul warned. "This trip could end with the loss of both the ship and its cargo, and people's lives will be in danger."

The captain did not respond to Paul's statement but turned back to Julius, "If conditions seem right in the near future, I will proceed, at least as far as Phoenix."

Julius weighed both sides of the argument. Since he represented the Roman state, his decision would be final. "You have guided many ships, using the stars, and are familiar with the winds. If your experience tells you it is safe to travel, I am in favor of going to Phoenix. I would like to transport my prisoners that far at least."

"Good advice," the captain declared as he nodded in agreement. "The harbor here at Fair Havens is a 'fair weather' harbor. It will expose the ship to storms. A safer port, Phoenix, is only 40 miles up the western coast of Crete."

October 10

"The conditions this morning are excellent for sailing," the captain said. "Light winds from the south will give us a good start."

"Yes, this is perfect," Julius agreed.

"These gentle breezes should push us straight west to Phoenix. We will be able to enter the bay from either the southwest or northwest inlet."

With great optimism the sailors pulled up anchor at Fair Havens and set sail toward the western end of the island. The ship again hugged the shoreline. It rounded Cape Matala and, without warning, the wind suddenly changed direction. A violent northeast wind, a Euroclydon, rushed down from the more than 8000-foot snow-capped Mount Ida in the center of the island. Fear clouded the eyes of the crew and passengers as the winds whipped the calm sea into choppy, white-crested waves. The captain shouted orders and sailors ran quickly around the deck tightening ropes and tying down crates.

For hours the crew fought to keep the ship on course while thick, black clouds swirled around them. A driving rain pounded the deck leaving passengers cold and wet. Daylight hours melted into night as gale force winds drove the ship up the crest of one wave only to crash down with a loud crack to meet the next. Paul's stomach churned whenever the ship rushed down the far side of a wave. Cold spray, running back and forth in little rivers, soaked the deck. The ship shuddered and creaked, threatening to fall apart.

Sailors fought to turn the vessel into the wind, but to no avail.

Finally, the exhausted crew stopped fighting and let the wind blow them. Fierce gusts strained the huge sail and drove them 25 miles out to sea. Squalls blew them down the east side of the small island of Clauda.

"Quickly!" the captain shouted. "While we are under the shelter of the island, lift the lifeboat out of the water onto the ship. The waves will smash it if we continue to tow it. Find as many helpers as you can."

Luke hurried to the side of the ship. Gripping one of the lines with his strong arms, he and Aristarchus helped the other men pull the lifeboat onto the deck.

"The ship is in danger of breaking apart," the captain yelled. As he spoke, the wind swallowed his words and snapped his clothes violently. The ship's boards creaked and groaned in loud chorus. "Tie the ship together," the captain again yelled, forcing the words out of his mouth. "The waves are loosening her timbers. Bring the cables to strengthen the hull."

The crew dropped thick loops of cable at the ship's bow, pulled them into place, and tightened them above deck. As they worked, the fierce wind blew gusts into their faces, stealing their breath away.

"The wind will drive the ship across the sea to the sandbars of Syrtis!" a panic-stricken passenger wailed. "I don't want to die in the shallow quicksands on the African coast!"

"If our ship hits the sandbanks, none of us will escape," a sailor commented. "It is the graveyard of the sea. But the captain will do all that he can to prevent such a disaster."

Turning to the crew the captain ordered, "Men, lower the top sails and set the storm sails. Drop the anchor. It will provide resistance as the ship rides the waves."

On the second day gale-force winds and mountainous waves continued to pound the helplessly rocking ship. Any loose articles slid heavily back and forth across the deck. Waves thundered and crashed over the ship's side. Salt water stung the passengers' eyes, and cold spray from the waves soaked their tents and bedding. Frightened travelers, their teeth chattering, huddled together trying to keep warm.

"The situation is desperate," the captain warned. "Throw part of the grain overboard. It may help save lives." On the third day he made more decisions. "In order to survive, the extra equipment must be thrown into the sea. Tell the passengers and crew to help."

Everyone worked together to push the heavy equipment off the ship to be swallowed in the angry water.

For eleven dark days and nights the terrible storm raged without a break. Heavy clouds blotted out the sun and stars. Winds howled; rain fell in torrents; mist and ocean spray clouded their vision. Because the captain could not guide the ship without stars for direction, the ship and passengers drifted further from their desired destination. The hope of survival was fading fast. Travelers gave in to seasickness and, in despair, refused to eat.

Paul had already been in three shipwrecks. He had even spent twenty-four hours in the open sea.

The fear of death and dying showed on the faces of the crew and passengers, but in the middle of this hopeless situation, Paul calmly stood before the crew. "Men, you never should have left Fair Havens. If you had listened to my advice, you would not have suffered all this damage and loss. However, now that we are here, I beg you to keep your courage. The ship will sink, but none of you will lose your lives!"

"How do you know that?" a man jeered.

"I worship the God who made heaven and earth. Last night, in the darkness of the storm, God sent His angel to tell me that I will arrive in Rome to stand trial before Caesar. God in His goodness has promised to save the lives of everyone on board this ship! Be encouraged. I trust in God, and everything will happen exactly as God's angel said it would. But this will include being shipwrecked on an island."

No one paid much attention to Paul as the storm continued driving them further across the Mediterranean Sea.

Near midnight on the fourteenth night a sailor called out, "Something has changed. The sound of land is in my ears."

"Are you sure it isn't a northeaster?"

"No! It is the sound of waves crashing against a shore."

"Quick – bring a line to test the depth."

A sailor ran to find a weighted line and lowered it into the water. A few minutes later he called, "The weight hit bottom. The water is 120 feet deep."

The crew repeated the test half an hour later. "90 feet!" an excited sailor called to the others.

"If the ship continues moving forward," another sailor warned, "the wind will drive us onto the coastal rocks."

"Throw out four anchors from the rear of the ship," the captain called. "It will keep the vessel steadier if the bow points toward the shore."

Tension increased as the passengers and crew waited anxiously for the first streak of daylight in the east.

During the long wait of the night Egyptian sailors on board conspired among themselves. "Lower the lifeboat," one of them whispered. "We will use it to escape from the ship."

"Great idea," a quiet voice responded from the shadows. "If anyone notices, we can pretend to be casting out anchors from the front of the ship. Then we can escape to shore in the lifeboat."

Paul, aware of the Egyptians' plans, turned to Julius, the commanding officer. "If the sailors do not stay on board, you will all die."

Julius had learned by now that Paul's advice was trustworthy, so he reacted quickly and issued orders to the soldiers, "Cut the ropes of the lifeboat."

Soldiers rushed over and wrestled with the escaping men.

Another soldier whipped out his sword to slice the ropes. The boat hit the water with a splash. It swirled around for a few minutes and then drifted quickly out of sight. Everyone settled down again to wait for morning.

Shortly before dawn Paul spoke to the crew and passengers. "You have been under a terrible strain for two weeks and you have eaten hardly anything. I encourage you to eat now for your own well-being. It will give you strength. As I have said, all of you will be safe. Not one of you will lose even a hair of your head."

After saying this, Paul took bread, raised his voice, and gave thanks to God. "Blessed are You, O Lord our God, the King of the world, who has produced this food and this drink from the earth and the vine." He broke off a piece of bread and ate it. Paul's confidence raised everyone's spirits, and all of them decided to eat. When each person had been satisfied, the crew lightened the ship by throwing the remainder of the wheat into the sea.

As darkness gave way to dawn, the coastline was faintly visible. "Where are we?" someone asked. "Is there a harbor?"

"No, and the land is unfamiliar in both directions."

"I see a bay," one of the sailors called out. "It has a beach."

The captain scanned the horizon hoping to find a more suitable place for the ship. His body tensed when he realized that he had very few options. "Steer the ship between the rocks – towards the sandy shore," he yelled, beads of perspiration rolling down his forehead.

The sailors cut away the anchors, abandoning them in the sea. They lowered the rudders and raised the topsail so the wind would catch it and drive them toward the shore.

As the big ship sailed forward, it shuddered and creaked. Suddenly it jerked to a halt. The dreadful sound of timbers tearing apart could be heard by all aboard. Passengers stumbled forward as the bow struck the sand with a jarring thud. No one had seen the reef. These treacherous underwater embankments are created where two currents meet. The ship lay helpless as the pounding waves smashed into it, breaking it into pieces.

The soldiers held a hasty discussion. "What should we do with the prisoners?"

"There is only one safe thing to do," an officer stressed. "All of the prisoners must be killed. It will keep them from swimming ashore and escaping!"

ITALY

Rome
Three Taverns
Ostia Appii Forum
Capua
Puteoli Mt. Vesuvius
Pompeii Brundisium

ILLYRICUM
DALMATIA

ADRIATIC SEA

TYRRHENIAN SEA

Volcanic
islands

SICILY Mt. Etna Rhegium

Syracuse

MALTA

Malta to Rome

Chapter
SEVENTEEN

Miracles

Malta, Puteoli, Rome

Late October, A.D. 59

"What about Paul?" Julius exclaimed with alarm. "Are you suggesting death for all prisoners?"

"Our own lives are in danger if even one prisoner escapes," a soldier reminded him. "Rome holds us responsible to keep every single one of them in custody."

"But Paul must live," Julius stated firmly. "He has helped us throughout this entire journey, and I am personally grateful to him. You will not end his life nor that of any other prisoner!"

Julius turned to the entire company of people, "Any of you who can swim, go ahead. If you cannot swim, hang onto a board or anything else from the ship that will float."

Julius had hardly finished speaking when the splash of people jumping overboard reached his ears. Kind-hearted ones stayed behind to help non-swimmers find floating objects. Within minutes the wreckage lay silent and deserted in the pounding surf.

Some swam easily. Others struggled and kicked furiously but made very little progress; they barely had enough strength to make it to the sandy shore. But when the people were counted, God had miraculously saved all 276 persons from the ship.

Malta

"I don't recognize this island," the captain said, "but there is a chance it could be Malta. The Phoenicians called it 'Melita,' Island of Refuge."

"If this is the Island of Refuge, it's well named," Luke commented to Paul through chattering teeth. Passengers milled about on the beach, shivering in the cool autumn air. Their dripping clothes clung to their bodies. Gritty sand stuck to their feet and legs.

Before long the Maltese who lived on the island arrived to welcome the survivors. Many of the islanders spoke a Phoenician dialect. They treated the new arrivals kindly and built a bonfire on the beach. The fire crackled invitingly, and the eager flames leapt into the air. Weary travelers held their hands up to the fire for warmth and comfort. When the smoke stung their eyes, they turned their bodies from front to back to absorb the heat. However, steady rains kept them soaking wet.

"The fire is almost reduced to ashes," Paul commented. "I will go and gather more wood." He searched along the beach, collecting armfuls of driftwood and dead branches. Returning with his load, Paul bent down to place the wood on the fire. The heat forced a poisonous snake out from under the wood. Its fangs sank deeply into Paul's hand.

"Look," one of the Maltese pointed. "A snake is hanging from that man's hand. He must be a murderer!"

Paul reacted instinctively, shaking the creature from his hand into the fire.

"Justice is being carried out," a bystander added. "He may have escaped death at sea, but his deeds have caught up with him."

"As soon as the snake poison goes throughout his body," another said, "he will swell up and drop dead."

The crowd kept their eyes on Paul as he continued to work.

"Why isn't he reacting to the poison?" one of them wondered.

"I don't know. He should be swelling by now."

"I don't understand why nothing happened when the snake bit his hand. He must be a divine man. Perhaps he is one of the gods!"

As the islanders talked, the governor, the representative of the Roman Empire, walked down to the water's edge. "Welcome to our Island," he said warmly to all the unexpected visitors. "My name is Publius. I invite you to come to my place as guests." With cold, shivering limbs the crowd followed Governor Publius up the gently sloping hill.

"Tell us about your island," the captain said as they walked.

"Malta is one of three islands and it has been inhabited for a long time. Ancient buildings and temples here date back hundreds of years."

Green fields and small clusters of trees dotted the countryside as the weary travelers made their way to Publius' home, which was made of a honey-colored limestone. He invited them in and gave them food and refreshing drinks from stone water pots. He hosted them kindly for three days, while the officials searched for another place to stay. During that time Publius' father fell ill with dysentery. Paul felt compassion for this man and asked if he could visit him. When given permission, he entered the room and found the sick man lying on a couch. An aroma of cloves, used as medicine, hung in the air.

"How are you feeling?" Paul asked, as he felt the man's forehead.

"Not good at all," the elderly man whispered between rapid breaths. "I have a high fever."

"Where do you have pain?"

"In my stomach," he replied weakly.

Paul laid hands on him and prayed. As he did so, God's healing power worked a miracle in the elderly man's life. The fever and pain left his body and he rose from his couch.

In the following days Publius told many people about the way

Paul had called on his God to heal his father. As the news spread, other sick islanders came to Paul. He spoke to them about the Lord and healed them through God's miraculous power.

February, A.D. 60

During the coldest winter months, November, December and January, the people of Malta continued to honor their guests. By early February the west winds blew again, bringing improved weather. The travelers could finally resume their journey to Rome. The people of Malta brought many gifts and supplies to help them on their way.

Julius arranged for the passengers of the original ship to travel on another Alexandrian ship that had spent the winter in a local harbor. This vessel carried a central mast with a large square sail. The front section swept upwards into carvings of the twin Roman gods, Castor and Pollux. These figures represented the ship's name. On the goose-necked back of the vessel stood a statue of the patron god of the ship's home port. These carved gods could not begin to compare with the powerful God who ruled the waves.

Julius and the prisoners in his care boarded the Castor and Pollux. Although sailing usually started later than February, gentle southerly breezes encouraged the captain and crew to set out early. The ship sailed away from the shore, leaving the fishing boats bobbing in the village harbor. Golden limestone buildings with bright red roofs seemed to grow smaller as the vessel made its way north toward Sicily, a large island near the southern tip of Italy.

After crossing open water for 80 miles, the ship docked at Syracuse, an important city on the east coast of Sicily. The next day dawned calm and beautiful but without a breath of wind. After waiting for three days, the winds picked up sufficiently to allow them to resume their journey north. The ship sailed past the volcanic Mount Etna. Wisps of smoke rose from the cone and floated into the air. Light winds were not strong enough for the ship to follow a straight course, so the captain resorted to sailing the vessel in a zigzag pattern. At last they arrived at

Rhegium, a city on the south end of Italy, right at the toe of the 'boot.' The next day a south wind allowed the captain to guide the ship through the Strait of Messina, a narrow channel of water with a dangerous whirlpool and the massive, jagged rock of Scylla. As the ship sailed up the coast, a cluster of small islands stood off in the distance to the west. Each one had formed from volcanic eruptions in the sea. A recurrent plume of gas rose from the cone of the most northerly volcano, Mount Stromboli.

Puteoli

The ship continued northward up Italy's west coast through the Tyrrhenian Sea until it passed the island of Capri and sailed into Puteoli, a main trading center in southern Italy. Puteoli lay sheltered in the northern part of the Bay of Naples across from the busy town of Pompeii and the towering volcanic Mount Vesuvius to the east.

Great crowds lined the wharf as the grain ship, Castor and Pollux, was towed into port guided by a smaller boat with many oars. Workers raised a gangplank. Travelers, including Paul, Luke, and Aristarchus, left the ship in the cool spring air.

"We must find the local Christians," Paul said to his companions. He looked down at his chains and prayed that Julius would allow him the freedom to do so. Approaching Julius, Paul asked, "How many days will we remain in Puteoli?"

"Seven," Julius responded.

"Would I be permitted to search for the Christians?"

"You may, but a soldier must accompany you."

Visiting the homes of Christians refreshed Paul's spirit. But as Paul and the Christians worshiped together at Puteoli, the week passed quickly.

Julius sent word that the prisoners would be traveling by land from Puteoli to Rome. The trip would last several days and would cover 130 miles.

Soldiers escorted Paul and the other prisoners along a road that led north. Luke and Aristarchus followed, carrying a few supplies. During the trip Paul had time to consider his actual arrival at Rome. How would the Roman Christians receive him?

After several miles they reached Capua where the roadway joined a great stone highway, the Appian Way, built three hundred years earlier. Julius found shelter where the prisoners could spend the night. From Capua the road ran either northwest to Rome or angled southeast to Brundisium in the heel of Italy's boot. The entire roadway stretched out more than 350 miles and connected travelers to the Greek world across the Adriatic Sea.

The Appian Way

Paul walked over the large, flat stones of the well-constructed Appian Way. Tidy curbstones lined the edges of the straight road. The group continued northwest until the road turned downhill into the Pontine Marsh. A chorus of frogs croaked their welcome. There the road ended temporarily, but workers had constructed a canal to allow a barge to pass through the reedy marsh. Julius loaded the prisoners onto the barge for the trip. Strong mules then pulled them through the waters. Passengers swatted at gnats as the irritating pests flew about. At the north end of the marsh Julius guided the prisoners safely back onto the road.

News of Paul's journey reached the Christians at Rome. A group of them left the big city and traveled south along the Appian Way with the idea of accompanying Paul back. Several miles south of Rome the Christians arrived at the town of Appii Forum, a well-known place for travelers to stop. The marketplace displayed brightly colored vegetables and fruit as well as meat and other produce. However, the Appii marketplace had a bad reputation from thieves and boatmen who came to the area.

Paul and the Christians spotted each other, and the group of Roman believers rushed toward him with excitement. "Paul," one of the Christians exclaimed, "we have wanted to meet you ever since you wrote us."

A warm feeling flooded Paul's heart as the Christians greeted him with kisses of pure affection. Julius did not interfere while Paul visited.

A few miles further north Julius and his prisoners stopped to rest at Three Taverns, a place with three shops – a general store, a blacksmith's shop, and a house where travelers could rest. There another group of Christians joined Paul and expressed their joy at seeing him face-to-face. While the group visited, hammering from busy ironworkers echoed into the street.

The Christians accompanied Paul as he traveled past lakes and through the emerald-colored Alban Hills to cover the last few miles to Rome. Near the city more monuments and marble tombstones appeared beside the busy roadway. Traffic increased and horse-drawn carts with wooden wheels clattered past pedestrians.

Rome had been founded on the eastern bank of the Tiber River seven or eight centuries earlier. This small collection of village huts gradually rose to power, becoming the world's greatest city. Now Rome covered seven hills and ruled the whole Mediterranean world.

Paul and the travelers on the Appian Way approached the Capena Gate. The city aqueduct with its many graceful arches crossed the road, carrying a plentiful supply of water to the citizens of Rome.

Rome

Four years earlier Paul had lived in Ephesus and had announced, "I must see Rome." Now he was passing through the Capena Gate and entering the city. An enormous arena for chariot races, the Circus Maximus, stood directly in front of him. It seated about 200,000 spectators. No one could imagine that in four short years this great racetrack would burn to the ground.

Paul's eyes caught sight of the palaces of the Caesars which were slightly east of the road and on top of Palatine Hill. Emperor Nero lived there, the Caesar to whom Paul had appealed while still in Caesarea. People in the streets whispered about their Emperor. He had developed an evil side and seemed to lack moral boundaries. He sometimes dressed as a common slave and wandered the streets at night with gangs who robbed people and carried off women.

The Roman Forum stood beyond the palaces between Palatine Hill and Capitoline Hill. Everything of importance in Rome was located close to the Forum – the Temple of Castor and Pollux, the senate, the palaces, circuses, baths, theaters, and the three-story Mamertine Prison.

The Christians stepped aside as Julius led the group of prisoners up the slope of Caelian Hill to the Camp of the Foreign Legion and delivered them to the officer in charge. "I have a letter from Governor Festus in Caesarea," Julius told the officer. "It concerns the prisoner Paul. He is a Roman citizen and stands out above the other prisoners. He has helped us greatly on this trip."

"All prisoners will be sent to local jails," the officer ordered, "except Paul. I will not send him to the barracks. We will keep him under arrest in a private house because he appealed to the Emperor. He is to be guarded at all times with his right wrist chained to the left wrist of a soldier."

Paul sent up a prayer of thanks to God for this small mercy. House arrest would allow him a certain amount of freedom to have visitors while he waited for his appearance before Nero.

Chapter
⪻EIGHTEEN⪼

Imprisoned Counselor

Rome

February, A.D. 60, Rome

During Paul's house arrest, he could expect no privacy. He would be chained night and day to a guard, who would hear everything Paul said and see everything he did. Although the guards came and went in shifts, Paul would have no relief from the chain or from the ever-present authority beside him.

Three days after arriving, Paul sent a message to the Jewish leaders asking them to meet with him. He would have gone to visit the synagogues in person had he been free to travel, but he could not.

When the men arrived, Paul introduced himself. "Brothers, I asked you to come here today because I am not at liberty to attend the synagogue. I want to explain to you why I'm in chains. Though I have done nothing hostile toward our people, the Jewish leaders in Jerusalem beat me and handed me over to the Roman government. The Romans tried me and wanted to set me free, but the Jewish leaders protested their decision. I felt I had no option but to appeal to Caesar. I stand here today only because of the fulfillment of God's promise to send the Messiah."

"Your coming to Rome is news to us," a spokesman said. "No one from Jerusalem sent either a letter or a bad report. But people everywhere are talking against those who believe as you do. No one has a good word to say about them. I suggest we set a date and time to hear more about this. That way we can invite others to evaluate what you have to say."

*   *   *   *   *   *   *

On the morning of the appointed day, a large number of people crowded into Paul's house. Chained to his guard, Paul stood in front of the group and explained the message of the Kingdom of God. He quoted from Moses and the prophets to prove that Christ was the long-awaited Messiah whom God had promised to send. Paul talked from morning until evening. He spoke urgently and convincingly.

A few believed Paul's words, but many did not. "How can you or anyone else fall for this teaching?" one of the men asked in an angry, mocking tone. "It sounds like pure imagination."

The men discussed the matter back and forth among themselves until a spokesman addressed Paul on behalf of the group. "We can't accept that Jesus is the promised Messiah."

Paul's heart sank. As the evening ended, he added a final warning. "The Holy Spirit was right when He said to our ancestors through Isaiah the prophet that you would hear His words, but would not understand; you would see, but would not recognize the meaning. Because your hearts are hardened, God's salvation will become available to others who will listen to it."

With Paul's final statement ringing in their ears the leaders left, but they continued to mull over what he had told them. One by one the men moved out into the starry night.

*   *   *   *   *   *   *

Emperor Nero, the Caesar to whom Paul hoped to make his appeal, lived in Rome on Palatine Hill in a magnificent palace. Several important people had influenced Nero's life: Seneca, his teacher; Burrus, a powerful military officer; and Agrippina, his mother. Six years earlier in A.D. 54, the teenaged Nero had come to power. Blond curls framed his deep-set blue eyes. Talented and artistic, he inspired confidence. However, he came from a family known for its cruelty and perversions. During the first five years of his rule he had accomplished much and made valuable improvements. But within a short time he developed a love of power and recognition. He soon acquired an evil reputation.

In A.D. 59, Nero turned twenty-one and rebelled against his powerful and popular mother. Shouting matches ensued. "I am tired of your interference, Mother! I do not want people to think of me as a mama's boy. Stop giving your opinion. I intend to govern the way I think best."

"How dare you speak to your mother that way," Agrippina retorted. "You have this position in Rome because I helped you to get it."

"That is not true," Nero responded angrily. "I want you to leave this palace! Go and live at one of your estates – just be sure it is far from here."

Typically their arguments would end with his mother storming out of the room. Eventually Nero came up with a plan to silence her forever. He tried to have her poisoned, but several attempts failed. Some time later he ordered workers to build a boat that would collapse. In that way she would drown, and it would look like an accident.

Nero traveled to his summer home at Baiae, on a hillside near the northern tip of the Bay of Naples. The clear, blue waters of the sea, the warm sun, the majesty of Mount Vesuvius – these would make a good setting for his plans. He sent a message inviting his mother Agrippina to a party, making an outward show of wanting to settle their differences. When she arrived, he fondly hugged and kissed her. At the end of the visit Nero sent her home across the Bay of Naples on the boat designed to collapse. During the voyage the boat fell apart and left her adrift in the water. She did not drown, however, but swam away from the disaster. Nero then acted quickly to finish the job before she could retaliate. At last he was free from her!

*   *   *   *   *   *   *

While Paul waited for his case to come up before Nero, he used every opportunity to preach and teach about the Lord Jesus Christ. He encouraged Christians, who once walked in darkness, to live as the Lord's people and to walk in the light.

Earlier Paul had written a letter to the Roman Christians sending greetings to many of the believers by name at Rome. Now he had the privilege of meeting them in person and of being reacquainted with others he already knew.

Paul also used his time as a prisoner to write to the churches of Asia to strengthen them.

A.D. 60, Rome

> *From: Paul, chosen by the will of God to be an apostle of Christ Jesus....*

> *To: God's holy people in Ephesus, who are faithful followers of Christ Jesus.*

> *May God our Father and the Lord Jesus Christ give you grace and peace.*

> *All praise to God, the Father of our Lord Jesus Christ, who has blessed us with every spiritual blessing in the heavenly realms because we are united with Christ....He is so rich in kindness and grace that he purchased our freedom with the blood of his Son and forgave our sins....God has now revealed to us his mysterious plan regarding Christ.... And this is the plan: At the right time he will bring everything together under the authority of Christ—everything in heaven and on earth....*

> *God's purpose was that we Jews who were the first to trust in Christ would bring praise and glory to God. And now you Gentiles have also heard the truth, the Good News that God saves you. And when you believed in Christ, he identified you as his own by giving you the Holy Spirit, whom he promised long ago. The Spirit is God's guarantee that he will give us the inheritance he promised and that he has purchased us to be his own people. He did this so we*

would praise and glorify him....

Once you were dead because of your disobedience and your many sins. You used to live in sin, just like the rest of the world, obeying the devil—the commander of the powers in the unseen world....God saved you by his grace when you believed. And you can't take credit for this; it is a gift from God. Salvation is not a reward for the good things we have done, so none of us can boast about it....He has created us anew in Christ Jesus, so we can do the good things he planned for us long ago.

Don't forget that you Gentiles used to be outsiders...but now you have been united with Christ Jesus. Once you were far away from God, but now you have been brought near to him through the blood of Christ....He made peace between Jews and Gentiles by creating in himself one new people from the two groups....

And this is God's plan: Both Gentiles and Jews who believe the Good News share equally in the riches inherited by God's children. Both are part of the same body, and both enjoy the promise of blessings because they belong to Christ Jesus....

Always be humble and gentle. Be patient with each other, making allowance for each other's faults because of your love....

He has given each one of us a special gift through the generosity of Christ....These are the gifts Christ gave to the church: the apostles, the prophets, the evangelists, and the pastors and teachers. Their responsibility is to equip God's people to do his work and build up the church, the body of Christ....

With the Lord's authority I say this: Live no longer as the Gentiles do, for they are hopelessly confused. Their minds are full of darkness; they wander far from the life God gives because they have closed their minds and hardened their hearts against him....

For once you were full of darkness, but now you have light from the Lord. So live as people of light! For this light within you produces only what is good and right and true....

Make the most of every opportunity in these evil days....Don't be drunk with wine, because that will ruin your life. Instead, be filled with the Holy Spirit, singing psalms and hymns and spiritual songs among yourselves, and making music to the Lord in your hearts....

And further, submit to one another out of reverence for Christ....Each man must love his wife as he loves himself, and the wife must respect her husband.

Children, obey your parents because you belong to the Lord, for this is the right thing to do....

Slaves, obey your earthly masters with deep respect and fear. Serve them sincerely as you would serve Christ....Masters, treat your slaves in the same way. Don't threaten them; remember, you both have the same Master in heaven, and he has no favorites.

A final word: Be strong in the Lord and in his mighty power. Put on all of God's armor so that you will be able to stand firm against all strategies of the devil. For we are not fighting against flesh-and-blood enemies, but against evil rulers and authorities of the unseen world, against mighty powers in this dark world, and against evil spirits in the heavenly places.

Therefore, put on every piece of God's armor so you will be able to resist the enemy in the time of evil....Stand your ground,

- *putting on the belt of truth and*
- *the body armor of God's righteousness.*
- *For shoes, put on the peace that comes from the Good News....*
- *Hold up the shield of faith to stop the fiery arrows of the devil.*

- *Put on salvation as your helmet, and*
- *take the sword of the Spirit, which is the word of God....*

I am in chains now, still preaching this message as God's ambassador. So pray that I will keep on speaking boldly for him, as I should....

Tychicus will give you a full report about what I am doing and how I am getting along. He is a beloved brother and faithful helper in the Lord's work....

May God's grace be eternally upon all who love our Lord Jesus Christ.

(Excerpts from Ephesians Chapter 1:1-3,7,9-10,12-14; Chapter 2:1-2,8-11,13,15; Chapter 3:6; Chapter 4:2,7,11-12,17-18; Chapter 5:8-9,16,18-19,21,33; Chapter 6:1,5,9-17,20-21,24 NLT)

Paul handed the letter to Tychicus for delivery to the Ephesians. Tychicus had been a trusted helper in the past when he traveled with Paul, Luke, and Timothy during Paul's third journey.

Paul was blessed to have many visitors at his prison-home. One day he expressed his appreciation to his co-workers. "Timothy, thank God for your companionship here in Rome." He turned toward the two Jewish men who worked with him in Rome to further the kingdom of God. "Jesus (Justus), you are a real comfort to me. And what can I say about you, Aristarchus? You traveled all the way to Rome with me and now you keep me company in prison."

"We have been through hard times together," Aristarchus mused. "Remember the riot at Ephesus?"

"How could I forget? It drove me out of town."

Paul turned to Mark, "You are a true helper."

Mark nodded and smiled. "The Lord has changed me since I first traveled with you and Barnabas. You were upset when I quit and did not finish that trip."

"Yes, I refused to give you another chance or to invite you on the next trip. In the end it resulted in two teams. You and Barnabas traveled by ship from Syrian Antioch to Cyprus, and Silas joined me to preach in other parts."

"Barnabas taught me patiently and encouraged me," Mark added. "Since that time I have grown in the Lord."

"I appreciate having you here in Rome. Tell me about your plans to travel to Asia Minor."

"I hope to go to Colosse."

"Good! Colosse is a church I have never visited, but I have had the privilege of meeting people from that city."

*   *   *   *   *   *   *

One day a young man came to the prison-house to visit Paul. "My name is Onesimus," he said nervously, eyes fixed on his shuffling feet. "I need to talk to someone."

"Come in. I have plenty of time. Tell me what's on your mind."

"Paul, I am a runaway slave. I traveled more than one thousand miles in my escape. I felt desperately unhappy working for my master in Colosse, so I stole money and left town. I came to Rome searching for happiness, but I have not found it. I feel as if my life is in danger, and I need a safe place to stay. What should I do?"

"You are welcome to stay here. Even though I am a prisoner, this is my rented house and you will be safe. But, Onesimus, while you are here, I want you to consider God's 'good news.' As a sinner you are controlled by the power of darkness. God punished His perfect Son for the sin of the whole world. Through the blood of Christ, He offers redemption, the forgiveness of sins. Christ died so that you would not be a slave to sin but instead would be free to serve God. God loves you and wants you to believe this in your heart. He wants you to repent of your sin and receive Christ as your Savior. If you do this, God will forgive you. You will not come under God's judgment, but you will be saved. As one of God's own children, you will be transferred from the kingdom of darkness to God's kingdom of light."

Onesimus had much to consider.

*   *   *   *   *   *   *

Epaphras, one of Paul's fellow-workers, had evangelized the three largest cities of the Lycus Valley during the time that Paul had lived and worked in Ephesus. He helped establish churches in Hierapolis, Laodicea, and Colosse, the home town of Onesimus.

Epaphras was now in Rome and he stopped to visit Paul. "I hope you are bringing news about the churches in the Lycus Valley," Paul said, as he greeted him with a warm smile.

The two men sat down to visit. The clanging of Paul's chain was a regular distraction. Soldiers worked in shifts, coming and going at different hours of the day. The ever-present soldier shackled to Paul's right hand restricted his movement and pulled at his wrist.

"Tell me," Paul said to Epaphras, as he adjusted the chain to a more comfortable position, "are the believers in Colosse growing?"

"What can I say? I am concerned...."

"What is the problem?"

"False teachers have entered the group and profess to know more than the apostles. These persuasive men claim that a person will not be happy unless he joins in their secret practices."

"That is serious!"

"That's only part of the problem. One group teaches that a person can live any way he pleases – that he doesn't have to worry about self-control. Another teaches that a person must give up all comforts. They say, 'Don't touch this! Don't do that! Follow the rules!'"

"That must be confusing. Speaking of rules – are there any at Colosse who insist on the Jewish law?"

"Yes, certain teachers promote Jewish religious rites. They condemn those who don't follow holy days or ceremonies."

"I suppose that includes following certain diets as well?"

"Yes, that too," Epaphras responded sadly. "But those who cause the greatest problems are false teachers who say that Christ is a lesser spirit coming from God."

"Oh, no! Christ is the exact representation of God!"

"These men teach that a person must approach God through angels – that Jesus is not the way to God. Using angels, they say, is a humbler way to approach God."

"What error!" Paul gasped. "That kind of teaching will result in the worship of angels instead of the worship of God."

"Yes," nodded Epaphras. "And you can add to those problems cultural differences – the Jews look down on the Greeks; the Greeks and Romans think everyone else is barbaric. And slaves have complaints against their masters."

"Oh, how I long to visit them," Paul said, as a wave of emotion flooded over him. "But I cannot." He glanced down at his hands. "I cannot – because of these chains. But what I could do would be to write them a letter to deal directly with these errors."

*   *   *   *   *   *   *

Because of Paul's earlier witness to Onesimus, that slave made a decision to follow Christ. He devoted himself to being Paul's helper by running errands for him.

One day Paul approached Onesimus, "It is time to talk about your situation."

Onesimus glanced uneasily at Paul and fidgeted nervously with his hands.

"We must talk," Paul continued, "about your run-away status. You are such a help to me, but you do not legally belong to me – you belong to Philemon. You are free in Christ, but the right thing to do would be to go back and face your earthly master. Roman law requires that I return you to your master or else I could be punished."

"But," Onesimus gulped, "if I return...he could beat me...or torture me!" Fear rose in his eyes, and he swallowed hard as he continued, "He might even kill me! As a slave I have no rights. I am not allowed to make any of my own decisions."

"This is true," Paul nodded. "But Philemon is our brother in the Lord, and he is a personal friend of mine. Through my preaching he became a Christian."

"But I would owe my master all that money. I could never repay it. He will throw me in jail."

"Will you return if I write him a letter explaining your situation?"

Onesimus trembled at the idea of returning. He considered his reply carefully. "Yes," he finally said in a quiet voice, "I will go."

"Good," Paul said emphatically. "Tychicus will be traveling to Colosse shortly. In fact, he plans to meet with the church that gathers in Philemon's house. You could travel with him. I will write a letter to the church at Colosse and a brief personal letter to Philemon."

*   *   *   *   *   *   *

Timothy sat down and arranged the papyrus so that the horizontal fibers were on the top side where he would write. The fibers would help guide his pen.

"Go ahead, Paul," Timothy said as he picked up his reed pen and dipped it into the ink. "I am ready."

From: Paul...and from our brother Timothy....

To: God's holy people in the city of Colosse....

May God our Father give you grace and peace....

You learned about the Good News from Epaphras, our beloved co-worker. He is Christ's faithful servant, and he is helping us on your behalf....We have not stopped praying for you since we first heard about you. We ask God to give you complete knowledge of his will and to give you spiritual wisdom and understanding....

Christ is the visible image of the invisible God. He existed before anything was created and is supreme over all creation, for through him God created everything in the heavenly realms and on earth. He made the things we can see and the things we can't see — such as thrones, kingdoms, rulers, and authorities in the unseen world. Everything was created through him and for him. He existed before anything else, and he holds all creation together. Christ is also the head of the church, which is his body. He is the beginning, supreme over all who rise from the dead. So he is first in everything. For God in all his fullness was pleased to live in Christ, and through him God reconciled everything to himself. He made peace with everything in heaven and on earth by means of Christ's blood on the cross....

I want you to know how much I have agonized for you and for the church at Laodicea, and for many other believers who have never met me personally....

Don't let anyone capture you with empty philosophies and high-sounding nonsense that come from human thinking and from the spiritual powers of this world, rather than from Christ. For in Christ lives all the fullness of God in a human body. So you also are complete through your union with Christ, who is the head over every ruler and authority....

Don't let anyone condemn you for what you eat or drink, or for not celebrating certain holy days or new moon ceremonies or Sabbaths....Don't let anyone condemn you by insisting on pious self-denial or the worship of angels, saying they have had visions about these things....You have died with Christ, and he has set you free from the spiritual powers of this world. So why do you keep on following the rules of the world?...Rules may seem wise because they require strong devotion, pious self-denial, and severe bodily discipline. But they provide no help in conquering a person's evil desires.

Since you have been raised to new life with Christ, set your sights on the realities of heaven, where Christ sits in the place of honor at God's right hand....

Put to death the sinful, earthly things lurking within you. Have nothing to do with sexual immorality, impurity, lust, and evil desires. Don't be greedy, for a greedy person is an idolater, worshiping the things of this world....But now is the time to get rid of anger, rage, malicious behavior, slander, and dirty language. Don't lie to each other, for you have stripped off your old sinful nature and all its wicked deeds. Put on your new nature, and be renewed as you learn to know your Creator and become like him....Since God chose you to be the holy people he loves, you must clothe yourselves with tenderhearted mercy, kindness, humility, gentleness, and patience....

Devote yourselves to prayer with an alert mind and a thankful heart....Live wisely among those who are not believers, and make the most of every opportunity. Let your conversation be gracious and attractive so that you will have the right response for everyone.

Tychicus will give you a full report about how I am getting along. He is a beloved brother and faithful helper who serves with me in the Lord's work....I am also sending Onesimus, a faithful and beloved brother, one of your own people. He and Tychicus will tell you everything that's happening here.

Aristarchus, who is in prison with me, sends you his greetings, and...make Mark welcome if he comes your way....

Luke, the beloved doctor, sends his greetings, and so does Demas. Please give my greetings to our brothers and sisters at Laodicea, and to Nympha and the church that meets in her house.

After you have read this letter, pass it on to the church at Laodicea so they can read it, too. And you should read the letter I wrote to them....

Paul stopped dictating, and Timothy handed him a pen to write a personal greeting. The chains on his right wrist clanked together and got in the way as he wrote.

Here is my greeting in my own handwriting – Paul.

Remember my chains. May God's grace be with you.

(Excerpts from Colossians Chapter 1:1-2,7,9,15-20; Chapter 2:1,8-10,16,18,20,23; Chapter 3:1,5,8-10,12; Chapter 4:2,5-7,9-10,14-16,18 NLT)

Timothy rolled up the letter. The vertical fibers of the papyrus would keep the outside of the roll strong. Then he prepared to write a shorter letter to Philemon.

From: Paul, a prisoner for preaching the Good News about Christ Jesus, and from our brother Timothy....

To: Philemon, our beloved co-worker, and to our sister Apphia, and to our fellow soldier Archippus, and to the church that meets in your house.

May God our Father and the Lord Jesus Christ give you grace and peace....

Consider this as a request from me—Paul, an old man and now also a prisoner for the sake of Christ Jesus. I appeal to you to show kindness to my child, Onesimus. I became his father in the faith while here in prison. Onesimus hasn't been of much use to you in the past, but now he is very useful to both of us. I am sending him back to you, and with him comes my own heart....

He is no longer like a slave to you. He is more than a slave, for he is a beloved brother, especially to me. Now he will mean much more to you, both as a man and as a brother in the Lord....If he has wronged you in any way or owes you anything, charge it to me.

I, Paul, write this with my own hand: I will repay it. ...

One more thing – please prepare a guest room for me, for I am hoping that God will answer your prayers and let me return to you soon.

Epaphras, my fellow prisoner in Christ Jesus, sends you his greetings. So do Mark, Aristarchus, Demas, and Luke, my co-workers.

May the grace of the Lord Jesus Christ be with your spirit.

(Excerpts from Philemon verses 1-3,9-12,16,18,19,22-25 NLT)

*   *   *   *   *   *   *

Tychicus and Onesimus took the letters and a supply of money, food, and water, and left to find a ship traveling east toward Asia Minor, where they would journey inland to Colosse, Onesimus' home town.

February, A.D. 62

While Paul sat in a Roman prison, burdened for the souls of men, the town of Pompeii to the south showed the first signs of coming disaster. Well-to-do people of Rome often traveled to Pompeii, a town located south of Mount Vesuvius, near the Bay of Naples. Vacationers flocked to this area to enjoy their country homes.

A Pompeii street with stepping stones, as it was during the first century A.D.

Though the mountain had once been an active volcano, local residents could not recall it ever being a danger to them or to their town.

Around noon on February 5, A.D. 62, the people of Pompeii heard a long roaring sound. Almost immediately the earth shook. Many people ran out of the buildings in panic. The earth opened up. The town's water reservoir broke, adding to the chaos. The temples of Jupiter and Apollo collapsed. Aftershocks continued all day. Thousands died in Pompeii and in the surrounding towns in southern Italy. News of the deadly earthquake reached Paul in the city of Rome shortly before spring.

The people who had survived the quake resolved to rebuild the town and make it more successful than before. Residents continued to cultivate their gardens on the slopes of Mount Vesuvius. No one had a premonition that seventeen years later their once quiet mountain would blow its top, shooting black smoke, flames, and red-hot stones into the air. Rolling mud would swallow homes and farms. Falling ash and deadly fumes would kill thousands, burying Pompeii and the surrounding towns under tons of volcanic matter.

In that coming day the pillar of smoke and ash would be visible even in Rome many miles away.

*   *   *   *   *   *   *

Spring, A.D. 62, Rome

Epaphroditus, a man from Philippi, traveled seven hundred miles from his home town to Rome. The Christians in Philippi had sent him with a gift of money for Paul. After a long and difficult trip he arrived in Rome and found him.

"Epaphroditus!" Paul exclaimed when he saw him at the door. "What a surprise! You have come a great distance. What brings you to Rome?"

"I have come to offer my help in whatever way I can."

"How are all the believers in Philippi?"

"Some are well and growing in the Lord."

"How are Euodia and Syntyche? I remember them fondly," Paul said. "Those two women worked hard with me to tell others the 'good news.'"

Epaphroditus cleared his throat. "There have been some recent clashes. They are fighting with one another."

"I hope they will reconsider and live in harmony once again."

"Legalistic Jews are another problem," Epaphroditus added. "They insist that everyone must keep the Law and that all men must be circumcised."

"Are the Philippians strong enough to withstand this pressure?" Paul asked.

"Generally, the believers are standing up to them, but you know what these men are like."

"Yes, they have dispositions like dogs."

"That is a fitting description!"

"I must write to the church at Philippi to thank them for their kindness and to address their current concerns."

It had been twelve years since God had called Paul to go to

Philippi in Macedonia. It was here on his second missionary journey that he had founded the first church in Europe. It was an important northern city on the great east and west highway. Lydia and the local jailer had been the first to come to Christ there.

*   *   *   *   *   *   *

"Timothy," Paul said, "I need to acknowledge the gift from the Philippians who are supporting my missionary work here in Rome. I did not ask them for this gift, but because I cannot work as a tentmaker, I am grateful for it. The Philippians have always been generous with money for the Lord's work. While I worked at Thessalonica, they sent money more than once. I also received gifts at Corinth."

"I will be happy to write while you dictate," Timothy said. He selected a new piece of papyrus, pulled out his pen and ink, and sat down waiting for Paul to speak.

From: Paul and Timothy, slaves of Christ Jesus....

To: all of God's holy people in Philippi who belong to Christ Jesus, including the elders and deacons.

May God our Father and the Lord Jesus Christ give you grace and peace....

Everyone here, including the whole palace guard, knows that I am in chains because of Christ....I fully expect and hope that I will never be ashamed, but that I will continue to be bold for Christ, as I have been in the past. And I trust that my life will bring honor to Christ, whether I live or die....

Have the same attitude that Christ Jesus had. Though he was God, he did not think of equality with God as something to cling to. Instead, he gave up his divine privileges; he took the humble position of a slave and was born as a human being. When he appeared in human form, he humbled himself in obedience to God and died a criminal's death on a cross.

Therefore, God elevated him to the place of highest honor and gave him the name above all other names, that at the name of Jesus every knee should bow, in heaven and on earth and under the earth, and every tongue confess that Jesus Christ is Lord, to the glory of God the Father....

Do everything without complaining and arguing, so that no one can criticize you. Live clean, innocent lives as children of God, shining like bright lights in a world full of crooked and perverse people....

I thought I should send Epaphroditus back to you. He is a true brother, co-worker, and fellow soldier. And he was your messenger to help me in my need....He risked his life for the work of Christ, and he was at the point of death while doing for me what you couldn't do from far away....

Watch out for those dogs, those people who do evil, those mutilators who say you must be circumcised to be saved. For we who worship by the Spirit of God are the ones who are truly circumcised. We rely on what Christ Jesus has done for us. We put no confidence in human effort....

We are citizens of heaven, where the Lord Jesus Christ lives. And we are eagerly waiting for him to return as our Savior. He will take our weak mortal bodies and change them into glorious bodies like his own, using the same power with which he will bring everything under his control....

I appeal to Euodia and Syntyche. Please, because you belong to the Lord, settle your disagreement. And I ask you, my true partner, to help these two women, for they worked hard with me in telling others the Good News. They worked along with Clement and the rest of my co-workers, whose names are written in the Book of Life.

Don't worry about anything; instead, pray about everything. Tell God what you need, and thank him for all he has done....

Fix your thoughts on what is true, and honorable, and

right, and pure, and lovely, and admirable. Think about things that are excellent and worthy of praise.

At the moment I have all I need – and more! I am generously supplied with the gifts you sent me with Epaphroditus. They are a sweet-smelling sacrifice that is acceptable and pleasing to God. And this same God who takes care of me will supply all your needs from his glorious riches, which have been given to us in Christ Jesus.

Now all glory to God our Father forever and ever! Amen.

(Excerpts from Philippians Chapter 1:1-2,13,20; Chapter 2:5-11,14-15,25,30; Chapter 3:2-3,20-21; Chapter 4:2-3,6,8,18-20 NLT)

*   *   *   *   *   *   *

One day that same spring a knock sounded at the door of Paul's rented house. A believer entered and got straight to the point. "Have you heard the news about James the Just?"

"No," Paul responded. "What is it?"

"The Jews have stoned James, the brother of our Lord, in Jerusalem! The high priest started the stoning, and others joined in."

Paul's eyes filled with tears. "What a faithful leader of God's people he has been. He spoke out boldly at the Jerusalem Council, insisting that centuries earlier the prophets had predicted Gentile conversions. He helped write the letter stating that Gentiles did not have to follow the Law of Moses. His death will be hard for his wife to bear, and a great loss to the Christians, but we can rejoice that he is with the Lord, which is far better."

As Paul mourned the death of James, his own uncertain future came to mind. What would be the outcome of his case when he was called to stand before Emperor Nero?

N

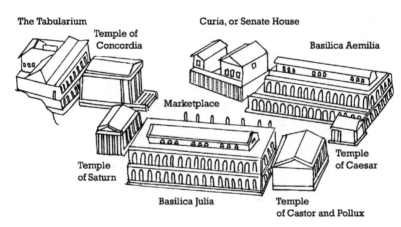

The Tabularium

Temple of
Concordia

Curia, or Senate House

Basilica Aemilia

Marketplace

Temple
of Saturn

Temple
of Caesar

Basilica Julia

Temple
of Castor and Pollux

The Roman Forum

Chapter
⟨NINETEEN⟩

Aging Shepherd

Rome, Asia Minor, Macedonia

Spring, A.D. 62, Rome

Paul had waited two years for a hearing of his appeal. He hoped that this time out of the public eye had put to rest the plans of religious leaders to have him killed. God had earlier assured him that he would stand before Caesar. As winter gave way to spring, Paul received news that the Roman Emperor was ready to judge his case.

A soldier led Paul through the narrow, disorganized streets of Rome, past overcrowded, fire-prone wooden apartment buildings. Families lived in small dwellings built around an inner courtyard. Each building was several stories high and stood barely an arm's length from the one next to it. The aroma of food sizzling on charcoal braziers drifted into the streets. Small shops at street level displayed brightly colored fruits and vegetables, and the strong odor of a fish market wafted through the air.

Green pines and cypresses waved in the breeze, displaying the new growth of spring on the Palatine, the center hill of the seven in Rome. The palace on the flat hilltop overlooked the Roman Forum. Many of the buildings in the Forum had been built centuries earlier at the foot of Capitoline Hill. Temples to the gods

Castor and Pollux, Saturn, Concord, and Julius Caesar surrounded the public square. From the bustling marketplace, patrons could enter the series of shops at the Basilica Aemilia. Roman Senators, known as the *curia*, hurried to the Senate House for the day's work. City officials entered the Tabularium, the official records' office. It was situated behind the Temple of Concord on the front slope of Capitoline Hill.

Paul and his guard walked up the steps into the Basilica Julia which housed the government offices and law courts.

Caesar's assistant judges sat at the far end of the room. Paul waited his turn. A young, blond-haired man entered the hall wearing a loose purple gown. Everyone rose in recognition of Emperor Nero.

Nero sat down and glanced at the unimpressive, older man who stood before him. "You are Paul of Tarsus?"

"Yes, your Excellency."

"Your citizenship?"

"Roman, by birth."

The prosecution handed Nero the sea-stained papyrus from Governor Felix. It listed the charges against Paul.

"You have three criminal charges against you," Nero stated, reading them slowly and deliberately:

- "a troublemaker who makes a habit of starting riots among the Jews all over the world and who encourages people to rebel against the Roman government,
- a ringleader of the sect called the Nazarenes,
- a rebel who tried to defile the Temple in Jerusalem."

After each charge the prosecution questioned Paul, but he denied the charges. As the hearing ended Paul added, "I did not encourage people to rebel against the Roman government. This is not true. In fact, five years ago I wrote a letter to followers in Rome and reminded them to obey those in authority."

When the last charge had been presented, Nero consulted with his assistant judges, and the group withdrew to a room to prepare the verdict.

After a considerable time Nero and his assistants returned. A spokesman announced, "The prisoner, Paul, is not guilty."

Paul sent up a quick prayer of thanks to God as guards removed the chains. Paul rubbed his wrist with a sense of relief.

Outside, melting snow trickled down the slopes of the Apennine Mountains to the east. Birds sang overhead. Tall oaks and beech trees provided shelter for nesting birds. Paul returned to the prison-house. He gathered his few belongings and went to say good-bye to his friends. As he walked through the streets, the sunshine warmed his skin. Horses and carts bumped their way past him.

When Paul and his traveling companions left Rome a short time later, they followed the road south, passing blossoming trees and breathing deeply of the fresh, spring air. He gave thanks to God for the opportunity to continue serving Him.

Spring, A.D. 62, Asia Minor

When Paul had written to Philemon, he had asked him to keep the guestroom ready for his upcoming trip to Colosse. He still hoped to travel east to visit the churches in Asia.

However, Paul went to Ephesus first, accompanied by Timothy. They worked side by side for several months. As warm summer temperatures changed to cooler autumn breezes, Paul felt an increasing urgency to pass the burden of the work to Timothy. "There are deep needs in the churches of Asia. Of all the young men I have worked with, you are the one who best understands my feelings for the believers. It is time for younger workers who love the people of God to shoulder more of the responsibility."

"I care for the believers, as you do," Timothy assured him.

Concern passed over Paul's face. "The church here at Ephesus is being divided by false teachers. I have dealt with them, but I would like you to stay here and help rebuild the work by teaching the Word and warning the Christians about the false teachers and their doctrine."

"I will stay. I agree that this will be best for the work."

"I do not want to go, but it is necessary. I must resume my travels before winter comes."

"It will not be the same without you," Timothy said, choking back tears. "I am young and inexperienced. You are decisive and handle troublemakers effectively."

"You can set an example to the believers by the way you live. Although you are young, focus on spiritual fitness. It will help you in both this life and the next. You must realize that you could easily be distracted with all the sports and competitions at the stadium in the north end of town. But remember, physical fitness lasts only for this life. Stay focused on eternal things."

Tears rolled down Timothy's cheeks as Paul packed up his few earthly goods and went down to the harbor to find a boat.

Autumn, A.D. 62, to spring, A.D. 63, Macedonia

Paul traveled from Ephesus to Macedonia where he and Luke spent time working together. Paul had a great desire to write to Timothy to give him further direction regarding the care of the church at Ephesus. During Paul's second missionary trip to Ephesus he had warned the Ephesians that vicious wolves would try to destroy the flock. Now it seemed to be happening right before their eyes. Timothy, however, was timid by nature and needed encouragement to handle problems that arose.

Luke agreed to write while Paul dictated.

> *From: Paul, an apostle of Christ Jesus, appointed by the command of God our Savior and Christ Jesus, who gives us hope....*
>
> *To: Timothy, my true son in the faith,*
>
> *May God the Father and Christ Jesus our Lord give you grace, mercy, and peace.*
>
> *When I left for Macedonia, I urged you to stay there in Ephesus and stop those whose teaching is contrary to the truth.... The purpose of my instruction is that all believers*

would be filled with love that comes from a pure heart, a clear conscience, and genuine faith.…

I used to blaspheme the name of Christ. In my insolence, I persecuted his people. But God had mercy on me because I did it in ignorance and unbelief.… This is a trustworthy saying, and everyone should accept it: "Christ Jesus came into the world to save sinners"—and I am the worst of them all. But God had mercy on me so that Christ Jesus could use me as a prime example of his great patience with even the worst sinners. Then others will realize that they, too, can believe in him and receive eternal life. All honor and glory to God forever and ever! He is the eternal King, the unseen one who never dies; he alone is God. Amen.

Timothy, my son, here are my instructions for you, based on the prophetic words spoken about you earlier. May they help you fight well in the Lord's battles. Cling to your faith in Christ, and keep your conscience clear. For some people have deliberately violated their consciences; as a result, their faith has been shipwrecked. Hymenaeus and Alexander are two examples. I threw them out and handed them over to Satan so they might learn not to blaspheme God.

I urge you, first of all, to pray for all people. Ask God to help them; intercede on their behalf, and give thanks for them.…For there is only one God and one Mediator who can reconcile God and humanity—the man Christ Jesus.…

And I want women to be modest in their appearance. They should wear decent and appropriate clothing and not draw attention to themselves by the way they fix their hair or by wearing gold or pearls or expensive clothes. For women who claim to be devoted to God should make themselves attractive by the good things they do.…

An elder must be a man whose life is above reproach. He must be faithful to his wife. He must exercise self-control, live wisely, and have a good reputation. He must enjoy having guests in his home, and he must be able to teach. He must not be a heavy drinker or be violent. He must be gentle, not quarrelsome, and not love money. He must manage his own family well, having children who respect and obey him. . . . An elder must not be a new believer, because he might become proud, and the devil would cause him to fall. Also, people outside the church must speak well of him so that he will not be disgraced and fall into the devil's trap.

In the same way, deacons must be well respected and have integrity. They must not be heavy drinkers or dishonest with money. . . . In the same way, their wives must be respected and must not slander others. They must exercise self-control and be faithful in everything they do. A deacon must be faithful to his wife, and he must manage his children and household well. . . .

Without question, this is the great mystery of our faith. Christ was:

* *revealed in a human body and*

* *vindicated by the Spirit. . .*

* *seen by angels and*

* *announced to the nations. . .*

* *believed in throughout the world and*

* *taken to heaven in glory.*

Now the Holy Spirit tells us clearly that in the last times some will turn away from the true faith; they will follow deceptive spirits and teachings that come from demons. . . . They will say it is wrong to be married and wrong to eat certain foods. But God created those foods to be eaten with thanks by faithful people who know the truth. . . .

Never speak harshly to an older man, but appeal to him respectfully as you would to your own father. Talk to younger men as you would to your own brothers. Treat older women as you would your mother, and treat younger women with all purity as you would your own sisters.

Take care of any widow who has no one else to care for her....

True godliness with contentment is itself great wealth....For the love of money is the root of all kinds of evil. And some people, craving money, have wandered from the true faith and pierced themselves with many sorrows....

At just the right time Christ will be revealed from heaven by the blessed and only almighty God, the King of all kings and Lord of all lords. He alone can never die, and he lives in light so brilliant that no human can approach him. No human eye has ever seen him, nor ever will. All honor and power to him forever! Amen....

Timothy, guard what God has entrusted to you. Avoid godless, foolish discussions with those who oppose you with their so-called knowledge. Some people have wandered from the faith by following such foolishness.

May God's grace be with you....

(Excerpts from 1 Timothy Chapter 1:1-3,5,13,15-20; Chapter 2:2,5,9-10; Chapter 3:2-4,6-8,11-12,16; Chapter 4:1,3; Chapter 5:1-3; Chapter 6:6,10,15-16,20-21 NLT)

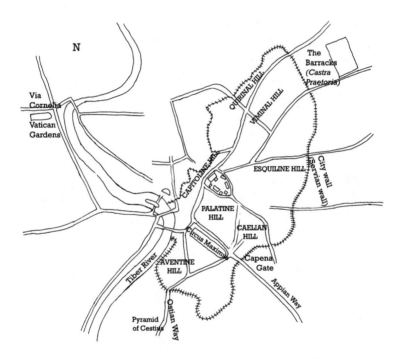

N

Via Cornelia

Vatican Gardens

The Barracks *(Castra Praetoria)*

QUIRINAL HILL

VIMINAL HILL

CAPITOLINE HILL

ESQUILINE HILL

City wall (Servian wall)

PALATINE HILL

CAELIAN HILL

Circus Maximus

Tiber River

AVENTINE HILL

Capena Gate

Appian Way

Pyramid of Cestius

Ostian Way

Rome at the time of the apostle Paul

Chapter
⌒TWENTY⌒

Fires of Rome

Rome

Summer, A.D. 64, Rome

Emperor Nero now practiced every kind of evil. Not only had he ordered his mother Agrippina killed, but also he had poisoned his stepbrother Britannicus, son of Claudius Caesar. This guaranteed that Nero would remain in power. Since his wife Octavia, a young woman in her early twenties, had not produced any children, he divorced her and banished her to a small island near the Bay of Naples. Within days of her arrival on the island, Nero sent men who killed her as she begged for her life.

After Octavia's death Nero married a woman of great beauty. He could not resist the large eyes, straight nose, and full lips of Poppea Sabina. She had been married to Otho, a friend of Nero's, but her husband did not have a chance against a suitor like Nero.

Hot, dry summer days in Rome scorched the grass to a sere brown. Emperor Nero found relief from the heat by visiting his seaside home in Antium about thirty-three miles south of Rome. But most of the remaining million or more residents of Rome had to endure the oppressive heat.

During the night of July 18, a fire crackled to life in a wooden booth in District 11. It quickly spread to surrounding huts. A hot, southeast summer wind fanned the flames till they leapt into the sky and surrounded the Circus Maximus at the foot of Palatine and Caelian Hills. The wooden bleachers of the enormous entertainment complex, the site of Rome's chariot races, provided fuel for the hungry fire.

The night-watch firefighters stationed on Aventine Hill in the southwest region of the city were the first to notice the orange glow in the sky. Firefighters hurried to the scene and put their efficient fire department to work. Water carriers formed bucket brigades between their water source and the site of the fire. Others squirted water on the flames with a pump. A third group used hooked weapons to wrestle with burning roofs and walls. But all the axes and ladders in Rome could not put out the fire. The southeast winds blew the flames faster and higher than anyone could have imagined. Firefighters could not keep up with the voracious appetite of this inferno.

Fire raced up Palatine Hill and gobbled up Nero's palace, including his art, his library, his musical instruments, and his costumes. His staff fled for their lives. "Hurry," a palace guard yelled at one of Nero's servants. "You must ride to Antium to break the news to Nero."

All night long the blaze burned, turning streets into rivers of raging fire. It swept northeast up the low cliffs of Esquiline Hill, changed direction, and moved southwest through Aventine Hill until it reached the Tiber River. Sparks jumped from building to building, and the resulting fires trapped people in the upper stories of their burning apartments. Firefighters' ladders could not reach them. Some jumped to the streets. Kind persons tried to break the fall of those jumping. An occasional person helped an invalid or elderly one. People ran in mad confusion and screamed in terror. But wherever anyone turned, he choked on smoke and the fire followed him.

Nero returned to Rome as quickly as possible, but he had no power to do anything. The fire burned for a week. Flames licked up everything in their path. Billowing columns of gray and black smoke hung heavily in the air.

At last the fire burned itself out. Almost immediately, however, another broke out north of Capitoline Hill in a less populated area, but the Viminal and Quirinal Hills seemed to escape. This second fire caused great damage to temples and public buildings, but fewer people lost their lives. After nine days of terror, the Great Fire of Rome exhausted itself. Of the city's fourteen districts, the fire had leveled three to the ground; seven lay scorched in ruins, and only four remained untouched. The fire had destroyed nearly two-thirds of the city. Half of Rome's population was homeless.

Nero met with Rome's leaders to talk about the future. "Plan relief efforts," he said with uncharacteristic compassion. "Offer the homeless shelter in the remaining public buildings and temples. I will set up food stations and order grain from the government storage at Ostia. Reduce the price of wheat to make it more affordable to those who have lost their homes. Rome must be rebuilt."

"With better streets, I presume?" one of them asked.

"Yes, of course. The narrow, crowded streets are gone. Rome's new streets will be wider and straighter. There will be open spaces between buildings and a limited number of stories."

"How do you plan to clear the land of all the charred material?"

"Well," Nero suggested, "it might be best to ship the burned rubble out of the city by barge, and dump it into the malaria-ridden marshes around Ostia."

"Great idea, Caesar!"

"There is something else," Nero confessed. "I have a dream." He turned to his chief advisor, Tigellinus. "It includes building a palace – one that will be bigger and better than any previous building in history. The fire left large areas of south-central Rome denuded of buildings. I will build my new palace there and call it 'The Golden House' (*Domus Aurea*). It will be surrounded by a beautiful park that includes gardens, lakes, fountains, and trees. I want the work to begin immediately – even if it means taking workers away from rebuilding other parts of Rome."

*   *   *   *   *   *   *

"Have you heard the news about Caesar's new project?" one of the citizens of Rome whispered to another.

"No, tell me."

"People are saying that he set the fire himself."

"Really?"

"Yes. They say he wanted to clear the area in order to build a new palace."

"That makes sense. The fire destroyed all those old, run-down buildings."

"Now there is land to build his Golden House in the center of Rome."

"That man is capable of anything! What will he do next?"

"Some say that while Rome burned, Nero played his lyre and recited poems!"

These rumors passed from person to person and persisted. Graffiti appeared on walls saying that Nero had purposely set fire to the city.

When Nero learned of the gossip, he complained to his staff. "People are accusing me of setting the fire. What should I do?"

"Find someone else to blame," one of them advised.

"There is one unpopular group that could be targeted," another suggested, "– the religious sect called Christians. A number of them live in this city. Some of them have houses on the Aventine near the area where the flames first broke out. Pin the blame on them, and the crowds will be satisfied."

"Good idea," Nero agreed. "Blame the Christians! Yes, that sounds good. The Christians set fire to Rome. Of course, they must be punished! I will order guards to find the Christians and arrest them. I will plan an event at the stadium where I race my horses and chariot."

"Wonderful," Tigellinus agreed enthusiastically. "The stadium at Vatican Gardens will be a good location."

"I will order all citizens to report any Christians to the authorities. The round-up will begin immediately."

Chapter
TWENTY-ONE

Arrests

Rome, Crete, Asia Minor, Nicopolis, Greece, Troas

The sound of approaching horses brought dread into the hearts of Christians. One by one, guards arrested them and dragged them to the *Castra Praetoria*, the Roman barracks. The Christians remained locked up until guards moved them to Vatican Gardens, the stadium built by Emperor Caligula west of Rome near the Tiber River.

Autumn, A.D. 64, Rome

After the authorities had arrested several hundred Christians, Nero invited the citizens of Rome to come and watch their punishment. On the day of the big event, tens of thousands filled the stadium. The towering obelisk that Caligula had brought from Egypt stood on a platform in the center of the racetrack. Nero arrived wearing his purple and gold tunic and sat in the emperor's section. His wife Poppea, his friends, and his advisors joined him. Settling himself comfortably, Nero signaled that the event should begin.

Christians who had been kept in prison were now marched into the stadium for the first event of the day. Grandparents, fathers, mothers, and children were paraded in front of the spectators. At a given signal, guards released lions from their cages. These ferocious creatures, maddened by hunger, prowled closer to the Christians who had no possible way of escape. One by one the tawny beasts hunted down their prey, their strong legs and sharp teeth leaving no doubt as to the outcome. Victims fell, screaming in pain. Having gorged on their victims, only bones remained to litter the ground.

With fanfare the spokesman announced the next event. More Christians were paraded into the stadium, but this time each one carried a wooden cross. The guards then nailed each Christian to a cross and left them hanging there as the remaining events unfolded.

One appalling event followed another. Guards strapped Christians to rotating iron wheels that dipped into fire, slowly roasting them alive. Others were tied to the horns of a wild bull. Each bull lunged around the stadium before charging into a wall to free itself of the aggravating burden.

Nero reserved the most spectacular punishment of the "accused arsonists" until the end of the day. In the darkness of the evening, the guards brought out dozens of wooden pillars that had been treated with resin and oil. They chained Christians wearing shirts soaked in nitrates, sulfur, and pitch, to the pillars. The guards then lit the bottom of the poles, and flames crept up toward the victims, torturing them in the fire. The posts served as giant torches, continuing to burn for several hours until the flames consumed the bodies tied to them.

A.D. 65, Rome

Nero's building project, the Golden House, became a costly undertaking. To finance the work he demanded that the rich leave their money to him in their wills. As soon as the rich had done as he asked, he would have them murdered and then he would take their money. He also taxed the provinces as a source of income to pay for the rebuilding of Rome.

From time to time Nero judged cases that came to trial. At one such time the governor of the region of Judea had sent several Jewish priests to Rome for trial. A young Pharisee named Josephus traveled with the men to intercede on their behalf. Josephus met Nero's wife, Empress Poppea, who showed sympathy to the Jews, and through her help they won their case.

Nero and Poppea had a daughter named Claudia Augusta, but she died as an infant. Now Poppea was pregnant again. One night Nero stayed out particularly late after watching several races. When he arrived home, Poppea scolded him. Angry words were hurled back and forth between them. Finally, Nero reacted with a fit of rage, kicking his wife. When he had finished, Poppea Sabina, Empress of Rome, lay motionless before him. She was dead and so was his child. For a short time Nero bemoaned her loss, but he soon found another wife, Statilia Messalina. Not content with her, Nero's increasing perversion showed itself when he held a public wedding ceremony with his slave boy, Sporus.

Nero's murderous inclination spread to anyone closely connected with him. He executed many of his friends and statesmen or forced them to commit suicide. Nero's victims included his Spanish-born tutor and adviser, the philosopher Seneca; Seneca's nephew, the poet Lucan; and Seneca's brother Gallio, who had made it possible for Paul to have an effective ministry in Corinth thirteen years earlier.

However, in spite of all of the evil and darkness in the Roman Empire, the Lord enabled the apostle Paul to continue to travel and to speak for Him.

Early summer, A.D. 66, Crete

As a prisoner on his way to Rome seven years earlier, Paul had been a passenger on an Alexandrian ship that had found shelter during a storm at Fair Havens on the south side of Crete. Now Paul again found himself on board ship, traveling with eager anticipation through crystal waters toward Crete, a large island located southeast of Greece.

Blue summer skies and calm waters contrasted with the stormy seas of his earlier trip. As the ship neared its destination, it passed long, sandy beaches that bordered the rocky cliffs.

The Romans had conquered the island in 67 B.C. and had made it part of the Roman Empire. The native Cretans were excellent seamen and were skilled with the bow and arrow. However, to their shame, many had become notorious for lying and immorality.

Upon arrival Paul left the ship and entered a city with narrow streets. A light breeze from the north gently stirred the palm branches. Paul was thankful to be working with his co-worker Titus for the summer months. Titus was one of Paul's earlier converts, and in September, A.D. 49, they had traveled together to the Council at Jerusalem to visit the elders. Titus had been an example to new believers that circumcision was not necessary for salvation. For several years after that, Titus helped at Corinth where he dealt with cases of immorality. He also assisted in the weekly collections for the poor saints at Jerusalem.

"There is a strong Jewish settlement in Crete," Titus observed.

Paul nodded. "Yes, and most of them have never heard the truth about Christ."

Island of Crete

Titus agreed. "Many Cretans worship the so-called king of the Greek gods, Zeus. There is a legend that he was born on Crete's highest peak, Mount Ida."

Paul and Titus traveled and preached in various places throughout this mountainous island. The mountain ranges ran from one end of Crete to the other, but fertile valleys nestled between them. When Paul preached the 'good news,' some became followers of Christ. Occasionally the pair would meet a Christian who had been in Jerusalem on the Day of Pentecost, but these individuals needed more teaching.

Some, however, were more interested in arguing about their genealogies than in learning about Christ. When Paul tried to clear up the questions they raised, the men went back to heatedly discussing minute details of the Law.

By the middle of the hot, dry summer, Paul sensed God's leading to leave Crete. "Titus," Paul said, "I must do more traveling before the autumn rains and cooler temperatures arrive. There is much to do before winter – so many places to go. Will you stay here in Crete?"

"Of course," Titus responded. "I will gladly continue teaching the new converts."

"Good! I am thankful to God for your service. When I leave, I want you to go to the different towns and appoint elders."

The day of Paul's departure arrived. Titus accompanied him to the harbor and stayed until Paul's ship sailed north into the open seas.

Late summer, A.D. 66, Asia Minor

Even after Paul arrived in Asia Minor, his burden for Crete continued to weigh on him. The churches there had problems similar to the ones that Timothy had dealt with in Ephesus. Paul dictated a letter with more specific instructions for Titus.

From: Paul, a slave of God and an apostle of Jesus Christ....

To: Titus, my true son in the faith that we share,

May God the Father and Christ Jesus our Savior give you grace and peace.

I left you on the island of Crete so you could complete our work there and appoint elders in each town as I instructed you. An elder must live a blameless life. He must be faithful to his wife, and his children must be believers who don't have a reputation for being wild or rebellious....He must have a strong belief in the trustworthy message he was taught; then he will be able to encourage others with wholesome teaching and show those who oppose it where they are wrong....

There are many rebellious people who engage in useless talk and deceive others. This is especially true of those who insist on circumcision for salvation. They must be silenced, because they are turning whole families away from the truth by their false teaching. And they do it only for money....

As for you, Titus, promote the kind of living that reflects wholesome teaching. Teach the older men to exercise self-control, to be worthy of respect, and to live wisely. They must have sound faith and be filled with love and patience....

Older women must train the younger women to love their husbands and their children, to live wisely and be pure, to work in their homes, to do good, and to be submissive to their husbands. Then they will not bring shame on the word of God.

In the same way, encourage the young men to live wisely....

Slaves must always obey their masters and do their best to please them....For the grace of God has been revealed, bringing salvation to all people. And we are instructed to turn from godless living and sinful pleasures....

Once we, too, were foolish and disobedient. We were misled and became slaves to many lusts and pleasures. Our lives were full of evil and envy, and we hated each other.

But—"When God our Savior revealed his kindness and love, he saved us, not because of the righteous things we had done, but because of his mercy. He washed away our sins, giving us a new birth and new life through the Holy Spirit...."

Do not get involved in foolish discussions about spiritual pedigrees or in quarrels and fights about obedience to Jewish laws. These things are useless and a waste of time....

I am planning to send either Artemas or Tychicus to you. As soon as one of them arrives, do your best to meet me at Nicopolis, for I have decided to stay there for the winter. Do everything you can to help Zenas the lawyer and Apollos with their trip. See that they are given everything they need. Our people must learn to do good by meeting the urgent needs of others; then they will not be unproductive.

Everybody here sends greetings. Please give my greetings to the believers—all who love us.

May God's grace be with you all.

(Excerpts from Titus Chapter 1:1,4-6,9-11; Chapter 2:1,2,4-6,9,11-12; Chapter 3:3-5,9,12-15 NLT)

*   *   *   *   *   *   *

Winter, A.D. 66-67, Nicopolis

Paul traveled from Asia Minor to Nicopolis for the winter season. The city was set on a peninsula along the west coast of Greece between the sea and a large gulf. It had been founded by Octavian almost one hundred years earlier to celebrate his victory over Anthony and Cleopatra at Actium. Its name meant 'city of victory.' Now three hundred thousand people from various countries lived there.

Paul had asked Titus to join him for the winter months. Although the cooler temperatures, rainfall, and sea winds had arrived, they did not prevent Paul, Titus, and fellow Christians from using every opportunity to tell others the 'good news.'

Spring to autumn, A.D. 67, Greece

During the spring Paul and his companions resumed their travels through Macedonia and Greece. In each town Paul spoke of the Lord and gave Him the credit for anything of value that was accomplished. He praised God for salvation and honored the Lord for His greatness, His power, and His perfect character.

While Paul was talking about the glorious work that God had done through Christ, Emperor Nero was traveling, promoting himself in a concert tour. He had set sail for Greece the previous autumn. Nero had invited his fan club to cheer and clap for his performances. Though he appeared in chariot races, he also performed in live theater where entertainers accompanied him on their stringed instruments, including lyres and the more professional seven-stringed kithara. While the musicians played, Nero would either recite his own poems or sing and play the lyre. For these performances this thick-necked, pot-bellied man with skinny legs and long, curly hair dressed himself up in masks, costumes, and buskins (laced boots that rose to the knee.)

Before coming to Greece, Nero had ordered the Isthmian Olympic Games of A.D. 65 to be delayed for two years in order that he might be their distinguished guest. The Games held drama and musical events as well as athletic competitions. No matter how Nero performed, the judges would always declare him the winner and present him with many trophies and prizes.

Nero and his troupe continued traveling from town to town during the autumn of A.D. 67. Paul and his companions, however, finished their travels in Greece and made plans to return to Asia Minor. Erastus did not go with them, remaining instead in Corinth. The others crossed the Aegean Sea to Miletus, a city located south of Ephesus. During this time at Miletus, Paul's fellow-worker Trophimus became sick and could not continue. Trophimus had been a loyal worker through the years. He had converted to Christ in Ephesus. Later he had gone with Paul to Jerusalem, where Jews had falsely accused Paul of taking him into the Temple. This caused the riot that resulted in Paul's arrest and his first trip to Rome.

Autumn, A.D. 67, Troas

Paul and his companions continued to travel north from Miletus to the seaport town of Troas. Paul had his writings, his parchments, and his coat with him since the weather would soon turn cold. At Troas he was welcomed into the home of Carpus, a fellow Christian.

One day a Roman officer came for him. "Are you Paul of Tarsus?"

"Yes."

"You are under arrest," the officer stated. "Come with me! You will need to answer a formal charge before the Roman governor of Asia."

The soldier escorted him to an office where the governor read the charges. In a few short moments Paul's circumstances had changed abruptly from a life of freedom to one of captivity once again.

The powers of darkness and the rulers of this world had applied pressure yet again to silence the voice that spoke for God. A soldier wrapped the inevitable chain around the prisoner's wrist. Paul and his guards left Troas for Rome where Paul would have to appear before Nero a second time. Paul sensed that his mission to make Christ known would soon be complete. He loved the work God had given him to do, but the finish line appeared to be near at hand.

Chapter
⌒TWENTY-TWO⌒

Voice of Welcome

Rome

Autumn, A.D. 67, Rome

The guard led Paul past the Roman Forum en route to the prison. When they entered the building, the guard pulled Paul across the room to a round opening in the floor. Removing the grated cover, rough hands lowered him into the semi-darkness below. The cold, stale air stung his nostrils as he descended into the dim light of the lower level. A guard, waiting for him at the bottom, shoved him to the floor and attached his chains to a post. Rats scampered to the edge of the room to escape the disturbance.

The dampness penetrated his body, and Paul shivered. Would he ever feel warm again? He had left his coat, his books, and his parchments in Troas when he was arrested. Carpus would keep the items safe, but now he really needed his coat in Rome. He had not even tried to take along his belongings at the time of his arrest because the soldiers would have helped themselves to whatever they wanted.

Not so long ago loving friends had surrounded Paul. Now he sat in the stale, low-ceilinged, musty cell surrounded by stone walls, with repulsive creatures to keep him company. Emotions battled inside him as he remembered the warmth, the kind words, and the loving touch of the Christians in Antioch, Asia, Greece, and Italy.

One day melted into the next. Each day he received a prisoner's ration of food when the guards lowered it through the hole in the ceiling.

Several days after Paul arrived, guards opened the grate. Shadows obscured the face of the one who was let down into the dim light of the damp, smelly dungeon. A guard pointed the visitor toward Paul.

"Is that you, Paul?" a voice asked as he peered into the darkness.

"Over here," Paul responded, his chains rattling as he tried to move.

"You are a hard man to find," Onesiphorus greeted. "I have traveled from prison to prison searching for you."

"Onesiphorus! Welcome!" Paul exclaimed with excitement, as he rose to greet him. "My friend from Ephesus – Oh, I am thankful that you have come! But are you not afraid to associate with me and my chains?"

"No, not at all; I am here to help in any way that I can."

"You are risking your life by coming here to visit me. The persecution under Emperor Nero is fierce."

"Yes, I am aware of that. There is much gossip in the streets. People are saying that Christians drink human blood and are plotting to overthrow the government."

"And," Paul added, "I am sure there must be informers everywhere who want all the Christians dead. The government once classified us under Judaism, but that is no longer true. I am now considered a criminal because I am a Christian."

"That is true," Onesiphorus nodded. "Many are afraid to suffer as you are suffering. Hurtful lies are circulating about Christians, and many are dying as a result of those lies."

"I am here today, chained as a criminal, because I preached the Good News."

"Yes, I remember when you preached in Ephesus."

"Timothy is there now, carrying on that work."

"Tell me," Onesiphorus inquired, "what caused your arrest this time?"

"Do you remember Alexander the coppersmith, the one who operates in Ephesus and Troas? He is an enemy of the gospel. I opposed him because of his false teaching, and he brought a formal charge against me before the Roman governor of Asia. As a result, the governor sent both of us to Rome. It seems that all those in Asia have turned their backs on me."

"Have courage, Paul. The guards may have chained you like a common criminal, but no one can separate you from God's love or God's purpose."

Paul spoke to Onesiphorus as his visitor prepared to leave. "There is little hope of release, but your coming has refreshed me. Thank you."

Onesiphorus retreated toward the grated opening to return to the main floor.

*   *   *   *   *   *   *

Within a short time Paul appeared before a judge for a first hearing. The second stage of his trial was set to take place in a few months. The Roman Empire considered him a leader of the sect accused of burning Rome. Alexander's false charges against Paul would stand.

During the cool days of autumn Paul, now in his mid-sixties, shivered constantly in the drafty cell. He pulled his garments closer, but he could not get warm. An occasional Christian came to visit him, but he often felt lonely and forsaken with too much time on his hands. Luke visited the most, and Eubulus, Linus, Pudens, and Claudia sent their greetings.

Paul hoped that Timothy would come before the second stage of his trial, but until then, he had to depend on letter writing as a way to encourage Timothy to live a steadfast Christian life. A flickering tallow candle shed a dim light across his piece of papyrus.

From: Paul, chosen by the will of God to be an apostle of Christ Jesus....

To: Timothy, my dear son,

May God the Father and Christ Jesus our Lord give you grace, mercy, and peace.

Timothy, I thank God for you—the God I serve with a clear conscience, just as my ancestors did. Night and day I constantly remember you in my prayers....

So never be ashamed to tell others about our Lord. And don't be ashamed of me, either, even though I'm in prison for Christ. With the strength God gives you, be ready to suffer with me for the sake of the Good News.... Through the power of the Holy Spirit who lives within us, carefully guard the precious truth that has been entrusted to you....

Endure suffering along with me, as a good soldier of Christ Jesus. Soldiers don't get tied up in the affairs of civilian life, for then they cannot please the officer who enlisted them. And athletes cannot win the prize unless they follow the rules. And hardworking farmers should be the first to enjoy the fruit of their labor....

Work hard so you can present yourself to God and receive his approval. Be a good worker, one who does not need to be ashamed and who correctly explains the word of truth....

In a wealthy home some utensils are made of gold and silver, and some are made of wood and clay. The expensive utensils are used for special occasions, and the cheap ones are for everyday use. If you keep yourself pure, you will be a special utensil for honorable use. Your life will be clean, and you will be ready for the Master to use you for every good work....

Gently instruct those who oppose the truth. Perhaps God will change those people's hearts, and they will learn the truth....

You should know this, Timothy, that in the last days there will be very difficult times. For people will love only themselves and their money. They will be boastful and proud, scoffing at God, disobedient to their parents, and ungrateful.

They will consider nothing sacred…You know how much persecution and suffering I have endured. You know all about how I was persecuted in Antioch, Iconium, and Lystra—but the Lord rescued me from all of it. Yes, and everyone who wants to live a godly life in Christ Jesus will suffer persecution.…

All Scripture is inspired by God and is useful to teach us what is true and to make us realize what is wrong in our lives. It corrects us when we are wrong and teaches us to do what is right.…

For a time is coming when people will no longer listen to sound and wholesome teaching. They will follow their own desires and will look for teachers who will tell them whatever their itching ears want to hear. They will reject the truth and chase after myths.…

As for me, my life has already been poured out as an offering to God. The time of my death is near. I have fought the good fight, I have finished the race, and I have remained faithful. And now the prize awaits me—the crown of righteousness, which the Lord, the righteous Judge, will give me on the day of his return. And the prize is not just for me but for all who eagerly look forward to his appearing.

Timothy, please come as soon as you can. Demas has deserted me because he loves the things of this life and has gone to Thessalonica. Crescens has gone to Galatia, and Titus has gone to Dalmatia. Only Luke is with me. Bring Mark with you when you come, for he will be helpful to me in my ministry.…When you come, be sure to bring the coat I left with Carpus at Troas. Also bring my books, and especially my papers [the parchments].

Alexander the coppersmith did me much harm, but the Lord will judge him for what he has done. Be careful of him, for he fought against everything we said.…

Give my greetings to Priscilla and Aquila and those living in the household of Onesiphorus.…

Do your best to get here before winter. Eubulus sends you greetings, and so do Pudens, Linus, Claudia, and all the brothers and sisters.

May the Lord be with your spirit. And may his grace be with all of you.

(Excerpts from 2 Timothy Chapter 1:1-3,8,14; Chapter 2:3-6,15,20-21,25; Chapter 3:1-2,11-12,16; Chapter 4:3-4,6-11,13-15,19,21-22 NLT)

*   *   *   *   *   *   *

While Paul suffered in jail, Nero journeyed from Greece toward Rome making elaborate plans with his advisors. "When I return to Rome," he ordered, "I want the people to recognize my great deeds. I will enter the city as an Olympic champion."

"You want to follow all the Olympic customs?" an advisor asked in disbelief.

"Yes, of course," Nero insisted, his chest swelling with pride. "I want the wall broken down so I can ride through it with my chariot. I expect the people of the city to welcome me and to celebrate my victories as I ride through the streets."

Winter, A.D. 68, Rome

On a cool January day, with all the pride of a returning Olympic hero, Nero rode through a portion of the city wall. Dressed in purple and gold, and crowned with a victor's wreath, he displayed his trophies as he rode through the city. Rome had prepared extensively for the event. Workers had decorated the streets with garlands, and the scent of incense filled the air. At the end of the long day of celebration, Nero retreated to his temporary quarters at the south end of Rome.

As soon as he could, he checked on his new palace, the Golden House. "It is progressing well," he told his advisors. "I am happy that the building and grounds are nearing completion."

Nero's youthful appearance had been replaced by that of a middle-aged man much older than his thirty years. He had gained weight and looked unhealthy. His drinking had increased, and at times he gave the impression of being out of touch with reality. He cared more about his singing, acting, and sports than he did about running the Empire.

*   *   *   *   *   *   *

Spring, A.D. 68

The rulers now called Paul for the second stage of his trial. They read the charges and heard the evidence.

It didn't take the judge long to make his decision. "The prisoner is guilty as charged! He is condemned to death by the sword! It is well known throughout the Empire that this man has many followers. His death will attract too much attention in Rome. Because of that, lead him outside the city under military escort to the place of execution."

Paul caught his breath as the judge spoke. His heart seemed loud enough for all to hear. But he had been expecting this verdict. His time had come. *"The Lord is my light and my salvation; whom shall I fear?"*

*   *   *   *   *   *   *

Roman soldiers, uniformed with helmet and sword, escorted the pale, aging apostle out of the courtroom and into the spring air. They traveled south, passing under a brick archway known as the Ostian Gate, and continued along the stone-paved Ostian Way. The road led to Rome's harbor. Along the way the group passed a tomb, The Pyramid of Cestius, built for a Roman official 80 years earlier. The bright sun reflected from the slabs of white marble on the 90-foot monument. Paul squinted to protect his eyes from the unaccustomed brightness. At the third milestone the travelers reached a level spot.

Stone Pine tree

The soldiers turned to the left and stopped under a Stone Pine tree where they set up a large wooden block, positioning it to make it level.

With quiet calmness Paul stepped up to the block, dropped to his knees, and bent forward. His heart beat wildly, and with every nerve in his body on alert, he waited for the moment. *"My life has already been poured out as an offering to God. The time of my death is near. To die is gain – to be with Christ...is far better."*

A soldier raised his sword with both hands. With a downward slash, Roman justice was served.

Who shall separate us from the love of Christ?

Shall sword? . . .

Neither death, nor life . . .

Nor powers . . .

Nor any other created thing,

Shall be able to separate us from the love of God,

which is in Christ Jesus our Lord.

God's voice of welcome to His eternal home, the city of light, would far outshine that of any Olympic hero entering the city of Rome.

For now we see through a glass, darkly; but then face to face.

Epilogue

Paul had been released from his physical body, and events in the Roman Empire continued to spiral out of control. A growing faction was agitating to remove Nero as Emperor. Leaders of the provinces in the northern parts of the Empire had long been dissatisfied and were ready to act. Governor Vindex of Gaul (France and Belgium) had one hundred thousand men prepared to march against Rome.

Nero spent his time in the coastal city of Naples, involved as usual in trivial entertainment. News of a revolt came first to the attention of Nero's advisors in Rome. One of them traveled to Naples with an urgent message for Nero that the northern province of Gaul was in revolt against Rome.

With an offhanded, "I'll deal with it later," Nero continued with his distractions. He allowed several days to slip by without paying attention.

Messengers began arriving from Rome with news of more threatening events. Spain and Lusitania (Portugal) were planning to join the revolution. Advisors finally convinced Nero to return to Rome, but even then he did not give the matter his total attention. His behavior clearly demonstrated that saving the Roman Empire was not a priority. His attention was absorbed with drinking and pursuing his acting career.

The Senate in Rome, increasingly concerned about uprisings in Spain, Gaul, and Lusitania, began to conspire behind closed doors as they made secret plans to depose Nero.

One day in early June, Nero searched for his palace guard. They were gone! He had been deserted! About the time Nero made this discovery, the Senate, meeting in another location, declared Nero 'an enemy of the state.' They condemned him to a slave's death – death by flogging. A warrant was issued for his arrest.

When Nero realized that his bodyguards and personal attendants had abandoned him, he was panic-stricken. He planned an immediate escape, but soldiers captured him on June 9, A.D. 68. Rather than face this shameful death sentence, he committed suicide.

Rome suffered through a further year of tumult after Nero's death. Several commanders tried their hand at ruling the Empire:

- Galba, a commander from Gaul, ruled for seven months.

- Otho, a commander from Lusitania, lasted for almost three months. This former friend to Nero had been married to Poppea before Nero enticed her to be his wife. In recent years Otho had been Governor of Lusitania under Nero.

- Aulus Vitellius, a commander from the Rhine, took charge for eight months.

- Vespasian, a capable military commander, finally took over as Emperor. He had been in Judea to put down a revolt ever since Nero's tour of Greece in A.D. 67. When Vespasian became Emperor, his son Titus took over in Judea. Under Titus, the Temple in Jerusalem was destroyed in A.D. 70. Vespasian had the Arch of Titus built in Rome to commemorate his son's victory. Vespasian ruled the Empire for ten years (A.D. 69-79) and a time of stability returned to Rome.

Even though it was still illegal to be a Christian, Emperor Vespasian did not actively persecute believers. Many, however, continued to suffer for their faith.

Notes

Preface (pages 11 to 14)
GALLIO, DATES OF THE PROCONSUL OF ACHAIA: (1) F. F. Bruce, *New Testament History*, p. 298. (2) Paul L. Maier, *The Flames of Rome*, Notes, p. 423.

Chapter 1 – Approving Bystander (pages 17 to 20)
Scripture for Further Study: Acts 6, 7.

COUNCIL, SANHEDRIN: *New Bible Dictionary*. The Sanhedrin was the highest tribunal of the Jews. It is believed to have originated with the seventy elders who assisted Moses, Numbers 11:16-24. Under the Romans this council had wide powers.

STEPHEN'S BLOOD: Acts 22:20.

STONING: (1) William MacDonald, *Believer's Bible Commentary*, p. 420; authority to order a stoning. (2) F. F. Bruce, *The Book of Acts*, pp. 159-160; description of a typical stoning of the 2nd century (Eusebius, HE 2.23.16). (3) Paul L. Maier, *Pontius Pilate*, pp. 213,364; description of the procedure for stoning (*Sanhedrin*, vi, 1-4). (4) Achan was told to confess before he was stoned, Joshua 7:19.

TEMPLE: Acts 6:13-14; 7:48.

Chapter 2 – Passionate Pharisee (pages 21 to 30)
Scripture for Further Study: Acts 22:3,28; 23:6; Romans 11:1; Philippians 3:5.

CHILDHOOD AND EDUCATION: (1) Tim Dowley, *Everyday Life in Bible Times*, p. 14. (2) Ralph Gower, *The New Manners and Customs of Bible Times*, p. 86. (3) Luke 1:63 demonstrates the use of a writing tablet. (4) 2 Timothy 3:15. Scripture during childhood. (5) Galatians 1:14. Paul advanced to the top of his class.

CYDNUS RIVER: Strabo, *Geography* 14.5.12.

DARKNESS OVER THE EARTH FROM NOON TO 3 P.M.: (1) Luke 23:44. (2) Paul L. Maier, *Pontius Pilate*, Endnotes, p. 366; Tertullian, *Apologeticus*, xxi, 20. This event was visible in Rome, Athens, and other Mediterranean cities.

FLAX: Tom H. Ratcliffe, *Bible Plants, Fruits & Products*, p. 86.

GAMALIEL: (1) F. F. Bruce, *Paul, Apostle of the Heart Set Free*, p. 43. (2) *New Bible Dictionary*, p. 395. (3) Ralph Gower, *The New Manners and Customs of Bible Times*, p. 83.

GOATS AND TENTS: (1) William M. Ramsay, *St. Paul: The Traveler and Roman Citizen*, p. 34. (2) F. F. Bruce, *Paul, Apostle of the Heart Set Free*, p. 35.

GREEK LANGUAGE, PRESSURE TO CONVERT TO GREEK: *Ibid.*, pp. 26-27.

HEBREW OF HEBREWS: (1) Marvin R. Vincent, *Word Studies in the New Testament*, vol. 3, p. 446. This expression refers to one who retains the Hebrew language and customs. (2) F. F. Bruce, *Paul, Apostle of the Heart Set Free*, p. 42.

HEBREW (OR ARAMAIC) LANGUAGE: *American Heritage Dictionary* (Houghton Mifflin), p. 123. This refers to the Semitic language widely used by peoples throughout southwest Asia from the 7th century B.C. to the 7th century A.D.

JESUS: Matthew 12:9,10,14; 15:8; 26:1-5; Mark 11:18; Luke 19:45-48.

JOHN THE BAPTIST: Matthew 3:1-4; John 1:23,29.

REED PENS, WOODEN INKWELLS: *Family Encyclopedia of the Bible* (Chancellor), p. 93.

RHEGMA'S HARBOR: *Strabo* xiv.672.

SAUL'S FAMILY AND SOCIAL STATUS: William M. Ramsay, *St. Paul: The Traveler and Roman Citizen*, p. 35. Citizenship shows that Paul's family was one of distinction and at least moderate wealth.

SAUL'S (PAUL'S) SISTER: Acts 23:16.

SAUL'S TRADE, TENT-MAKING: Acts 18:3.

TARSUS: *New Bible Dictionary*, p. 1154.

TEN COMMANDMENTS: The complete version is found in Exodus 20.

VESTA, GODDESS OF FIRE: F. R. Cowell, *Everyday Life in Ancient Rome*, p. 38.

Chapter 3 – Voice in the Darkness (pages 31 to 38)

Scripture for Further Study: Acts 8:1-4; Acts 9:1-23; 22:6-16; 26:13-18.

ABANA RIVER: also known as Nahr Barada River.

ANTI-LEBANON MOUNTAINS: J. Carl Laney, *Concise Bible Atlas*, p. 218. Damascus is located east of these mountains.

ARABIA: *New Bible Dictionary*, p. 65; Galatians 1:17-18.

DAMASCUS, CHRISTIANS LIVED AT PEACE AMONG THEIR KINSMEN: William M. Ramsay, *St. Paul: The Traveler and Roman Citizen*, p. 43; Acts 22:12.

DAMASCUS HAD A LARGE JEWISH POPULATION: F. F. Bruce, *The Book of the Acts*, p. 181.

MOUNT HERMON: *Israel's Tourism Guide*. Hermon's highest point is 9230 feet (2814 meters) above sea level.

SAUL PERSECUTED THE CHURCH: Galatians 1:13; 1 Timothy 1:13; Philippians 3:6.

SAUL'S CONVERSION. It is recorded three times: Acts 9:3-19; Acts 22:6-16; Acts 26:13-18. Each time different details are given. (1) Acts 26:13, all fell to the ground. (2) Acts 9:7, the men stood speechless; therefore they must have risen to their feet. (3) Acts 22:9, all saw the light but did not understand articulate speech.

SAUL'S CONVERSION AND HIS RETURN TO JERUSALEM: *New Bible Dictionary*, p. 198. The three years in Arabia were probably two part-years and one complete year.

STEPHEN'S BURIAL: Ralph Gower, *The New Manners and Customs of Bible Times*, p. 72. Burial.

SYRIAN-ARABIAN DESERT: *New Bible Dictionary*, p. 251. Damascus is located west of this desert.

TRIBE OF BENJAMIN, THEIR FIGHTING SPIRIT: Genesis 49:27.

WAY OF THE SEA: William M. Ramsay, *St. Paul: The Traveler and Roman Citizen*, p. 43. 'The way of the sea' refers to the Sea of Galilee.

Chapter 4 – Escapes (pages 39 to 45)
Scripture for Further Study: Acts 9:24-30; 2 Corinthians 11:32-33; Galatians 1:18-19.

BASKET: W.E. Vine, *Vine's Expository Dictionary*, p. 99, notes 2 and 3.

GOVERNOR OF DAMASCUS: ruled under King Aretas, 2 Corinthians 11:32.

SAUL VISITS JAMES (KNOWN AS JAMES THE JUST): Galatians 1:19.

SAUL VISITS PETER IN JERUSALEM: Galatians 1:18.

SAUL'S TRIP FROM DAMASCUS TO JERUSALEM: F. F. Bruce, *The Book of the Acts*, p. 192; Acts 9:25.

TRIP FROM JERUSALEM TO CAESAREA: *New Bible Dictionary*, p. 153; about 60 miles or 100 km.

Chapter 5 – The Roman Empire (pages 46 to 50)
Scripture for Further Study: Acts 9:30; Galatians 1:21-24.

AGRIPPINA, RICH AND BEAUTIFUL: *World Book Encyclopedia*, Agrippina the Younger.

AUGUSTUS: (1) *Ibid.* When Caesar Augustus became the first Roman Emperor in 27 B.C., the Roman Republic ended and the Roman Empire began. After his death the people worshiped him as 'Divine Augustus.' (2) Merrill F. Unger, *The New Unger's Bible Dictionary*, pp. 125-126.

CALIGULA: (1) GAVE AGRIPPA GALILEE AND PEREA: *New Bible Dictionary*, p. 472. (2) REAL NAME, GAIUS: *World Book Encyclopedia*. (3) PLAN TO KILL THE ROMAN SENATE MEMBERS: *Ibid.* (4) HIS SECRET NOTEBOOKS: Paul L. Maier, *Pontius Pilate*, p. 323. (5) HIS STATUE IN THE TEMPLE AT JERUSALEM: (a) F. F. Bruce, *New Testament History*, p. 254. "Agrippa was able to dissuade Gaius (Caligula) from his foolish policy, although he took his life in both hands to do so." (b) F. F. Bruce, *Paul, Apostle of the Heart Set Free*, p. 232.

CLAUDIUS CONQUERED BRITANNICUS (BRITAIN): A.D. 43.

CLAUDIUS IMPROVED CONDITIONS IN THE ROMAN EMPIRE: *World Book Encyclopedia*.

HAIL CAESAR: Paul L. Maier, *Pontius Pilate*, p. 290.

JAMNIA ALTAR: F. F. Bruce, *Paul, Apostle of the Heart Set Free*, p. 232.

PILATE RECALLED TO ROME: Paul L. Maier, *Pontius Pilate*, p. 368; quoted from Josephus, *Antiq.*, xviii 4, 2-3.

PILATE REPLACED BY GOVERNOR FELIX: *New Bible Dictionary*, p. 929.

ROMAN EMPIRE: *World Book Encyclopedia*.

SAUL PREACHED IN SYRIA AND CILICIA: Galatians 1:21-24.

Chapter 6 – Christians (pages 51 to 59)
Scripture for Further Study: Acts 11:19-30; 12:1-25.

AGRIPPA: (1) AGE AT HIS DEATH: *New Bible Dictionary*, p. 472.

(2) AGRIPPA'S' CLOTHING DESCRIBED: Josephus, *Antiquities of the Jews*, xix, viii, 2.

ANTIOCH – IMAGES OF THE GODDESS ISIS IMPRINTED ON FLOOR MOSAICS: *Thompson Chain Reference Bible*, G. Frederick Owen's Archaeological Supplement, 1993 ed.

ANTIOCH OF SYRIA, POPULATION: J. Carl Laney, *Concise Bible Atlas*, p. 219. Antioch was the third largest city in the Roman Empire after Rome and Alexandria.

ANTIOCH'S COLONNADES: *Ibid.*, p. 224. In Antioch, Herod the Great provided colonnades on either side of its main street and paved the street with polished stone.

BARNABAS, A NATIVE OF CYPRUS: Acts 4:36.

BARNABAS AND JOHN MARK: Colossians 4:10.

CAESAREA, GOVERNMENT OFFICES UNDER THE ROMANS: F. F. Bruce, *The Book of Acts*, p. 240.

CHRIST-PEOPLE: *Ibid.*, p. 228. Christ-people became known as Christians.

DAPHNE: *International Standard Bible Encyclopedia*, p. 787; a suburb of Antioch on the Orontes, a place of great natural beauty.

FAMINE, GRAIN FROM EGYPT, FIGS FROM CYPRUS: William M. Ramsay, *St. Paul: The Traveler and Roman Citizen*, pp. 56-60.

GREEKS TURN TO CHRIST: A.T. Robertson, *Word Pictures of the New Testament;* Acts 11:20. The use of 'Greeks' is undoubtedly the correct reading of this verse. Some manuscripts use 'Greek-speaking Jews.'

JERUSALEM AND AGRIPPA: *Ibid.*; Acts 12:19. "Herod Agrippa made his home in Jerusalem, but went to Caesarea to the public games in honor of Emperor Claudius."

MARY – MOTHER OF JOHN MARK: Acts 12:12.

Chapter 7– Voice for God (pages 60 to 74)
Scripture for Further Study: Acts 13:1-52; 14:1-19.

ABRAHAM AND GOD'S PROMISE: Genesis 12:3; Isaiah 49:6.

ANTIOCH OF PISIDIA: *International Standard Bible Encyclopedia*, pp. 156-157.

CYBELE: *Ibid.*, Antioch of Pisidia.

ELYMAS: His Jewish name was Bar-Jesus.

EUNICE AND LOIS, THEIR FAITH: 2 Timothy 2:5; Acts 16:1.

IMPERIAL ROAD: A.T. Robertson, *Word Pictures of the New Testament*, Acts 14:6.

JOHN MARK'S RETURN TO JERUSALEM: Acts 13:13.

MALARIA: (1) William M. Ramsay, *St. Paul: The Traveler and Roman Citizen*, p. 88. Paul's illness mentioned in Galatians 4:13 may have started in Perga. (2) *Strong's Concordance*, G769 - as-then'-i-ah (from G772): feebleness (of body or mind); by implication malady; disease, infirmity, sickness, weakness.

MEDITERRANEAN: William M. Ramsay, *St. Paul: The Traveler and Roman Citizen*, p. 72. Currents flow between Seleucia and Cyprus in the spring.

PAPHOS: (1) *International Standard Bible Encyclopedia*, p. 2238. Paphos. (2) Basil Mathews, *Paul the Dauntless* (Partridge), pp. 138,144. (3) William M. Ramsay, *St. Paul: The Traveler and Roman Citizen*, p. 74.

PERGA: (1) *New Bible Dictionary*, p. 901. (2) *International Standard Bible Encyclopedia*, p. 2322. (3) F. F. Bruce, *The Book of Acts*, pp. 250-251.

SALAMIS, EXPORTATION: *International Standard Bible Encyclopedia*, p. 2662.

SAUL'S NAME CHANGE: (1) Merrill F. Unger, *The New Unger's Bible Dictionary*, p. 968. The name Paul means "little" and Paul wanted to be known as the "little one" in Christ's service. (2) William M. Ramsay, *St. Paul: The Traveler and Roman Citizen*, p. 80. The name change is a case of applying 1 Corinthians 9:20-21, "I became all things to all men."

SERGIUS PAULUS: (1) *International Standard Bible Encyclopedia*, p. 2292. Paulus, Sergius. (2) *New Bible Dictionary*, p. 246. As the proconsul, Sergius Paulus would answer directly to Rome. (3) F. F. Bruce, *The Book of Acts*, p. 248. This man may be identical with Quintus Sergius Paullus who held office in Cyprus under Claudius.

ZEUS, PRIEST, OXEN: *Ibid.*, p. 275.

ZEUS' TEMPLE: (1) William M. Ramsay, *St. Paul: The Traveler and Roman Citizen*, p. 105. (2) Basil Mathews, *Paul the Dauntless* (Partridge), p. 170.

Chapter 8 – Defender of Truth (pages 75 to 87)
Scripture for Further Study: Acts 14:20-28; 15:1-39a; Galatians.

AGRIPPINA THE YOUNGER: *World Book Encyclopedia*.

BLOOD: Leviticus 3:17. Israelites were to eat neither fat nor blood.

CIRCUMCISION NOT REQUIRED FOR TITUS: Galatians 2:1-3.

DICTATION OF THE LETTER TO GALATIANS: (1) Marvin R. Vincent, *Word Studies of the New Testament*. Paul took the pen from an amanuensis at Galatians 6:11-14. (2) However, William MacDonald's *Believer's Bible Commentary* at Galatians 6:11 suggests Paul had written the letter himself. The large letters suggest Paul's eyesight was poor.

DISTANCE TRAVELED DURING FIRST MISSIONARY TRIP:
J. Carl Laney, *Concise Bible Atlas*, p. 226.

FALSE BRETHREN WHO CAME FROM JUDEA: Galatians 2:4; Acts
15:1.

FOURTEEN YEARS AFTER PAUL'S CONVERSION: Robert Jamieson,
A.R. Fausset, and David Brown, *Commentary on the Whole Bible*, Galatians
2:1.

JEWISH PEOPLE IN PHOENICIA AND SAMARIA AFTER
PERSECUTION: Acts 11:19.

KEEPING THE LAW: James 2:10; Galatians 3:10.

NERO: *World Book Encyclopedia.*

PAPYRUS OR PARCHMENT: Experts do not always agree whether the
letters of Paul were written on papyrus or parchment. (1) A.T. Robertson,
Word Pictures of the New Testament, 2 Timothy 4:13. He mentions two available materials: (a) books – these were probably papyrus rolls. (b) parchments
– these membranes were dressed skins. Parchment would be more expensive
than papyrus. (2) William M. Ramsay, *St. Paul: The Traveler and Roman
Citizen*, p. 141. Papyrus was used for letters of antiquity.

PETER ATE WITH GENTILES AT CAESAREA: Acts 10.

PETER'S REFUSAL TO EAT WITH GENTILES: Galatians 2:12.

Chapter 9 – Team Leader (2nd Journey) (pages 88 to 101)
Scripture for Further Study: Acts 15:39 - 17:8; 1 Corinthians 1:14;
Philippians 4:15; Colossians 4:10-14; 2 Thessalonians 3:8-9;
1 Timothy 4:14.

EGNATIAN WAY TO ROME: (1) J. Carl Laney, *Concise Bible Atlas*,
p. 229. (2) F. F. Bruce, *In the Steps of the Apostle Paul*, p. 32.

FORECASTING THE FUTURE: F. F. Bruce, *Paul, Apostle of the Heart Set
Free*, p. 226. Predicting the future was forbidden by Augustus in A.D. 11.
Tiberius added the death penalty to this decree in A.D. 16. In spite of that,
Paul taught the truth of the second coming to the Thessalonians.

ISSUS: (1) Barry J. Beitzel, *Moody Atlas of Bible Lands*, p. 179. (2) Charles F.
Pfeiffer, *Baker's Bible Atlas*. The modern name for Issus is Iskenderun.
Spelling is varied: Issus, Issos.

JERUSALEM DECREE: In each city they read the decree to the churches,
Acts 16:4.

JOHN MARK'S FATHER: "Mary's house" in Acts 12:12 infers that John
Mark's father was no longer living.

LUKE: (1) A GENTILE: Paul distinguishes Luke from those of the
circumcision, Colossians 4:14. The Jewish men are Aristarchus, Mark, and
Jesus Justus, Colossians 4:10-11. The Gentiles are Epaphras, Luke, and
Demas, Colossians 4:12-14. (2) LUKE IS NOT LUCIUS of Acts 13:1:
(a) William M. Ramsay, *St. Paul: The Traveler and Roman Citizen*, p. 168;
(b) *International Standard Bible Encyclopedia*, Luke, p. 1936.

(3) LUKE TRAVELS WITH PAUL: Luke, the writer, joins Paul's company and uses the word "we" instead of "they," Acts 16:8-10. (4) LUKE'S HOME TOWN: (a) William M. Ramsay, *St. Paul: The Traveler and Roman Citizen*, pp.162-163. Luke was a man from Macedonia; (b) *International Standard Bible Encyclopedia*. "Philippi is the home town of Luke." (c) Other commentators believe Luke was from Syrian Antioch, e.g., F. F. Bruce, *New Testament History*, p. 307.

LYDIA, TRADER OF PURPLE DYE: F. F. Bruce, *The Book of Acts*, p. 311; Acts 16:14.

LYSTRA AND DERBE LOCATED IN GALATIA: William M. Ramsay, *St. Paul: The Traveler and Roman Citizen*, p. 145.

PHILIPPI: (1) CHRISTIANS GIVE MONEY TO PAUL: Philippians 4:15. (2) PRISON COURTYARD: F. F. Bruce, *The Book of Acts*, p. 318. (3) SECURING PRISONERS: William M. Ramsay, *St. Paul: The Traveler and Roman Citizen*, p. 176. (4) ACROPOLIS: F. F. Bruce, *In the Steps of the Apostle Paul*, p. 33. (5) ARCHWAY: *Thompson Chain Reference Bible*, G. Frederick Owen's Archaeological Supplement, 1993 ed. Philippi. (6) LACK OF A SYNAGOGUE: F. F. Bruce, *The Book of Acts*, p. 310. (7) SCHOOL OF MEDICINE: J. Carl Laney, *Concise Bible Atlas*, p. 229. (8) THE FORUM: *Thompson Chain Reference Bible*, G. Frederick Owen's Archaeological Supplement. 1993 ed. The forum in Philippi measured 300 by 150 feet (92 x 46 meters). It had a speaker's platform in the center of the north side and a marketplace on the south side.

POLICE ATTENDANTS: F. F. Bruce, *The Book of Acts*, p. 315. These police attendants were lictors who attended the chief magistrates in Rome.

ROMAN MILITARY GOVERNORS: magistrates.

SILAS: (1) SILAS WAS A ROMAN CITIZEN: Acts 16:37-39. (2) SILAS BAPTIZED THE JAILER: This is an assumption. Paul said he only baptized Crispus, Gaius, and the household of Stephanas, 1 Corinthians 1:14,16.

STOCKS: Merrill F. Unger, *The New Unger's Bible Dictionary*.

TIMOTHY: (1) CIRCUMCISION: F. F. Bruce, *The Book of Acts*, p. 304; Acts 16:3. (2) HIS COMMISSION: *Ibid.*, p. 304; 1 Timothy 4:14.

Chapter 10 – Discouraged Evangelist (pages 102 to 119)
Scripture for Further Study: Acts 17:7 - 18:18; 1 Corinthians 1:14-16; 9:15; 16:17,19; 1 and 2 Thessalonians

ACHAIA: *New Bible Dictionary*, p. 10. Achaia is a small region of Greece on the south coast of the Gulf of Corinth. When the Romans defeated Greece in 146 B.C., they used the name Achaia to refer to Greece in general. Corinth was the capital of Achaia, and it is always in connection with Corinth that the name Achaia appears in the New Testament.

APOLLO'S VIEW ON RESURRECTION: F. F. Bruce, *New Testament History*, p. 313; quoted from Aeschylus, *Eumenides*, 647f.

AREOPAGUS: The traditional location, Mars' Hill, was a rocky hill called the Areopagus (Hill of Ares). (1) F. F. Bruce, *In the Steps of the Apostle Paul*, p. 39.

Paul was brought before the Court of the Areopagus, because it met originally on the Areopagus, the hill of the war-god Ares, which rises on the west side of the Acropolis. By the first century A.D., however, except on solemn occasions, the court is believed to have met in the Royal Colonnade in the *agora*. (2) *New Bible Dictionary*, p. 79. "Except for investigating homicides, the Areopagus usually met in the Royal Porch in the Athenian market-place (*agora*) and it was probably here that Paul was brought before the Areopagus." (3) William M. Ramsay, *St. Paul: The Traveler and Roman Citizen*, p. 19. "To say that 'Paul stood in the middle of the hill' is in Greek absurdity. He stood in the middle of the council." (4) *Thompson Chain Reference Bible*, G. Frederick Owen's Archaeological Supplement, 1993 ed., p. 2024. "The actual site of the council meetings has been increasingly questioned."

ATHENA: (1) *Ibid.* (2) *Illustrated Encyclopedia of Bible Facts* (Nelson). (3) Philip Ardagh, *Ancient Greece*. Athena was 39 feet (12 meters) tall.

ATHENS: (1) UNKNOWN GODS: *International Standard Bible Encyclopedia*. Paul came from the harbor toward the city by road, along which were altars to the unknown God. (2) CITY OF ATHENS: *Ibid.*, pp. 319-320. (3) HOME OF WRITERS AND PHILOSPHERS: F. F. Bruce, *The Book of Acts*, p. 329. (4) PARTHENON: *World Book Encyclopedia*, Parthenon; made of white marble. (5) POETS: F. F. Bruce, *The Book of Acts*, p. 338. 'In Him we live and move and have our being.' Paul quoted this phrase from a poem attributed to Epimenides the Cretan. "*We are His children.*" *Ibid.*, p. 339. The 5th line of the Phainomena of the Greek poet Aratus. (6) THEATER OF DIONYSUS: www.cs.utk.edu/.../Classes/US210/theater.html.

BEREA: F. F. Bruce, *The Book of Acts*, p. 327.

CORINTH: (1) APHRODITE, GODDESS OF LOVE: *The Veil is Torn*, vol. 1: *The Christians*, p. 135. Latin name, Venus. (2) *BEMA*: *International Standard Bible Encyclopedia*, p. 1778. Judgment Seat. (3) CONVERTS: 1 Corinthians 1:14-16; 6:9-10. (4) GALLIO: (a) F. F. Bruce, *The Book of Acts*, p. 352; (b) William M. Ramsay, *St. Paul: The Traveler and Roman Citizen*, p. 199; (c) F. F. Bruce, *Paul, Apostle of the Heart Set Free*, p. 253. (5) PAUL'S PREACHING STYLE: 1 Corinthians 2:3-4. (6) PAUL TURNS TO THE GENTILES: Acts 18:6. (7) PLAYING THE CORINTHIAN: *Ibid.*, p. 249. (8) RACES: 1 Corinthians 9:24-27. (9) RACES EVERY SECOND YEAR: *Ibid.*, p. 249. (10) RACES, IN HONOR OF SEA-GOD: F. F. Bruce, *In the Steps of the Apostle Paul*, p. 41. (11) THE CORINTHIAN DISEASE: *The Veil is Torn*, vol. 1: *The Christians*, p. 135. (12) THIEVES NEAR CORINTH: *Ibid.*, p. 135.

EPICUREANS: 1) *International Standard Bible Encyclopedia*. Epicureans. Section 7, Atomic theory. (2) *World Book Encyclopedia*.

HOT DRINKS IN THE MARKETPLACE: Philip Ardagh, *Ancient Greece*.

IDOLS AND ATHENS: A.T. Robertson, *Word Pictures of the New Testament*.

IDOLS AND DEMON WORSHIP: 1 Corinthians 10:20.

MAN CREATED TO LIVE FOR GOD: 2 Corinthians 5:15.

MAN TO HAVE JOY: John 17:13.

SOSTHENES: Mentioned in Acts 18:17. He was the leader of the synagogue at Corinth. Sosthenes, our brother, mentioned in 1 Corinthians 1:1, may be the same man who converted to Christianity after the events of Acts 18.

STOICISM: Founded by Zeno, born on Cyprus. The dates of Zeno's life remain controversial according to Apollodorus, as quoted by Philodemos. Zeno's birth: 334/3 B.C; death: 262/1 B.C.

THESSALONIANS, PAUL'S DESIRE TO SEE THEM: 1 Thessalonians 3:6-10.

THESSALONICA, TIMOTHY WENT THERE TO ENCOURAGE: 1 Thessalonians 3:1-3.

Chapter 11 – Capable Co-workers (3rd Journey) (pages 120 to 135)
Scripture for Further Study: Acts 18:19 - 19:31; Romans 15:25-28;
    1 Corinthians; 2 Corinthians 8:9; 10:10; 12:18; Colossians 1:7; 2:1;
    4:12-13; Deuteronomy 18:9-12.

AMPHITHEATER LOCATED ON MT. PION: *The Veil is Torn*, vol. 1: *The Christians*, p. 153.

ANTIOCH OF PISIDIA: (1) ELEVATION: 3500 feet (1066 meters) above sea level. (2) ANTIOCH OF PISIDIA TO EPHESUS: F. F. Bruce, *The Book of the Acts*, p. 362; Acts 19:1; trip through the upper country.

APOLLOS, TRAVELING MERCHANT: F. F. Bruce, *Paul, Apostle of the Heart Set Free*, p. 256.

ARISTARCHUS: William M. Ramsay, *St. Paul: The Traveler and Roman Citizen*, p. 215. In the phrase "Gaius and Aristarchus a Macedonian," 'Macedonian' is singular referring to Aristarchus. Gaius was a native of Derbe, Acts 20:4.

ARTEMIS: *Ibid.*, p. 212. Artemis' temple, also known as "The Artemesium" during the New Testament period, was actually the 5th temple (Temple E) built on the site in Ephesus. It was built in the 4th century B.C. after Temple D was burned to the ground by a man named Herostratus. ARTEMIS: called Diana by the Romans. ARTEMIS' TEMPLE: Selahattin Erdemgil, *Ephesus*. The temple measured 180 x 377 feet (55 x 115 meters). "There were 127 pillars – each 57.91 feet high (17.65 meters)." Selahattin Erdemgil, archaeologist, Director of the Ephesus Museum.

CONSUL: *World Book Encyclopedia*. The title 'consul' was given to the two highest magistrates of the Roman Republic. The distinguishing signs of office were the purple-bordered toga, a staff of ivory, and an ornamental chair. The Empire retained the title but not the function.

CURETES STREET: William M. Ramsay, *St. Paul: The Traveler and Roman Citizen*, p. 205.

DEMETRIUS: F. F. Bruce, *Paul, Apostle of the Heart Set Free*, p. 293.

EPAPHRAS' WORK AT LAODICEA AND HIERAPOLIS: Colossians 1:7; 2:1; 4:12-13. EPAPHRAS AND THE LYCUS VALLEY: *The Veil is*

Torn, vol. 1: *The Christians*, p. 155. The Lycus Valley was 100 miles east of Ephesus.

EPHESUS: (1) A DAY'S WAGE: *The New Living Translation, Holy Bible,* Acts 19:19 (footnote). "Greek 50,000 pieces of silver, each of which was the equivalent of a day's wage." (2) CUSTOM'S HOUSE: Brandon Wason, *Paul's Ephesus.* (3) HARBOR STREET: Selahattin Erdemgil, *Ephesus,* p. 98. There were stores along Harbor Street. After Paul's time it was known as the Arcadian Way. (4) BOOKS OF MAGIC: F. F. Bruce, *The Book of the Acts*, p. 369. Books refer to papyri. (5) MARKETPLACE: Bibleplaces.com. The Commercial *Agora*, also known as the "Square *Agora*" (360 feet square), was built in the Hellenistic period. It is quite possible that Paul worked here with Priscilla and Aquila in their tent-making business. (6) POPULA-TION: *So That's Why! Bible* (Thomas Nelson), p. 1536. A quarter of a million lived in Ephesus. (7) TERRAIN NORTHEAST OF THE CITY: *International Standard Bible Encyclopedia.*

MEDIUMS FORBIDDEN: Deuteronomy 18:9-12.

MONEY FOR JERUSALEM: 1 Corinthians 16:1-4; 2 Corinthians 8:1-9; Romans 15:25-28.

PAUL: (1) WEAK APPEARANCE: 1 Corinthians 2:3; 2 Corinthians 10:10. (2) HOURS AT THE LECTURE ROOM OF TYRANNUS: F. F. Bruce, *The Book of Acts*, p. 366. According to the Western text, Paul had use of the building from 11 a.m. to 4 p.m. (3) TENTMAKER: William M. Ramsay, *St. Paul: The Traveler and Roman Citizen*, p. 207. Paul defined his own work hours. "You remember our labor and toil, working day and night," 1 Thessa-lonians 2:9. There, as often in ancient literature, the hours before daybreak are called "night" and his rule at Thessalonica may be extended to Ephesus. (4) INSTRUCTS CO-WORKERS: 2 Corinthians 12:18. (5) TEARS WHEN WRITING THE LETTER OF 1 CORINTHIANS: 2 Corinthians 2:4.

PETER: also known as "Cephas."

PRISCILLA AND AQUILA: William M. Ramsay, *St. Paul: The Traveler and Roman Citizen*, p. 201. Priscilla and Aquila remained in Ephesus for several years, but in A.D. 56 they returned to Rome, 1 Corinthians 16:19, and were there in the early part of A.D. 57, Romans 16:3.

TRIBUNE: *World Book Encyclopedia.* Tribunes were elected to protect the rights of the commoner. They held the office for one year but could be re-elected. Their powers did not extend past the city of Rome.

Chapter 12 – Enemies Everywhere (3rd Journey continued) (pages 136 to 153)
Scripture for Further Study: Acts 19:32-41; Acts 20; Acts 21:1-12; Romans 15:19,25; 16:1,21-23; 1 Corinthians 1:14; 2 Corinthians 1:1,8,9; 2:12; 7:5-7; 11:24-26; Colossians 4:10.

COS: A mountainous island where Hippocrates founded a medical school in the 5th century B.C.

DAY OF PENTECOST, MAY 29, A.D. 57: F. F. Bruce, *The Book of Acts,*
p. 387.

EPHESUS: (1) DANGER AND DISCOURAGEMENT: 2 Corinthians
1:8-9. (2) JEWS AT EPHESUS: A.T. Robertson *Word Pictures of the New
Testament,* Acts 19:33. Some of the Jews grew afraid that the mob would
turn on the Jews as well as on the Christians. Paul was a Jew and so was
Aristarchus. The Jews were as strongly opposed to idolatry as were the
Christians. (3) EPHESUS: *The Companion Bible* (Kregel). The town clerk
was a recorder. (4) EPHESUS TO TROAS: William M. Ramsay, *St. Paul:
The Traveler and Roman Citizen,* p. 218. Ramsay suggests that Paul took a
coasting vessel from Ephesus to Troas.

GREECE: *New Bible Dictionary,* p. 435. The reference to Greece in Acts 20:2
must refer to the Roman province of Achaia.

MEDITERRANEAN TRAVEL: William M. Ramsay, *St. Paul: The Traveler
and Roman Citizen,* p. 218.

MERCHANT SHIP: Max Schwartz, *Machines, Buildings, Weaponry of Biblical
Times,* p. 177. A typical merchant ship might be 140 feet long, 36 feet
broad, and 33 feet deep with a capacity of three tons. Some used oars, but
most relied on sail power.

MILETUS HARBORS: *Holylandphotos.org.* Eventually the four harbors of
Miletus silted up and today the site, instead of being seaside, is located 6
miles (10 km) inland from the Aegean Sea.

PHILIPPI: F. F. Bruce, *The Book of Acts,* p. 383. Paul celebrated the Feast of
Unleavened Bread.

TRAVEL DOWN THE WEST COAST OF ASIA: William M. Ramsay,
St. Paul: The Traveler and Roman Citizen, p. 222. Traveling in the early
morning.

TROAS TO MACEDONIA: 2 Corinthians 2:12-13.

TYRE: Residents of Tyre and Sidon traveled to hear Jesus, Luke 6:17.

Chapter 13 – Courageous Servant (pages 154 to 162)
Scripture for Further Study: Acts 21:13 - 22:23; Deuteronomy 16: 9-12.

HORSES: (1) F. F. Bruce, *The Book of Acts,* p. 402. "It has been inferred from
Luke's language that animals were provided for them so that they might
ride rather than go by foot." (2) William M. Ramsay, *St. Paul: The Traveler
and Roman Citizen,* p. 230. ". . . we find the verb which means in classical
Greek, 'to equip or saddle a horse.'"

MNASON'S HOME: *New Bible Dictionary,* p. 775. There is some uncertainty
as to where Mnason actually lived.

PASSOVER: Also known as The Feast of Unleavened Bread.

PENTECOST: Also known as The Feast of Weeks. It was a time to
remember the poor, Deuteronomy 16:9-12.

PENTECOST, MAY 29, A.D. 57: F. F. Bruce, *The Book of Acts,* p. 387.

PRISON CONNECTED TO THE OUTER COURT OF THE
TEMPLE BY TWO FLIGHTS OF STAIRS: *Ibid.,* p. 411.

PURIFICATION: *Ibid.*, pp. 406-407. Paul would be purifying himself from ritual defilement after returning from a long residence in Gentile lands. The others would be performing the Nazirite purification.

TEMPLE SIGN PROHIBITING FOREIGNERS FROM ENTERING THE INNER COURT: *Ibid.*, p. 409. These words are written on a tablet discovered from Herod's Temple.

Chapter 14 – Roman Citizen (pages 163 to 169)
Scripture for Further Study: Acts 22:24 - 23:35.

ANTIPATER: Josephus, *Antiquities of the Jews* 16.143; BJ 1.417.

COMMANDER: *Ibid.*, p. 411; commander of 760 foot soldiers and 240 cavalry.

COUNCIL (SANHEDRIN) MEETINGS: (1) F. F. Bruce, *The Book of Acts*, p. 423; p. 91, footnote 13. (2) *New Bible Dictionary*, pp. 1060-1061, Sanhedrin.

HIGH PRIEST AND PAUL'S LACK OF RECOGNITION: William M. Ramsay, *St. Paul: The Traveler and Roman Citizen*, p. 243.

OATH: F. F. Bruce, *The Book of Acts*, p. 431. Their solemn oath probably took a familiar form. It would be similar to one found in the Old Testament.

WHIPPING (BODY STRETCHED OVER A FRAME): Merrill F. Unger, *The New Unger's Bible Dictionary*, p. 1141.

WHIPPING (SCOURGING): F. F. Bruce, *The Book of Acts*, p. 420. The instrument used was probably a scourge.

Chapter 15 – Faithful Witness (pages 170 to 179)
Scripture for Further Study: Acts 24:1 - 26:32.

AGRIPPA II: *Ibid.*, pp. 455-457; also known as Marcus Julius Agrippa, born A.D. 27.

BERNICE: born A.D. 28.

BRITANNICUS: Paul L. Maier, *Josephus, the Essential Works*, p. 279.

BRITANNICUS SECRETLY BURIED: *World Book Encyclopedia*, Nero.

DRUSILLA: *New Bible Dictionary*, p. 263. Drusilla was born A.D. 38 (Josephus, *Ant.* 19.354.)

FELIX: (1) *New Bible Dictionary*, p. 283. This is usually believed to have been Antonius Felix, p. 367. (2) F. F. Bruce, *The Book of Acts*, pp. 447-449. Felix used the word "felicity" as a play on his name.

FELIX AND DRUSILLA: Albert Barnes, *Notes on the Bible*, Acts 24:25. Felix and Drusilla intended that Paul should provide some entertainment.

FELIX AND HIS WIVES: F. F. Bruce, *The Book of Acts*, p. 437. His three wives were all of royal birth, according to Suetonius, *Life of Claudius* 28; the third was Drusilla, youngest daughter of Herod Agrippa I.

FELIX, HIS FIRST WIFE – GRANDDAUGHTER OF ANTHONY AND CLEOPATRA: *Ibid.*, p. 437; quoted from Tacitus, *History* 5.9.

FELIX SENT TROOPS INTO CAESAREA AND MANY JEWISH LEADERS DIED: *Ibid.*, p. 449.

NERO BECAME EMPEROR ON OCT. 13, A.D. 54: F. F. Bruce, *Paul, Apostle of the Heart Set Free,* p. 295.

PAUL PREACHED RIGHTEOUSNESS, SELF-CONTROL, AND FUTURE JUDGMENT: Acts 24:25. Ideas for Paul's message came from Acts 17:31; Romans 2:16; 2 Corinthians 6:2; Philippians 2:9-11; Hebrews 9:27; 1 Peter 4:5.

PAUL'S CHAINS: Acts 26:29.

PAUL'S GREETING: F. F. Bruce, *The Book of Acts,* p. 461. Paul raised his hand in salutation.

TERTULLUS: A.T. Robertson, *Word Pictures of the New Testament,* Acts 24:1. The employment of a Roman lawyer (Latin 'orator') was necessary since the Jews were not familiar with Roman legal procedure and it was the custom in the provinces (Cicero, *pro Cael* 30).

Chapter 16 – Voice in the Storm (pages 180 to 191)

Scripture for Further Study: Acts 27:1-42; Acts 11:19; Matthew 15:21-28; 2 Corinthians 11:25.

ANCHOR: *New Bible Dictionary,* p. 1096, Ships and Boats. The weight of the anchor was 1322 lbs. (600 kg).

ANCHOR FOR RESISTANCE: Although some commentaries (Barnes, Gill) suggest the top sails were lowered, F. F. Bruce (*The Book of Acts,* p. 486) suggests that they dropped an anchor for resistance.

ANDRIAKE, PORT OF MYRA: A.T. Robertson, *Word Pictures of the New Testament,* Acts 27:5.

CAESAREA'S HARBOR: (1) F. F. Bruce, *In the Steps of the Apostle Paul,* p. 51. (2) *International Standard Bible Encyclopedia,* p. 536. Stones 50 x 18 x 9 feet (15.2 x 5.4 x 2.7 meters) were set down 20 fathoms under the sea, i.e., 120 feet (36.58 meters).

CANAANITE WOMAN: *New Bible Dictionary,* p. 1100, Sidon; Matthew 15:21-28.

CENTURION: Merrill F. Unger, *The New Unger's Bible Dictionary,* p. 217. A centurion was a captain of one hundred men in the Roman legion. He carried a staff of vinewood as a badge of office.

CLAUDA: called "Cauda" in some manuscripts.

GIVING THANKS FOR FOOD: Albert Barnes, *Notes on the Bible,* Matthew 14:19; Acts 27:35. The custom among the Jews was universal. The form of prayer which they used in the time of Christ has been preserved by their writers, the Talmudists.

MOUNT IDA: (1) F. F. Bruce, *The Book of Acts,* p. 484; located in the center of the island. (2) Google Earth, the height of Mount Ida, 8057 feet (2456 meters).

PHOENICIA: Acts 11:19.

SHIPS AND MEALS: *The Veil is Torn,* vol. 1: *The Christians,* pp. 178-179.

SHIPS TO ITALY USE LARGER PORTS: A.T. Robertson, *Word Pictures of the New Testament,* Acts 27:2.

SHIPWRECKS AND PAUL: 2 Corinthians 11:25.

Chapter 17 – Miracles (pages 192 to 200)

Scripture for Further Study: Acts 27:43-44; 28:1-16.

APPII MARKETPLACE: Simon Jenkins, *Bible Map Book* (A Lion Book), p. 106; a quote from Horace.

AQUEDUCT: (1) Paul Lawrence, *The IVP Atlas of Bible History*, p. 166. (2) Albert G. MacKinnon, *The Rome of St. Paul*, p. 26.

CAPENA GATE: (1) *Atlas of the Bible Lands*, revised edition (Broadman Press), p. 24. (2) Paul Lawrence, *The IVP Atlas of Bible History*, p. 167.

CASTOR AND POLLUX: *New Bible Dictionary*, p. 1096, Ships and Boats.

CLOVES: one of the ancient remedies for dysentery.

MALTA: F F. Bruce, *The Book of Acts*, p. 497. It has been suggested that when Luke wrote "we learned that the island was called Malta (Melita)" he really meant, "we recognized that it was well named." Melita is the Canaanite word for "refuge." (The word "we" in Acts 28:1 is found in F. F. Bruce's translation of the Greek text, as well as in most versions of the Bible.)

MALTA'S GOVERNOR: Robert Jamieson, A.R. Fausset, and David Brown, *Commentary on the Whole Bible*, Acts 28:7-8. The governor was the representative of the Roman Empire.

NERO: Paul L. Maier, *The Flames of Rome*, pp. 162-168,424; quoted from Tacticus, *Annals*, xiii, 25; Suetonius, *Nero*, xxvi; *Dio Cassius*, lxi, 8-9.

PONTINE MARSH: Description of Pontine Marshes from *Satires I*, by the poet Horace (65-8 B.C.). (Quoted from Basil Mathews, *Paul the Dauntless*, (Partridge) p. 413.)

PUTEOLI: J. Carl Laney, *Concise Bible Atlas*. Puteoli is modern Pozzuoli.

PUTEOLI AND APPIAN WAY: *New Bible Dictionary*, p. 992.

SAILING: A.T. Robertson, *Word Pictures of the New Testament*, Acts 28:13. The ship had to tack to reach Rhegium and was not able to make a straight course. (Tacking can mean: (1) Zigzagging so as to sail directly toward the wind (and for some rigs also away from it). (2) Going about.)

SAILING, LARGE VESSELS WERE GUIDED INTO PORT: *The Veil is Torn*, vol. 1: *The Christians*, p. 179.

THREE TAVERNS: Forbes' *Footsteps of St. Paul*, p. 20.

Chapter 18 – Imprisoned Counselor (pages 201 to 219)

Scripture for Further Study: Acts 28:17-31; Ephesians 6:21; Philippians 1:1; 4:2,3,18; Colossians 1:1; 4:7-14; Philemon 2,10,24.

AGRIPPINA'S DEATH: *The Veil is Torn*, vol. 1: *The Christians*, p. 218. After Agrippina survived the boating accident, Nero sent an assistant and three military men to her home to beat her with clubs and finish her with a sword (Tacitus).

BARBARIC OR UNCIVILIZED: A.T. Robertson, *Word Pictures of the New Testament*, Colossians 3:11. An uncivilized person was called a Scythian and was considered the climax of barbarity. The term was used for any rough person like "Goths and Vandals".

DISPOSITIONS LIKE DOGS: Philippians 3:2-3.

EPAPHRAS: Colossians 1:7; 4:12-13.

FALSE TEACHERS WHO TAUGHT THAT CHRIST WAS A LESSER SPIRIT: *Believer's Study Bible, NKJV* (Thomas Nelson Publishers), Colossians 1:18, footnote.

JAMES THE JUST WAS MARRIED: 1 Corinthians 9:5.

JESUS, SURNAMED JUSTUS: Colossians 4:10-11.

MARK'S PLANS TO VISIT COLOSSE: Colossians 4:10.

ONESIMUS, THE SLAVE: F. F. Bruce, *Paul, Apostle of the Heart Set Free*, pp. 399-400. Athenian law permitted a slave in danger of his life to seek sanctuary at an altar (including the hearth of a private family).

PAUL'S WORDS TO THE JEWS AT JERUSALEM: Isaiah 6:9-10; Acts 28:25-27.

PHILIPPI: Merrill F. Unger, *The New Unger's Bible Dictionary*, p. 788. Luke also accompanied Paul to Philippi, Luke 16:10-11; 16:25 - 17:1, but did not leave the city, because after that time, the third person "they" is used. During the intervening years it is supposed that Luke spent his time at Philippi. The first person "we" reappears when Paul comes to Philippi at the end of his third journey, Acts 20:6 - 21:18.

PHILIPPI AND GIFTS SENT TO PAUL: Philippians 4:16; 2 Corinthians 11:9.

SYNAGOGUES IN ROME: *The Veil is Torn*, vol. 1: *The Christians*, p. 220. A dozen synagogues existed in Rome during Paul's time.

TYCHICUS AND COLOSSE: Colossians 4:7-9.

TYCHICUS TRAVELED WITH PAUL: Acts 20:4-5.

Chapter 19 – Aging Shepherd (pages 220 to 227)
Scripture for Further Study: Philippians 2:24; 1 Timothy.

COURT PROCEDURE: Paul L. Maier *The Flames of Rome*, Endnotes, p. 428; known court procedures.

EPHESUS: William MacDonald, *Believer's Bible Commentary*, p. 2075. It seems probable that after Paul's first imprisonment at Rome, he visited Ephesus with Timothy, 1 Timothy 1:3.

EPHESUS' STADIUM: Selahattin Erdemgil, *Ephesus*, p. 105.

FOOD, COOKING: *The Veil is Torn*, vol. 1: *The Christians*, pp. 224,228.

LUKE WAS PAUL'S AMANUENSIS FOR 1 TIMOTHY: F. F. Bruce, *Paul, Apostle of the Heart Set Free*, p. 443.

TEMPLE OF CONCORD LOCATED ON THE FRONT SLOPE OF CAPITOLINE HILL: It is described in Pliny the Elder's *Natural History*.

TIMOTHY'S TEARS: 2 Timothy 1:4.

TREES OF ROME: Pliny - *Hist. Nat.* xvi. 177.

TRIAL: (1) F. F. Bruce, *Paul, Apostle of the Heart Set Free*, p. 441. It is probable that Paul's appeal did come up for hearing at the end of his two years in Rome. (2) It is not known precisely where Paul was tried. (3) The 3 charges would be the same as during Paul's first hearing before Felix, Acts 24:1-9.

TRIAL AND ACQUITTAL: William MacDonald, *Believer's Bible Commentary*, p. 1665, Acts 28:31. It is generally believed that after his 2 years in Rome, his case came before Nero and the verdict was acquittal.

WOLVES: Acts 20:29-30.

Chapter 20 – Fires of Rome (pages 228 to 232)

CHRISTIANS ACCUSED OF SETTING THE FIRE: (1) Tacitus, *Annals*, xv, 44: "To put an end to the rumor that he had set fire to Rome, Nero substituted as culprits, and punished with cruelty, those called Christians." (2) Albert G. MacKinnon, *The Rome of St. Paul*, pp. 71-74, 112, 118-119. The church that met in Priscilla's and Aquila's home was located on the Aventine. Some of the earliest Christians lived in that area.

GUARDS: The Praetorian Guard.

NERO'S GOLDEN HOUSE: Larry F. Ball, *The Domus Aurea and the Roman Architectural Revolution* (Cambridge University Press). "Nero's palace, the *Domus Aurea* (Golden House), is the most influential known building in the history of Roman architecture." It was 833 x 610 feet (254 x 186 meters).

ROME'S DAMAGE IN THE FIRE OF A.D. 64: Tacitus, *Annals*, xv, 40.

ROME: (1) THE FIRE: *Great Disasters*, pp. 42-45; the burning of Rome (from the historian Tacitus). (2) DISTRICT 11: *Ibid.*, p. 44. Rome had 14 administrative districts.

ROME'S FIRE DEPARTMENT: It had been in operation since a disastrous fire in A.D. 6.

ROME'S POPULATION: F. R. Cowell, *Everyday Life in Ancient Rome*, p. 16; 1,000,000 inhabitants.

Chapter 21 – Arrests (pages 233 to 240)

Scripture for Further Study: Acts 2:11; Philemon 22; 2 Timothy 4:13, 20; Titus.

CARPUS: 2 Timothy 4:13.

CRETANS AT PENTECOST: Acts 2:11. Cretans were in attendance at the Day of Pentecost.

CRETE: *World Book Encyclopedia*; an island 185 miles long.

ERASTUS STAYED IN CORINTH: 2 Timothy 4:20.

JOSEPHUS AND NERO: Paul L. Maier, *Josephus, Essential Works*, pp. 9,280.

NERO AT OLYMPIC GAMES: http://www.ancientlibrary.com/smith-bio/2273.html (Lucian, *Nero*, vol. iii, p. 642, ed. Hemst).

PERSECUTION IN ROME: Paul L. Maier, *The Flames of Rome*, pp. 320-338; persecution described by Suetonius, Tacitus, and other early historians.

TITUS, A CONVERT OF PAUL: inferred in Titus 1:4.

TROPHIMUS BECAME SICK: 2 Timothy 4:20.

VATICAN GARDENS OR VATICAN CIRCUS: Albert G. MacKinnon, *The Rome of St. Paul*, pp. 194-195. Vatican Circus was located outside of the city on the Via Cornelia.

Chapter 22 – Voice of Welcome (pages 241 to 248)
Scripture for Further Study: 2 Timothy.

ALEXANDER THE COPPERSMITH: (1) Paul L. Maier, *The Flames of Rome*, p. 439; quotes from *1 Clement* v, 2, who says that it was through jealousy that Paul was delivered up to death. (2) William MacDonald, *Believer's Bible Commentary*, p. 2127. Conybeare and Howson translate: "Alexander the coppersmith charged me with much evil." The Alexander mentioned in 2 Timothy 4:14 may have been the same one referred to in 1 Timothy 1:20.

BOOKS AND PARCHMENTS: *Ryrie Study Bible*, 2 Timothy 4:13, notes. Books refer to papyrus rolls; the parchments would be skins of vellum used for more precious documents, in this case probably Paul's personal copies of portions of the Old Testament.

CHAINS: 2 Timothy 1:16.

DALMATIA: *Ryrie Study Bible*, 2 Timothy 4:10, notes. Titus was sent to Dalmatia, the former Yugoslavia. However, tradition says Titus returned to Crete and died there.

LETTER OF 2 TIMOTHY: Paul may have dictated this letter to Luke, 2 Timothy 4:11.

OSTIAN WAY: Robert Jamieson, A.R. Fausset, and David Brown, *Commentary on the Whole Bible*, p. 1373; quoted from Eusebius, *Ecclesiastical History*, 2.25.

PAUL'S DEATH BY THE SWORD: (1) F. F. Bruce, *Paul, Apostle of the Heart Set Free*, p. 441. "That Paul's life was brought to an end in Rome by the executioner's sword may be confidently accepted." (2) *Ibid.*, p. 450; according to "Acts of Peter and Paul, 80", Paul was executed beneath a stone pine. Excavations at the site of Paul's death found a number of fossilized pine-cones with a mass of Neronian coins. (3) Robert Jamieson, A.R. Fausset, and David Brown, *Commentary on the Whole Bible*, p. 1373; quoted from Orosius, *Hist.*, 7.7.

PRISON IN ROME: Some believe the prison to have been the Mamertine. It is mentioned by several commentators including F. F. Bruce (*In the Steps of the Apostle Paul*, p. 60). It was located on the northeast slope of Capitoline Hill. It was a plain-looking building located near the Forum. The prison had been built 400 years earlier, with a lower level and a second lower level. The description of Paul's entry into the prison is based on conditions at the Mamertine Prison. Others believe that Paul would not have had access to visits from friends at that location, so would have been held at the *Castra Praetoria* on the north end of Rome.

PYRAMID OF CESTIUS ON THE OSTIAN WAY: (1) Albert G. MacKinnon, *The Rome of St. Paul*, p. 214.

STONE PINE TREE: *Red List of Threatened Species*, IUCN, 2006. The (Italian) Stone Pine (or Umbrella Pine) is a native of Southern Europe. The tree has edible pine nuts and can grow taller than 82 feet (25 meters), but is usually 39-66 feet (12-20 meters) tall.

TALLOW CANDLE: F. R. Cowell, *Everyday Life in Ancient Rome*, p. 28. Candles made from tallow fat rolled round a twisted wick were used by the poor in ancient Rome.

THIRD MILESTONE: F. F. Bruce, *In the Steps of the Apostle Paul*, p. 60.

VERSES USED NEAR THE END OF PAUL'S LIFE: Psalm 27:1 (NKJV); 1 Corinthians 13:12 (KJV); 2 Timothy 4:6 (NLT); Philippians 1:21,23 (NKJV); Romans 8:35,38,39 (NKJV).

Epilogue (pages 251 to 252)

NERO CONDEMNED TO DEATH BY FLOGGING: *Great Disasters*, p. 45.

Selected Bibliography

Ardagh, Philip. *Ancient Greece*. History Detectives series. London, UK: Macmillan Books, 2000.

Backhouse, Robert. *The Temple*. Grand Rapids, MI: Kregel Publications, 1996.

Barnes, Albert. *Notes on Acts of the Apostles*. London, UK: George Routledge, 1847.

Beitzel, Barry J. *Moody Atlas of Bible Lands*. Chicago, IL: Moody Press, 1985.

Bruce, F.F. *The Book of Acts*, revised ed. Grand Rapids, MI: Eerdmans, 1988.

_____. *In the Steps of Our Lord*. Grand Rapids, MI: Kregel Publications, 1996.

_____. *In the Steps of the Apostle Paul*. Grand Rapids, MI: Kregel Publications, 1995.

_____. *New Testament History*. Garden City, NY: Doubleday, Anchor Books, 1972.

_____. *Paul, Apostle of the Heart Set Free*. Grand Rapids, MI: Eerdmans, 1977.

Christian History Project. *The Veil is Torn*. Vol. 1: *The Christians*. [n.p.]: Christian History Project Canada, 2002.

Cowell, F. R. *Everyday Life in Ancient Rome*. New York, NY: Perigree Books, 1980.

Dowley, Tim. *Everyday Life in Bible Times*. Grand Rapids, MI: Kregel Publications, 1999.

Erdemgil, Selahattin. *Ephesus*. Translated by Nüket Eraslan. Istanbul, Turkey: NET, Turistik Yayinlar, 1986.

Frank, Harry Thomas, ed. *Atlas of the Bible Lands*. Maplewood, NJ: Hammond Inc., 1990.

Gower, Ralph, *The New Manners and Customs of Bible Times*. Chicago, IL: Moody Press, 1987.

Great Disasters. Pleasantville, NY: Reader's Digest, 1989.

Herbert, David. *Eternity Before Their Eyes*. London, ON: D & I Herbert Publishing, 2007.

International Standard Bible Encyclopaedia. Edited by James Orr. Chicago, IL: Howard-Severance, 1915.

Jamieson, Robert; Fausset, A.R.; and Brown, David. *Commentary on the Whole Bible*. Grand Rapids, MI: Zondervan, reprint of 1870s ed.

Laney, J. Carl. *Concise Bible Atlas*. Peabody, MA: Hendrickson Publishers, Inc., 1999.

Lawrence, Paul. *The IVP Atlas of Bible History*. Downers Grove, IL: InterVarsity Press, 2006.

MacDonald, William. *Believer's Bible Commentary*. Nashville, TN: Thomas Nelson, 1995.

MacKinnon, Albert G. *The Rome of Saint Paul*. London, UK: Religious Tract Society, 1930.

Maier, Paul L. *The Flames of Rome*. Grand Rapids, MI: Kregel Publications, 1981.

_____. *Josephus, The Essential Works*. Grand Rapids, MI: Kregel Publications, 1988.

_____. *Pontius Pilate*. Garden City, NY: Doubleday, 1968.

New Bible Dictionary, 3rd ed. Downers Grove, IL: InterVarsity Press, 1996.

Packer, J. I.; Tenney, M. C.; and White, W., Jr. *Illustrated Encyclopedia of Bible Facts*. Nashville, TN: Thomas Nelson, 1995.

Pfeiffer, Charles F. *Baker's Bible Atlas*. Grand Rapids, MI: Baker Books, 1961.

Ramsay, William M. *St. Paul: The Traveler and Roman Citizen*. Edited by Mark Wilson. Grand Rapids, MI: Kregel Publications, 2001.

Ratcliffe, Tom H. *Bible Plants, Fruits & Products*. Bristol, UK: Christian Year Publications, 2002.

Robertson, A.T. *Word Pictures of the New Testament*. [n.p.]: Broadman Press, 1932.

Schwartz, Max. *Machines, Buildings, Weaponry of Biblical Times*. Grand Rapids, MI: Fleming H. Revell, 1990.

Stalker, James. *The Life of St. Paul*. Edinburgh: T. & T. Clark, 1885.

Unger, Merrill F. *The New Unger's Bible Dictionary*. Chicago, IL: Moody Press, 1988.

Vincent, Marvin R. *Word Studies in the New Testament*. 4 vols. New York: Charles Scribner's Sons, 1887.

Vine, W.E. *Vine's Expository Dictionary of Old and New Testament Words*. Old Tappan, NJ: Fleming H. Revell Co., 1981.

World Book Encylopedia. Chicago, IL: Field Enterprises Educational Corporation, 1972.

Picture and Map Sources

Chapter	Description	Photos and Map Credits
Front	Map, Roman Empire	Ron Letkeman, Della Letkeman
Chapter 1	Map, Tarsus, Jerusalem and Damascus	Ron Letkeman, Della Letkeman
Chapter 1	Street in old Jerusalem	Noel Bondt
Chapter 2	Cleopatra's gate	Ric and Tülin Munro
Chapter 3	Damascus walls	© Holger Mette / iStockphoto.com
Chapter 4	Caesarea, the ancient port	© Alex Gulevich / Dreamstime.com
Chapter 5	Caesar Augustus (Chart of the Roman Emperors in the first century)	© Hedda Gjerpen /iStockphoto.com
Chapter 5	Tiberius Caesar (Chart of the Roman Emperors in the first century)	Rome, Ara Pacis museum: cast of a portrait of Emperor Tiberius. From the collection of casts of busts showing the members of the Julio-Claudian dynasty. The original art work is exhibited in the Ny Carlsberg Glyptotek (Copenhagen). Picture by Giovanni Dall'Orto, March 28, 2008. The copyright holder of this file allows anyone to use it for any purpose, provided that the copyright holder is properly attributed. Redistribution, derivative work, commercial use, and all other use is permitted.
Chapter 5	Gaius (Caligula) (Chart of the Roman Emperors in the first century)	http://www.livius.org/archive.html Most (but not all) photos were taken by Marco Prins and Jona Lendering. You can download their pictures and use them for non-commercial purposes. High resolution photos are available on request. http://www.livius.org/ei-er/emperors/emperors01.html Small bust of Caligula (Palazzo Massimo alle terme, Roma)
Chapter 5	Claudius (Chart of the Roman Emperors in the first century)	http://upload.wikimedia.org/wikipedia/commons/b/b4/Claudius_Uffizi.jpg Claudius – from the bust in the Uffizi Gallery, Florence. Source: Ferrero, Guglielmo (1911). *The Women of the Caesars*, p. 247, New York: The Century Company. Date: 1911. Author: Unknown. This work is in the public domain in the United States because it was published before January 1, 1923. Public Domain-Canada – for Crown Copyright images first published over 50 years ago, photographs created before 1949 and other works where the author has been dead for over 50 years.

Chapter 5	Nero (Chart of the Roman Emperors in the first century)	Description: Nero pushkin.jpg – Emperor Nero. Plaster cast in Pushkin museum after original in British museum, London. Date: November 2007; Author: shako *This file is licensed under the Creative Commons Attribution ShareAlike 3.0 License. In short: you are free to share and make derivative works of the file under the conditions that you appropriately attribute it, and that you distribute it only under a license identical to this one.*
Chapter 6	Caesarea, the amphitheater	© Kushnirov Avraham / Dreamstime.com
Chapter 7	Map, 1st Missionary Journey	Ron Letkeman, Della Letkeman
Chapter 7	Cyprus beach on the Karpass Peninsula	Ric and Tülin Munro
Chapter 8	Map, city of Antioch, Syria	Della Letkeman
Chapter 9	Map, 2nd Missionary Journey	Ron Letkeman, Della Letkeman
Chapter 10	Athens, the Parthenon	© Valeria Cantone / Dreamstime.com
Chapter 10	Athens, the Tower of the Winds	© Pavlos Rekas / Dreamstime.com
Chapter 10	Corinth, the marketplace	© Tim Nichols / Dreamstime.com
Chapter 11	Map, city of Ephesus	Della Letkeman
	Ephesus, Harbor Street	Ric and Tülin Munro
Chapter 11	Ephesus, Curetes Street as it slopes downhill toward the commercial marketplace, the amphitheater, and the harbor.	Ric and Tülin Munro
Chapter 11	Ephesus, triple arches of the commercial *agora*, the main marketplace of Ephesus.	Ric and Tülin Munro
Chapter 11	Ephesus, amphitheater facing the harbor.	Ric and Tülin Munro
Chapter 12	Map, 3rd Missionary Journey	Ron Letkeman, Della Letkeman
Chapter 12	Troas, eastern gate and wall	© Alexander Khripunov / Dreamstime.com
Chapter 13	Jerusalem, the Temple	Painting by Ron Letkeman
Chapter 14	Caesarea, the aqueduct	© Kushnirov Avraham / Dreamstime.com
Chapter 15	Chart of Herod's Family Tree	Information for Herod's Family Tree taken from (1) *New Bible Dictionary* and (2) *The New Unger's Bible Dictionary*. Chart by Della Letkeman.
Chapter 16	Map, voyage to Rome	Ron Letkeman, Della Letkeman
Chapter 16	Caesarea, harbor	Noel Bondt
Chapter 17	Map, Malta to Rome	Ron Letkeman, Della Letkeman
	Rome, Appian Way	© Giuseppe Lancia / iStockphoto.com
Chapter 18	Pompeii Street	Alago – Public Domain
Chapter 19	Roman Forum illustration	Della Letkeman
Chapter 20	Map, city of Rome	Della Letkeman
Chapter 21	Crete	© Richard Kittenberger / Dreamstime.com
Chapter 22	Stone Pine Tree	© Candace Beckwith / Dreamstime.com

Conversion Charts

Miles	Approximate Kilometers	Found in:
1 mile	1.6 km	Chapters 9, 11
3 miles	5 km	Chapter 16
4 miles	6 km	Chapter 6
5 miles	8 km	Chapter 10
7 miles	11 km	Chapter 7
10 miles	16 km	Chapter 9
15 miles	24 km	Chapter 7
16 miles	25 km	Chapter 6
18 miles	29 km	Chapter 9
20 miles	32 km	Chapter 12
25 miles	40 km	Chapters 12, 16
27 miles	43 km	Chapter 14
30 miles	48 km	Chapters 2, 5, 12
33 miles	53 km	Chapter 20
35 miles	56 km	Chapters 10, 14
40 miles	64 km	Chapter 16
60 miles	96 km	Chapters 2, 8, 10, 13
70 miles	112 km	Chapter 16
80 miles	129 km	Chapters 7, 17
90 miles	150 km	Chapter 9
100 miles	160 km	Chapter 7
120 miles	193 km	Chapter 9
130 miles	209 km	Chapters 7, 17
185 miles	298 km	Notes, Chapter 21
200 miles	321 km	Chapter 10
300 miles	500 km	Chapter 6
350 miles	563 km	Chapter 17
500 miles	805 km	Chapter 9
700 miles	1126 km	Chapter 18
1000 miles	1600 km	Chapter 18
1250 miles	2012 km	Chapter 8

Fahrenheit	Celcius	Found in:
40 degrees	5 degrees	Chapter 11
90 degrees	32 degrees	Chapter 11

Feet	Meters	Found in:
3 feet	1 meter	Chapter 2
40 feet	12 meters	Chapters 10, 11
60 feet	18 meters	Chapter 11
90 feet	27 meters	Chapters 16, 22
120 feet	36 meters	Chapter 16
200 feet	61 meters	Chapter 16
250 feet	76 meters	Chapter 10
750 feet	228 meters	Chapter 12
1000 feet	305 meters	Chapter 9
4000 feet	1220 meters	Chapter 9
8000 feet	2456 meters	Chapter 16
9000 feet	2743 meters	Chapter 3

Index of Quoted Scripture

Index of Places and People

The abbreviations N, S, E, and W are used for north, south, east, and west.
The mark ' indicates the main accent of a word, and " indicates a weaker accent.